Maths Links

A Classroom Guide to School Mathematics and Published Resources

Joanna Turnbull

NARE Publications

First published 1981

ISBN 0 906730 03 1

Published under the auspices of the
NARE Publications Sub-committee
Publications Editor: Roy Edwards
The National Association for Remedial Education,
Central Office,
2 Lichfield Road,
Stafford ST17 4JX.

Further copies of this book, details of NARE's other classroom handbooks and of NARE membership may be obtained from Central Office.

Printed and bound by T. Stephenson & Sons Ltd., Prescot.

Contents

Acknowledgements

This book has evolved over a considerable time and owes much to John Armstrong who, as headmaster of The Mulberry Bush School in Standlake, Oxfordshire, provided the initial creative impetus.

The author gratefully acknowledges the help and guidance given by members of the NARE Publications Sub-committee; particular thanks are due to Alec Williams whose constructive comments at all stages in the development of this project have been invaluable.

The author joins with the publisher in gratefully acknowledging the permission of Norman Cawley and the Inner London Education Authority to print a revised version of *Worth Considering? Looking more analytically at new schemes and books* in Appendix III.

The author would like to thank her mother for helping with the proof reading, and both parents with Mary and Richard Giles for their constant support throughout.

Finally, warm appreciation is due to Marion Williams who typed the manuscript from a very difficult final draft.

1 General Introduction

What does *Maths Links* offer?

Maths Links is intended to *support and extend* existing mathematical programmes for pupils aged between 5 and 12 years and of all abilities, as well as those designed for low attainers at the secondary stage.

It does so by providing a developmental guide to topics — i.e. concepts and skills — generally considered to form the basis of the curriculum offered to the younger age group; in addition themes focused on the mathematical demands of adult life are integrated into the plan. The resultant scheme is finally linked to a wide range of current published resources. Figure 1 summarises the topics and also provides qualifying notes regarding their structuring and ordering.

Though published by NARE, *Maths Links* is not specifically designed for teachers of low attaining pupils, apart from the secondary extension. It offers a structured approach to the subject and this may be equally helpful to all teachers of maths.

How can *Maths Links* help?

1. By providing teachers with practical support
Because of the complexity of the subject and the varied attainments of children within most classes, maths is difficult to plan and teach effectively, and particularly so for the non-specialist and inexperienced teacher. *Maths Links* is practical in emphasis, offering teachers support and guidance closely related to the immediate task of providing appropriate experience for individual children in a class or group.

2. By facilitating a more conceptual approach to mathematics
There is a national concern about maths teaching and the attainment of children in schools, highlighted by research conducted by the British Government's Assessment of Performance Unit (APU).

(a) Primary level.
  The first report from the APU found that, though most 11 year olds tested could do simple arithmetical operations when presented in abstract form, performance declined when pupils were required to apply them to practical or unusual contexts (APU, 1980 a).

(b) Secondary level.
  The APU also found that a significant number of the 15 year olds tested had not acquired the concepts and skills generally considered to be part of the primary school curriculum, or had such a tenuous hold on the concepts that they had difficulty applying them to everyday situations (APU, 1980 b).

Taken together, these studies imply that there may be insufficient emphasis on concept acquisition and also the provision of experience for transferring learning to new situations, particularly to everyday applications. *Maths Links* assumes a conceptual approach to the subject, and offers teachers sources of applied maths.

3. By helping teachers to identify learning difficulties at an early stage
There are obvious advantages in detecting learning difficulties before they escalate into a repeated pattern of failure. All children have difficulties at some time, and *Maths Links* provides suggestions supported by a framework for identifying these, alongside appropriate experience to overcome them. The need for remedial education as a separate provision for particular children might be reduced if difficulties could be detected and remedied as they arose.

4. By helping to provide continuity of mathematical experience
If the mathematical experience of a child is to be coherent and not disjointed, teachers in different classes within a school, and between schools, should understand and take account of each other's approaches to the subjects as well as the child's previous experience and attainments. *Maths Links* might form the basis for general discussion about the teaching of maths as well as providing a structure for recording and communicating each child's attainments to the next teacher or school.

5. By permitting flexibility in the use of published materials whilst maintaining structure and continuity
Most schools already use published material, but teachers may have difficulty using a particular series selectively according to the needs of individual children or in using a range of different publications to support and extend a maths programme. The selective use of a range of approaches to, and printed presentations of the same concept or skill may help to consolidate learning. *Maths Links* should make this flexible use of the published material a lot easier.

What are the principles and assumptions in *Maths Links*?

1. The nature of maths and its teaching

(a) *A conceptual approach* is assumed with the acquisition of concepts preceding and accompanying the learning of skills and facts. The ability to transfer learning to new situations including everyday problems depends on conceptual understanding at all stages.
  (See Appendix II: Mathematical concepts, skills and facts.)

(b) *Maths is essentially developmental*, with the learning of new concepts and skills depending and building on the firm foundation of earlier ones.

(c) *Maths is an integrated body of knowledge.* Any school syllabus should reflect the inter-relationships between the various parts of maths if it is to be experienced as an integrated whole rather than as fragmented parts.

The example in Figure 2 demonstrates the developmental nature of maths and the inter-relationships between different aspects of the subject.

2. The importance of adapting to individual children.

(a) *The maths programme or syllabus.*
  Ideally, a programme of mathematical concepts and skills should be devised so that it meets the needs of individual children. A programme of mathematical objectives is selected and adapted so that it is realistic and related to the child's present level of understanding and perceived potential. The age of a child may be no indication of his level of understanding. With low attainers and particularly slow learners, a realistic programme will inevitably be selective. Only teachers who know the children are equipped to make this selection.
  The overall framework of topics is, therefore, not intended to provide an inflexible programme to be followed by all children, but rather a basis from which teachers can select topics and devise programmes that effectively meet the needs of particular pupils.

(b) *Teaching method.*
  There is no single 'best' teaching method for all children as different children learn at different speeds and in different ways. The choice of teaching method

Figure 2. An example of the developmental nature of mathematics and the interrelationships between different aspects of the subject. (See p.5 and Figure 1)

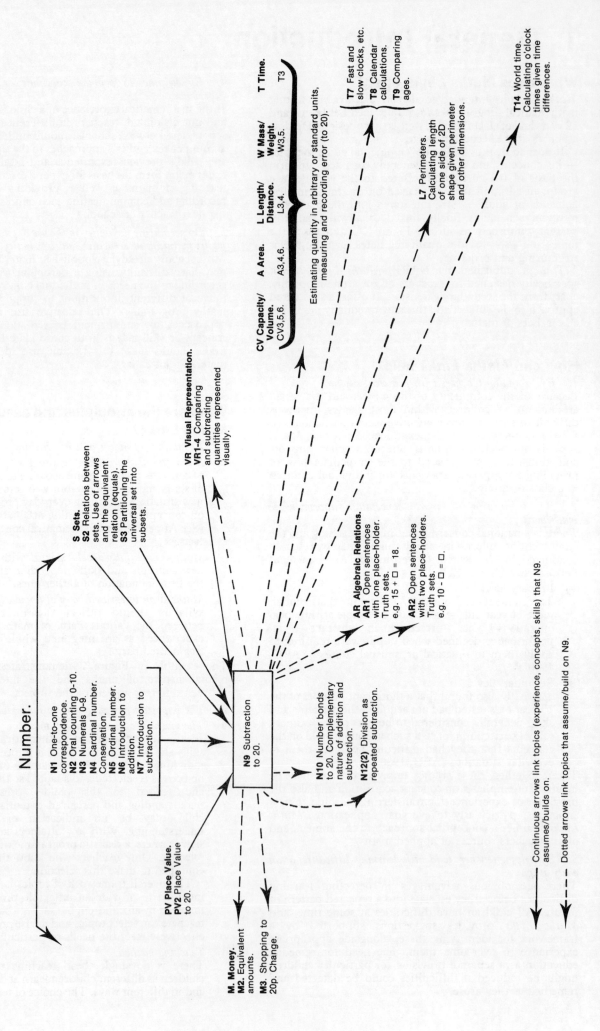

and the planning of experience most conducive to effective learning must be done by the teacher with the individual children in mind. Their varied rates of learning, interests and such emotional characteristics as their level and source of motivation and relative need for support and encouragement are some of the factors that teachers should bear in mind.

Therefore no particular method is advocated here; though conceptual learning and the systematic planning for pupil success, both of which impose constraints on method, are assumed to have paramount importance.

What information is given for each topic?

Each topic in Figure 1 is considered separately in the book, and in each case the format is as follows.

1. A description of the topic
Concepts and skills are specified together with the associated language and notation. The variation in length of these descriptions relates to the complexity of the topic and the probable needs of the inexperienced or non-specialist teacher.

2. A list of conceptually related topics ('See also' section.)
As maths is an integrated body of knowledge (see Figure 1) conceptually related topics have been listed. These are of two kinds.
(a) Topics that are approximately equivalent developmentally, referring to experience that might contribute to a greater conceptual understanding, applications of the concepts and skills or simple extensions of the ideas. Such topics could be introduced more or less concurrently, thereby extending the variety and interest of the curriculum as well as demonstrating important inter-relationships within the subject.
(b) Topics that are not developmentally equivalent, referring to concepts and skills that are assumed or topics that themselves assume and develop the ideas. In most cases it would be inappropriate to introduce these topics concurrently, but teachers' awareness of them may help in the planning of an integrated and coherent long-term programme.

3. Detailed reference to published pupil's books, cards and worksheets that offer experience of that topic
The complete list of included publications may be found in Appendix V. The material is listed in three groups, labelled **P**, **S** and **SM**.

P   refers to material written for *primary and/or middle* school children, and planned as a general course in maths, encompassing most aspects of the subject.

S   refers to material written particularly for low attaining *secondary* school children. Generally, though not always, these have a high interest and low

mathematical level. Here there are three kinds of books: those whose content emphasizes 'social' everyday maths, those with a traditional maths programme and those which combine both types of material. Many teachers find books in group **P** useful with secondary school children.

SM   refers to *support material* which does not offer a comprehensive maths course but can be used to stimulate experience and practice in particular topics with a variety of age groups.

Note that:
(a) In some cases the entire page, card or worksheet listed is devoted to the topic; whereas in others only a part of it may be.
(b) The inclusion of a published series or a reference does not imply a recommendation of its quality or value. The various materials adopt a wide range of approaches and emphases and some may be more appropriate and helpful than others.
(c) Likewise, the fact that a particular series has not been included does not imply anything derogatory. **It has been impossible to include all publications; and sufficient space has been left for a teacher to include any other material considered helpful.**

4. Detailed reference to teachers' books that offer more information about the topic and practical suggestions for the planning and implementation of learning experiences. The list of included publications may be found in Appendix V.

Note that:
(a) Preference for one teachers' book or another is a highly personal matter, reflecting the knowledge, experience and orientation of the teacher. Some teachers may already have their own preferred book and this could be incorporated if required.
(b) Some teachers' books, supporting a particular published pupil scheme, offer detailed suggestions of experiences that supplement and extend work included in the pupil material. The teachers' guides of this kind included here are limited to those whose formats make them useful to teachers not using the pupil material.
(c) Some topics are not accompanied by a reference to a teachers' book, and in these cases teachers are recommended to consult *Primary Mathematics Today* (Williams and Shuard, 1970).
(d) The listed books were selected with the needs of the inexperienced or non-specialist teacher in mind. For more detailed account of all aspects of primary-level maths, together with many practical suggestions, *Primary Mathematics Today* (ibid) is highly recommended; it has an excellent index which helps to make it a very accessible reference book.

2 The classroom use of published materials: one series or several?

Most schools already use published material. Many schools use one main commercial scheme; children may be matched to the appropriate part of that scheme and thereafter work through it as they pass from class to class through the school. The extent to which that one scheme determines the child's mathematical experience varies from school to school and from class to class. It may be used in close association with an accompanying teachers' guide offering suggestions for supplementary experience and/or supported by other material whether published or personally designed by teachers themselves. Some schools are not committed to one main published scheme, preferring to use a range of different publications and/or material produced by teachers within the school or education authority.

There will always be financial constraints on the purchase of published material. Schools should decide whether money is better spent on numerous copies of one particular series or on fewer copies of a wider range of publications.

The advantages of the availability of a range of different publications.

1. The strengths of a series may be used without suffering from its weaknesses.
All published materials have their strengths and weaknesses. Though a particular scheme may in general accord with a school's collective view of the teaching of maths, including the relative importance of different topics and how staff think children learn most effectively, in such a complex subject there will inevitably be aspects of that scheme that do not fit. The availability of a range of alternative publications allows the teacher to use the strengths of a scheme without having to endure its weaknesses. For example, a series that offers a well structured developmental approach to the four operations on number, but little or no experience of their everyday applications, could be supported by real-life problem material.

2. The options for selecting and using material according to the needs and interests of individual children are extended
Published schemes usually offer a general course in maths, designed for an age range, ability range or both. They obviously cannot take account of individual differences within the range. The availability of alternative publications, offering different approaches to the subject and its teaching, extends the options available to teachers when trying to select and plan experiences most conducive to effective learning with individual children. *Maths Links* aims to help teachers using material in this way.

Developing the range of classroom materials.

If a school decides to extend its range of publications, two immediate questions arise.
1. Which publications will best extend and complement the material already used?
Teachers will probably be aware of weaknesses and gaps in the published material they use. These weaknesses should be listed so that the gaps to be filled by new purchases are clearly defined. If a series is included here, *Maths Links* should help the teacher to identify any important topics not covered by that series at all, as well as those that are only partially covered. To assess the content of a series in more detail, teachers may find it helpful to follow up all its references to one or two crucially important topics; by

doing this they should gain an overall view of how those topics are presented throughout the series and where the weaknesses lie in relation to the needs of a particular school, class or group.

Maths Links may similarly facilitate the selection of publications that best extend and complement this material. With publications included here, a preliminary selection of those that cover the necessary topics could be followed by a more detailed comparative assessment of teaching method, presentation, etc. at a teachers' centre library, book exhibition or educational bookshop. Most publishers will send inspection copies if requested. Cawley's article *Worth Considering?* - reproduced in Appendix III - provides a useful structure of questions to facilitate analysis of published materials and the extent of their potential usefulness within a particular school.

2. How might a range of publications best be organised and stored so that they are readily accessible to both teachers and children?
The most practical way will depend in part on the size and organisation of the particular school and of classes within the school, as well as the number of copies of each publication available. Broadly there are two possible ways, though many variations within each.

(a) *Publications stored and used in their published form*
Books, cards and worksheets could be pooled within a school or group of classes and stored at a central point. Alternatively each class could have a number of copies of the material. In either case publications should be stored on shelves that are clearly labelled and appropriately levelled so that both teachers and children are able to find and return them easily.

The use of material organised in this way relies on the day-to-day identification by teachers of appropriate parts of that material, and either the presentation of the material itself to the child or a detailed reference to it, enabling him or her to fetch and subsequently return it.

(b) *The material stored and used as workcards*
A teacher or group of teachers could, with the help of *Maths Links*, select potentially useful pages from published books and worksheets and present them in workcard form, with a detailed reference to the source publication inserted on the card. These cards and material already published in this form could be classified and coded using the topic headings and codings offered in *Maths Links*. Self-adhesive peel-off labels may help with this coding. Workcards personally prepared by teachers could be similarly classified and stored with the published material.

Though time consuming, this practice carries the advantage of ultimately making a great deal of different material more accessible than when in book form, as well as demonstrating quite concretely any topics that are inadequately covered. Moreover, though it may not be considered financially feasible for a child to use a number of different consumable workbooks selectively, this possibility might be more realistic if they are cut up and classified in this way.

Well planned published schemes contain inbuilt reinforcement; earlier learning is consolidated over a considerable period of time by offering further practice and applications of it alongside new learning. If publications are to be organised and stored as workcards, it becomes solely the teacher's responsibility to intersperse new learning with reinforcement experiences.

3 Implementing a classroom programme

1. Assessing the child's present level of understanding.

In order to be able to extract from a broad maths programme appropriate learning objectives for each child, the teacher must first have a clear idea of the child's present level of understanding. Though this may be difficult in a busy classroom, it is time and effort well spent and likely ultimately to avoid time-wasting experiences that either cover learning already well established or learning that is too distant from the child's present understanding to be mastered. Lack of precision in assessment is probably the most important single factor contributing to pupil failure, and this can so easily spiral into a repeated pattern of failure with a growing dislike of the subject.

The teacher needs to find out
(a) What the child has mastered i.e. learned and generalised.
(b) What the child has learned in one form but not yet generalised.
(c) What the child has partially learned and what are the specific areas of difficulty.
(d) What the child has not learned at all.

There are several possible ways of making this assessment.
(a) Analytic observation of the child's previous work: old books, discussion with previous teacher etc.
(b) Individual assessment; presenting the child with tasks, observing his response and further discussion with him or her. *Checkpoint Assessment Cards* (ILEA) offer assessments of this kind, supported by learning experiences to remedy specific difficulties thereby discovered.
(c) Use of a group criterion referenced test i.e. a test that can be administered to a group, and is designed to assess the extent of a child's understanding in relation to specified concepts and skills.
Teachers may either
i) Use a published group criterion referenced test; e.g. *O. and B. Maths Test* (Oliver and Boyd) *Profile of Mathematical Skills* Norman France (Nelson) *Yardsticks* (Nelson); or
ii) Devise their own group criterion referenced test. This test could related closely to selected topics in *Maths Links*.
Any test should take account of the different levels of understanding possible for a single concept or skill if specific areas of weakness are to be detected. It is unlikely that a single question will indicate this.
Appendix IV offers an example of this kind of assessment.
Knowledge gained by assessment should be recorded for each child. See Record-keeping p10.

2. Formulating short-term learning objectives.

Figure 3 suggests how knowledge gained by assessment may be used in formulating short-term learning objectives. The crucial importance of objectives concerned with generalisation of previous learning is referred to in Appendix II. Objectives relating to new learning need to be very carefully planned; the identification and appropriate sequencing of small learning steps, building gradually towards the realisation of a learning objective, is particularly important for children with learning difficulties.

3. Planning and implementing learning experiences.

These clearly stated short term objectives may now be implemented by selecting mathematical experiences most conducive to their realisation. The teacher who knows the children is the best judge of what experiences are most likely to be effective. See pages 5 and 7.

Maths Links tries to help a busy classroom teacher to attain these objectives, firstly by reminding her of useful back-up publications, some of which may well be already in the school, so that children may have lots of material with which to practise and apply their knowledge, and secondly by suggesting published teachers' guides and pupils' materials for introducing and then reinforcing new maths ideas. *Maths Links* may also make the individualisation of programmes easier.

4. Classroom organisation.

The organisational problems in implementing a maths programme designed for individual children are obviously greatest in a large class containing children with a wide range of attainments. Yet this is the reality for most teachers.

Decisions about classroom organisation are largely a question of personal preference. There are however several principles that may help.

(a) *Grouping*
Though individual assignments may be necessary at times, there is value in two or more children working on the same assignment and discussing together strategies and discoveries. Individualisation does not necessarily mean working alone, though if children are to work together careful thought should be given to their grouping.
i) There is often a discrepancy between a child's attainment in maths and his attainment in other subjects, e.g. in reading, relative to the rest of the class. Thus if a class is grouped by reading attainment, regrouping will be necessary for maths.
ii) In maths no two children's present level of attainment in all aspects of the subject will be identical, nor will they learn in the same way or at the same rate. Grouping should therefore be flexible, allowing for the possibility of regrouping for different learning objectives or as the discrepancy between the attainments of different children in a group becomes evident.
Use of the class record sheets in Appendix VI may help the teacher to group children appropriately.

(b) *Teachers' personal participation*
The size of the class as well as the needs of individual children within it will obviously affect how much personal help can be given to each pupil. Classroom organisation should ideally allow the teacher to oversee the learning process and be available to help children with particular difficulties.

i) Children should be encouraged to work independently. If resources - equipment, workcards and published material - are stored on clearly labelled shelves, at appropriate heights, most junior and certainly secondary-aged children should be able to fetch and return these resources themselves, once they know which assignment to follow. Younger children will obviously need more training. On page 8, there are suggestions for organising and storing published material to maximise its accessibility to children.

ii) Children on new learning will need the teacher's intervention more than those practising known skills. It is advisable, therefore, not to have too many children on new work at any one time.

5. Checking up on learning.

When marking work, discussing it with children and helping particular children with difficulties, a teacher should continuously assess the effectiveness of learning and respond to indications of wrong learning or learning difficulties by providing supplementary experience or even revising learning objectives if this is necessary.

Before mastery is assumed, a teacher should be confident that concepts and skills have been generalised; the use of an individual or group criterion referenced test may help a teacher with this.

Some published series include periodic assessments of the effectiveness of previous learning, and these are generally intended to determine whether a child has mastered this learning and is ready to proceed to the next section or book. Some of these assessments are particularly designed to highlight specific areas of difficulty, e.g. The Moon Book (Book 6) at the end of each module in *Hey Mathematics*.

6. Record-keeping.

Records monitoring a child's mathematical experiences and attainments are important. Firstly, they support the teachers in individualising a developmental programme, helping in the continual process of identifying appropriate learning objectives for each child, remedying difficulties as they arise and revising learning objectives when necessary. Maths is too diverse a subject for a teacher to hold in mind each child's level of understanding. Secondly, records help to ensure continuity of experience from class to class and from one school to the next.

The developmental categorisation of topics in *Maths Links* provides a structure for record-keeping. If records are to be passed from class to class, the staff should meet together and decide the exact form the records should take. The possibilities to be found in Appendix VI could be considered at such a meeting.

(a) *Records for individual children*
i) Summary chart of the child's mathematical attainments.

Topics introduced and those mastered (i.e. learned/generalised) are indicated and added to periodically using a simple code, thus providing an up-to-date summary of attainment which could accompany a child through one school and on to the next.

ii) Detailed record sheet of the child's experiences and attainments. .

Here the teacher records daily or weekly significant aspects of the child's mathematical experience. The amount of detail recorded is obviously limited by the time available for it. A brief daily record of pertinent information that can be sustained is obviously preferable to a very detailed account which lapses when the teacher's initial enthusiasm flags.

This form of record will help the teacher to isolate the different concepts/skills within a topic and implement a step by step programme building towards full understanding of the topic, and this may be particularly useful with small groups of low-attaining pupils. When a child has mastered a whole topic, this could be recorded on the individual and/or class summary charts.

(b) *Class record sheets*
Separate sheets are offered for two different age ranges.
i) 5-8 years: Topics listed here, with minor additions, are those which the various publications of The Nuffield Foundation suggest might be introduced, but not necessarily mastered, during the first three school years (Nuffield/British Council, 1970; Moore, 1979; Williams and Moore, 1979; Latham and Truelove, 1980).
ii) 8-12 years: In order to cover the wide range of attainments within most classes at this level, two charts, each including different aspects of the subject, are provided. These sheets could also be used for groups of low attaining pupils at the secondary level, though in this case M(money)11, 12 and 13 which are concerned with adult money management, should be added.

On these charts topics introduced and those mastered are indicated using a simple code. This gives the teacher a 'bird's eye view' of the attainments of children in a class, showing where teaching is needed and helping in the flexible grouping of children by attainment or learning objective.

It is not suggested that all these forms of record-keeping should necessarily be used. Here, as throughout *Maths Links*, the intention is to offer teachers a range of practical alternatives that may be accepted, rejected or adapted according to their particular situation and thinking. There is no universally accepted 'right way' in mathematics.

Figure 3. The use of knowledge gained by assessment in formulating short-term learning objectives.

Knowledge gained by assessment.

1. Concepts firmly acquired and skills mastered, i.e. learned and generalised.

2. Skills learned in one or more forms but not generalised.
   e.g. A child may be able to calculate 100 ÷ 10 but unable to apply it *confidently* to a new situation such as how many 10p choc-bars can be bought for £1 (or 100p).

3. Concepts and skills partially acquired or learned and specific areas of difficulty.

4. Concepts and skills not covered at all.

Short-term learning objectives.

1. Objectives relating to
   a. practice/reinforcement of previous learning.
   b. generalisation of previous learning i.e. experience of new contexts, applications, problems, etc.

2. Objectives relating to new learning.

Money

Contents

M1 Concept of exchange. Extension of vocabulary.

Concept of exchange (or swopping) through real experience in shops, supplemented by varied shopping play.

Introduction to, and extension of, vocabulary associated with money: spend, cost, worth, buy, sell, how much, shop, money, coin, note, cash, earn, save, pay, price, charge, poor, rich, cheap, expensive, swop, fare, amount, bill, afford etc.

See also   S1,3   Sorting and classifying.
           S2   Relations between sets. The equivalent relation.

Books for teachers
    Early Mathematical Experiences   'Home Corner. The Family'. 'Outdoor Activities. The Environment'.
    Mathematics: the first 3 years   p59-60, 62.

M2 Recognition of coins 1p, 2p, 5p, 10p and ½p. Counting money to 20p. Equivalent amounts.

Recognition of these coins and the symbols.

Counting sums of money to 20p.

Different ways of making up a sum of money to 10p and later 20p. Relationships between the coins.

See also   PV2   Place value to 20.
           N3   Numerals 0-9.
           N5   Ordinal number.
           N6,8   Addition to 20.
           N10   Number bonds to 20, etc.
           F1,2   Half and whole one. Addition of halves.
           S1,3   Sorting and classifying.
           S2   Relations between sets. The equivalent relation.
           Sh2   Sorting and naming circles.

P   *Ready for Alpha and Beta (new ed.)*   p7, 16.
     Beta (new ed.)   Beta 1 p9, 10, 14, 26-27.
     Hey Mathematics   Mod 1. Book 3 p3. Book 4 p18.
     Key Maths   Level 1. Book 3 p58-59. Book 4 p48, 49, 51. Book 5 p41-43, 44.
                 Level 2. Book 1 p3, 31.
     Making Sure of Maths   Blue Book p12. Introductory Book p22.
     Mathematics for Schools   Level 1 (2nd ed.). Book 5 p37-39. Book 7 p12.
     Maths Adventure   1. Pupil's Book p25-26.
     Nuffield Maths 5-11   1. Worksheets M1. 1·1-1·2, 2·1-2·2, 3·1-3·3, 4·1.
                    2. Worksheets M2. 1·2, 2·1, 2·2, 3·1-3·4.
                    3. Pupils' Book p25-27, 30.
     Numbers and Words   Book 2 p21-24. Book 4 p14-17. Book 5 p15-17. Book 6 p2-4, 30-32.
     Our First School Maths   Book 3 p7-9. Book 4 p18-20. Book 5 p14-15.
     Oxford Middle School Mathematics   Book 1 p68.
     Primary Mathematics (SPMG)   Stage 1. Workbook 1 p13-20.
                               Stage 2. Workbook 1 p11.
                               Stage 4. Card 54.
     Towards Mathematics   Core Unit 4 p13, 14.

S   *Headway Maths*   Book 1 p12.
     Impact Maths   Pupil's Book 1 p17.
     Mathematics for Life   Book A2 p8-9.
     Maths (Holt)   Book 2 p51.

SM   *Check it Again*   Book 1 p30-31. Book 2 p26.
        Four a Day series   Book 4 p48, 55-56. Book 5 p24-25, 34-35. Book 6 p37-38, 40.

Books for teachers
     Nuffield Maths 5-11   1. Teachers' Handbook p142-145.
                    2. Teachers' Handbook p128-132.
                    3. Teachers' Handbook. Chapter 6.

Shopping to 20p. Change.

Simple shopping activities without change giving. One item and later more, exchanged for money to 10p and later 20p.

Shopping to 20p giving and checking change by 'adding on' (i.e. shopkeepers' method) and 'counting back'.

Simple bills. Addition and subtraction of money to 20p.

See also N6,8　Addition to 20. Vertical addition.
　　　　　N7,9　Subtraction to 20; 'difference' and 'taking away' aspects.
　　　　　F2　　Addition and subtraction of halves.

P　*Ready for Alpha and Beta (new ed.)*　p8.
　　Beta (new ed.)　Beta 1 p10, 15, 26.
　　Basic Mathematics　Book 1 p37.
　　Hey Mathematics　Mod 2. Book 1 p39. Book 2 p39.
　　Key Maths　Level 1. Book 3 p53, 60. Book 4 p50, 51. Book 6 p53, 54.
　　Making Sure of Maths　Blue Book p12-13. Introductory Book p23-24.
　　Mathematics for Schools　Level 1 (2nd ed.). Book 5 p40-43. Book 6 p30-31, 57.
　　Maths Adventure　1. Pupil's Book p59, 80.
　　Nuffield Maths 5-11　2. Worksheets M2 $4 \cdot 1$, $4 \cdot 4$, $5 \cdot 2$, $6 \cdot 1$, $6 \cdot 2$.
　　Numbers and Words　Book 2 p25. Book 4 p20-23, 27. Book 7 p16-17. Book 8 p24-25.
　　Our First School Mathematics　Book 5 p16. Book 6 p12-13.
　　Primary Mathematics (SPMG)　Stage 1. Workbook 2 p5-9. Workbook 3 p8. Workbook 4 p10.
　　　　　　　　　　　　　　　　　Stage 2. Workbook 1 p12.

S　*Headway Maths*　Book 1 p13.
　　Mathematics for Life　Book A2 p12-13.

SM　*Blackie's Practice Workbooks*　Book 1 p22-26. Book 2 p7-8.
　　Check it Again　Book 1 p30, 32-33. Book 2 p25.
　　Four a Day series　Book 4 p47, 49. Book 5 p19-20.

Books for teachers
　　Nuffield Maths 5-11　1. Teachers' Handbook p146-148, 149-152.
　　　　　　　　　　　　　2. Teachers' Handbook p132-137.
　　　　　　　　　　　　　3. Teachers' Handbook p41, 98-99.

Recognition of 50p coin and £1 note. Counting money to £1.
Equivalent amounts.

£1 as 100p.

Counting sums of money over 20p.

Different ways of making up a sum of money over 20p. Relationships between coins to £1.

(Any references below which involve sums of money over £1 are indicated (over £1).)

See also PV2　Place value to 100.
　　　　　N15　Addition to 100. Number bonds to 100.
　　　　　F2　　Addition of halves.
　　　　　Sh2,16 50p coin as a regular heptagon.

P　*Ready for Alpha and Beta (new ed.)*　p19.
　　Alpha (new ed.)　Alpha 1 p27, 28. Alpha 2 p8. Alpha 4 p11 (over £1).
　　Beta (new ed.)　Beta 1 p40-41, 48. Beta 2 p6-7, 11. Beta 3 p6 (over £1), 7. Beta 5 p6.
　　Basic Mathematics　Book 1 p36, 38, 39, 65. Book 2 p60.
　　Hey Mathematics　Mod 1. Book 3 p19. Book 4 p29.
　　　　　　　　　　　Mod 2. Book 1 p12-13.
　　　　　　　　　　　Mod 3. Book 1 p3. Book 2 p6-7 (over £1).
　　　　　　　　　　　Mod 4. Book 1 p1.
　　Key Maths　Level 1. Book 5 p45. Book 6 p52.
　　　　　　　　Level 2. Book 1 p32, 38. Book 6 p14 (over £1).
　　Making Sure of Maths　Introductory Book p45. Book 1 p34-36, 54. Book 2 p27, 91.
　　Mathematics for Schools　Level 2 (2nd ed.). Book 1 p33-34. Book 2 p43.
　　　　　　　　　　　　　　Level 2 (1st ed.). Book 3 p42. Book 4 p1.
　　Maths Adventure　2. Pupil's Book p10-11.
　　Nuffield Maths 5-11　2. Worksheets M2. $1 \cdot 1$.
　　　　　　　　　　　　3. Pupils' Book p25, 28-29, 30, 72-73.

Our First School Maths   Book 6 p14 (over £1).
Oxford Middle School Mathematics   Book 1 p69.
Primary Mathematics (SPMG)   Stage 1. Workbook 3 p9-10.
                                Stage 2. Workbook 1 p4.
                                Stage 4. Card 55.
Towards Mathematics   Core Unit 4 p14. Core Unit 9 p15 (over £1).

S   *Impact Maths*   Pupil's Book 1 p17, 63 (over £1).
Inner Ring Maths   Book 1 p22.
Maths (Holt)   4th Year p12-13.
Understanding Money   Book 2 p24 (over £1).

SM   *Check it Again*   Book 5 p14-15.
Four a Day series   Book 5 p29-32, 35. Book 6 p38-39, 40-41, 42, 43, 44 (over £1).
                       Book 7 p41-42, 43-44, 45, 49-50 (over £1). Book 8 p34-36, 37-38.
                       Book 9 p53 (over £1), 55 (over £1).

Books for teachers
Nuffield Maths 5-11   2. Teachers' Handbook p127-128.
                        3. Teachers' Handbook p97-98.

M5   Shopping to £1.

Extension of buying and change giving to 50p and later £1, giving and checking change by 'adding on' and 'counting back' methods.

Bills. Addition and subtraction of money to £1, focusing on applications.

See also   M8   Unit pricing.
           N15   Addition to 100.
           N16   Subtraction to 100.
           F2   Addition and subtraction of halves.

P   *Alpha (new ed.)*   Alpha 1 p29-30. Alpha 2 p8, 20.
Beta (new ed.)   Beta 1 p47, 48. Beta 2 p11. Beta 3 p7.
Basic Mathematics   Book 1 p63-64, 66.
Hey Mathematics   Mod 2. Book 1 p38. Book 2 p30-31. Book 3 p8. Book 4 p26-27.
                    Mod 3. Book 2 p22. Book 3 p24.
Key Maths   Level 1. Book 5 p46-47. Book 6 p55. Book 7 p25, 26, 27.
              Level 2. Book 1 p39. Book 2 p9.
Making Sure of Maths   Book 1 p36, 37, 55. Book 2 p28, 31.
Mathematics for Schools   Level 2 (2nd ed.). Book 1 p35-36. Book 2 p41-42, 44, 45.
                            Level 2 (1st ed.). Book 3 p43. Book 4 p2-3.
Maths Adventure   1. Pupil's Book p94.
Nuffield Maths 5-11   2. Worksheets M2. 4·2, 4·3, 5·1.
                        3. Pupils' Book p31, 74-76.
Primary Mathematics (SPMG)   Stage 1. Workbook 4 p17.
                               Stage 2. Workbook 1 p8, 9, 10, Card 4.
                               Workbook 3 p19, Card 4a.

S   *Headway Maths*   Book 1 p35, 57.
Impact Maths   Pupil's Book 1 p29.
Mathematics for Life   Book A2 p10-11, 14-15. Book A3 p12-19.
Maths (Holt)   Book 1 p41.
On Our Own Two Feet   Book 4 p3-4.

SM   *Check it Again*   Book 4 p18, 19-20, 21-22. Book 5 p12.
Four a Day series   Book 5 p45-47. Book 6 p44-45, 46, 47-48. Book 7 p53-54.
                      Book 8 p42-43. Book 9 p57. Book 10 p54.
Problems   Second Problems p10.

Books for teachers
Nuffield Maths 5-11   3. Teachers' Handbook p98-99.

Decimal notation of the pound (e.g. £1·25).

Changing pounds to pence and vice versa.

See also PV4 Place value. Grouping in 100's.
          PV6 Place value. Hundredths as decimals.
          S2   The equivalent relation.

P *Alpha (new ed.)* Alpha 1 p48. Alpha 2 p8, 9. Alpha 3 p6.
Beta (new ed.) Beta 2 p40, 84. Beta 3 p19. Beta 4 p7. Beta 5 p7.
Basic Mathematics Book 2 p27, 28, 58.
Hey Mathematics Mod 3. Book 2 p5. Book 5 p6.
                   Mod 4. Book 1 p33.
Key Maths Level 2. Book 3 p19-20. Book 5 p14. Book 6 p14.
Making Sure of Maths Book 1 p57. Book 2 p29-30, 92. Book 3 p17.
Mathematics for Schools Level 2 (1st ed.). Book 4 p4-5.
Maths Adventure 2. Pupil's Book p68.
                   3. Pupil's Book p11.
Oxford Middle School Mathematics Book 1 p91.
Primary Mathematics (SPMG) Stage 4. Textbook p31.
Towards Mathematics Core Unit 4 p14. Core Unit 9 p14, 15.

S *A World of Mathematics* Book 2 p37-38.
Headway Maths Book 2 p9.

SM *Check it Again* Book 3 p21-23.
Four a Day series Book 6 p44. Book 7 p45-47, 48-49, 50. Book 8 p38-39, 40-41, 42.
                     Book 9 p52-53, 54-55, 56. Book 10 p53.
Number Workbook Decimals p16.

Shopping over £1.

Buying and change giving involving amounts over £1.

Bills. Addition and subtraction of money over £1 focusing on applications.

Efficient shopping habits. Opening times of different shops, efficient use of department stores, etc.

See also M8   Unit pricing.
          N8,9,15,16,20,21 Addition and subtraction of whole numbers.
          N22   Addition and subtraction of decimals.
          F2   Addition and subtraction of halves.
          T5,7   Opening days and times of shops.

P *Alpha (new ed.)* Alpha 1 p49, 80. Alpha 2 p34. Alpha 3 p47. Alpha 4 p11, 24.
Beta (new ed.) Beta 2 p41. Beta 5 p6, 7.
Basic Mathematics Book 2 p29, 57, 58, 59. Book 3 p51, 53. Book 4 p57.
Hey Mathematics Mod 2. Book 2 p29. Book 3 p19.
                   Mod 3. Book 1 p25. Book 2 p24. Book 3 p26, 27.
                   Mod 6. Book 1 p29. Book 2 p23.
Key Maths Level 2. Book 3 p25, 28. Book 5 p14, 21, 31. Book 6 p15, 16.
Making Sure of Maths Book 2 p36-37. Book 3 p18.
Mathematics for Schools Level 2 (1st ed.). Book 4 p6-7. Book 6 p62. Book 7 p6.
Oxford Middle School Mathematics Book 1 p91-93.
Primary Mathematics (SPMG) Stage 5. Textbook p118. Card 6.
Towards Mathematics Core Unit 14 p7, 10.

S *A World of Mathematics* Book 3 p59. Book 6 p37-39, 48-49.
Headway Maths Book 1 p58, 75. Book 2 p24-25. Book 3 p8-9. Book 4 p18-19.
Mathematics for Life Book A3 p20-29, 30-31. Book B2 p30-31.
                        Book B3 p12-15, 24-25, 26-27, 28-29. Book C2 p8-9.
Mathsworks Book 1 p6.
On Our Own Two Feet Book 2 p18, 23. Book 3 p11-13, 17. Book 4 p2, 18, 24. Book 5 p18, 20-21, 25-26.
Understanding Money Book 2 p21-25.

SM *Check it Again* Book 5 p13.
Four a Day series Book 7 p54-56, 57-58. Book 8 p43-44, 44-45. Book 9 p58, 60. Book 10 p54-55, 56-57.
Problems Second Problems p6, 11. Third Problems p53.

M8 Unit pricing. Best buys.

Money is related through multiplication and division to number, capacity and volume, area, length, weight and time. Ready reckoners. e.g. cost of 5 kg of carrots at £0·26 a kg.
cost of 100 nails at 2½p each.
cost of ½ metre of wire if 5 metres cost £2·40.

Value for money and best buys. Value for money of different brands of the same product compared by calculating the common price for equivalent units of quantity: e.g. which is the best buy, 450 grams for 22p or 500 grams for 30p?

Multiplication and division of money, focusing on applications (problems).

See also M3,5,7 Shopping.
M11 Household bills etc. involving unit pricing.
M12 Pay — piecework, timework, etc.
N17,18,19(3),29,30,33,34 Multiplication and division of whole numbers.
N23 Ratio, rate and proportion.
N31,32 Multiplication and division of decimals.
F2,4 Multiplication of halves by whole number.
AR4 Straight line graphs.
CV10, A10, L10, W8, T12 Unit pricing. Applications involving multiplication or division of money.

P *Alpha (new ed.)* Alpha 1 p81, 82, 83, 84. Alpha 2 p34, 49. Alpha 3 p22, 47, 49. Alpha 4 p24.
Beta (new ed.) Beta 2 p50. Beta 4 p34, 41. Beta 5 p12. Beta 6 p40, 41.
Basic Mathematics Book 2 p85. Book 3 p52, 70, 71, 96, 97. Book 4 p58, 59. Book 5 p20.
Hey Mathematics Mod 2. Book 4 p24. Book 5 p17.
Mod 3. Book 1 p10, 22. Book 2 p34, 37. Book 3 p28, 29. Book 4 p3, 26.
Mod 5. Book 4 p2. Book 5 p14.
Mod 6. Book 1 p30-32. Book 2 p21-22.
Key Maths Level 2. Book 2 p33. Book 3 p52, 60. Book 4 p51-53. Book 5 p40, 41, 42, 43, 44, 50.
Book 6 p28, 29, 89, 106.
Making Sure of Maths Book 2 p31. Book 3 p19. Book 4 p28-29.
Mathematics for Schools Level 1 (2nd ed.). Book 6 p32-34, 58-59.
Level 2 (2nd ed.). Book 2 p42, 44, 45.
Level 2 (1st ed.). Book 3 p43-44. Book 4 p2, 21. Book 5 p64.
Book 6 p46, 63. Book 7 p38. Book 8 p40-43.
Maths Adventure 2. Pupil's Book p69.
3. Pupil's Book p26.
4. Pupil's Book p30-31 Cards 3, 22.
5. Pupil's Book p41.
Nuffield Maths 5-11 3. Pupils' Book p74.
Our First Schools Maths Book 6 p13.
Oxford Middle School Mathematics Book 2 p44-45, 64-65.
Primary Mathematics (SPMG) Stage 2. Workbook 3 p21 Card 4b.
Stage 3. Textbook p8, 9, 34-35, Card 12, 13, 14, 15.
Stage 4. Textbook p9, 61-62, 66-67, 69-70, 111, 113, Card 38.
Stage 5. Textbook p3, 41, 81-83, 118.
Towards Mathematics Core Unit 19 p4.

S *Focus Mathematics* Book 1 p74-77.
Headway Maths Book 1 p62. Book 3 p22-23. Book 4 p10-11, 32, 33. Book 5 p63-64.
Mathematics for Life Book B1 p4-5, 6-7. Book B2 p30-31. Book B3 p10-11, 20-23, 30-31.
Maths (Holt) Book 1 p28. Book 2 p84. 4th Year p18. 5th Year p83. 5th Year Workbook p26.
Maths Matters Book 1 p23. Book 3 p2, 8-9.
Mathsworks Book 1 p7-9, 24-25, 42, 44, 51, 77, 103, 104. Tryouts 1 p11, 21-25.
Book 2 p67. Tryouts 2 p39.
Maths You Need p7-8, 36-37.
On Our Own Two Feet Book 2 p17. Book 4 p1, 19-20.
Understanding Money Book 2 p21-25, 69.

SM *Check it Again* Book 1 p32. Book 2 p27. Book 3 p24, 25. Book 4 p20-21, 24-28. Book 5 p13-14.
Four a Day series Book 6 p49-51, 51-52. Book 7 p51-52, 59-60, 60-61, 64.
Book 8 p46-47, 47-48, 48-49, 50-52, 56, 69. Book 9 p60-61, 62-64, 65-66, 81.
Book 10 p58-59, 60-61, 72.
Problems Second Problems p31, 53, 59. Third Problems p8, 48.

Simple money management. Discounts and increases in price.

Simple management of money including planning and costing trips, budgeting pocket money. Saturday or holiday jobs.

Percentage or fractional discounts (e.g. in sales) and increases in price.

Changing values and the practical implications of inflation.

Advertising and trading stamps.

See also M11,12,13 Percentage VAT, other tax, interest, etc.
N22,31,32 Operations on decimals.
N23 Ratio, rate and proportion.
N24 Percentages.
N36,37,38 Statistics and advertising.
F3,4 Multiplication of fraction by whole number.

P *Beta (new ed.)* Beta 4 p74.
Hey Mathematics Mod 6. Book 2 p22, 23, 38-40. Book 3 p35, 36, 39, 40.
Key Maths Level 2. Book 6 p68.
Mathematics for Schools Level 2 (1st ed.). Book 7 p63. Book 8 p22. Book 9 p43.
Oxford Middle School Mathematics Book 3 p81.
Primary Mathematics (SPMG) Stage 5. Textbook p14-15, 74-76.

S *Focus Mathematics* Book 10 p39-40.
Headway Maths Book 4 p60-61, 64, 69.
Mathematics for Life Book A2 p16-17. Book B3 p4-5, 16-17, 18-19. Book C3 p28-29.
Maths Matters Book 2 p18-19.
Mathsworks Book 1 p12. Tryouts 1 p1. Book 2 p42, 48.
Maths You Need p1-3, 40-41, 42-43.
On Our Own Two Feet Book 5 p22.
Understanding Money Book 1 p45-46.

Foreign currency.

Foreign currency and currency conversion.

Costing and planning holidays abroad when foreign currency is involved.

Travellers' cheques.

See also M13 Banks, cheques, etc.
PV1,3 Number bases.
N14 Multibase arithmetic.
N23 Ratio, rate and proportion.
AR4 Conversion graphs.
L12, T14 World distances and world time.

P *Alpha (new ed.)* Alpha 4 p13.
Beta (new ed.) Beta 5 p65.
Hey Mathematics Mod 6. Book 4 p39.
Making Sure of Maths Book 4 p85. Book 5 p29-30.
Mathematics for Schools Level 2 (1st ed.). Book 6 p47.
Primary Mathematics (SPMG) Stage 5. Card 7.

S *Headway Maths* Book 5 p67-68.
Maths (Holt) Book 1 p87. 5th Year Workbook p34-35.
Maths You Need p114-115, 116-117, 118.
Understanding Money Book 1 p64-65.

SM *Check it Again* Book 5 p19-20.

M11 Post-school money management: I Household bills, etc.

Budgeting for self or household. Planning and costing decorations etc.

Understanding and paying household bills: rent, rates, electricity, gas, telephone, car bills, doctor's prescriptions, etc.

The Post Office services: stamps, parcels, telephone, telegrams, licences, etc.

Invoices and keeping accounts.

VAT and percentage service charges.

See also   M5,7   Addition and subtraction of money. Bills.
           M8   Unit pricing. Multiplication and division of money.
           M9   Percentage discounts and increases.
           N22,31,32   Operations on decimals.
           N23   Ratio, rate and proportion.
           N24   Percentages.
           W8, T12   Parcel and telephone STD charges.
           T5   Daily, weekly, monthly.

P   *Beta (new ed.)*   Beta 6 p41.
       Primary Mathematics (SPMG)   Stage 4. Textbook p112.
       Towards Mathematics   Core Unit 19 p4.

S   *Focus Mathematics*   Book 10 p44, 46, 47-48.
       Headway Maths   Book 5 p62-64, 77-79.
       Mathematics for Life   Book A3 p2-3, 4-5, 6-7, 8-11, 24-25. Book B2 p18-19. Book B3 p2-3, 8-9.
                         Book C1 p24-25. Book C2 p16-19, 20-23. Book C3 p2-7, 10-13, 18-23, 24-27, 28-29.
       Maths Matters   Book 2 p18-19.
       Mathsworks   Book 1 p4-5, 13, 16, 52-54. Tryouts 1 p8. Book 2 p44, 48. Tryouts 2 p23, 25.
       Maths You Need   p7, 25, 56-58, 67-69, 72-73, 74-80, 81-83.
       On Our Own Two Feet   Book 2 p1, 24-27. Book 3 p21-24, 27-28. Book 4 p7-9, 13-17, 20-21, 25. Book 5 p3-4.
       Understanding Money   Book 1 p37-45, 53-54, 56-65, 69-70, 71-73.
                        Book 2 p2-15, 19-20, 26-29, 29-31, 32-34, 34-36, 42-46, 68-77, 80-81.

M12 Post-school money management: II Pay, payslips, etc.

Pay. Piecework, timework, bonus schemes, commission.

Payslips: take home pay, income tax and tax forms. National Insurance and graduated pension contribution.

Benefits: unemployment, sickness, industrial injury, maternity, child, family income supplement, social security.

Union membership.

Insurance and assurance: household, motor, life, unit trusts, etc.

See also   M5,7   Addition and subtraction of money.
           M8   Unit pricing. Multiplication and division of money.
           M9,11   Percentage discounts and increases. VAT.
           N22,31,32   Operations on decimals.
           N23   Ratio, rate and proportion.
           N24   Percentages.
           T5   Daily, weekly, monthly.
           T12   Time and unit pricing.

S   *Focus Mathematics*   Book 9 p30-37, 37-38, 39-42.
       Headway Maths   Book 4 p70, 86, 87, 88, 89-90. Book 5 p35-37, 80-83.
       Mathematics for Life   Book C1 p3-15, 16-17, 18-19, 20-21, 22-23, 28-29, 32. Book C2 p28-31.
       Maths Matters   Book 2 p5.
       Mathsworks   Tryouts 1 p2-3, 4-5. Book 2 p44, 45.
                Tryouts 2 p23.
       Maths You Need   p12-18, 19-20, 21, 22, 23, 24, 70-71, 87.
       On Our Own Two Feet   Book 1 p10-22, 23-26, 27-29. Book 4 p21-23. Book 5 p13-14.
       Understanding Money   Book 1 p1-18. Book 2 p37-61.

Concept of profit, and relevant considerations for the self-employed e.g. growing vegetables for profit.

Bank and other accounts. Cheques and bank statements. Giro.

Saving money. Deposit accounts, building societies etc. Interest.

Borrowing money. Bank and other loans. Interest payable.

Buying outright as opposed to renting.

Hire purchase, mortgages, credit cards, mail order catalogues.

Gambling.

See also   M5,7   Addition and subtraction of money. Bills.
           M8   Multiplication and division of money. Unit pricing.
           M9,11,12   Percentage discounts and increases. VAT and other tax.
           M10   Travellers' cheques.
           N22,31,32   Operations on decimals.
           N23   Ratio, rate and proportion.
           N24   Percentages.
           N27,35   Directed numbers (overdrawn accounts, profit/loss).
           N38   Probability and gambling.
           A10   Area/profit relationships.
           T5   Daily, weekly, monthly.

P   *Beta (new ed.)*   Beta 4 p75. Beta 5 p7. Beta 6 p30.
      Hey Mathematics   Mod 5. Book 1 p16-18.
      Mathematics for Schools   Level 2 (1st ed.). Book 6 p64. Book 9 p29, 44-45, 46, 48.

S   *A World of Mathematics*   Book 6 p30-33.
      Focus Mathematics   Book 10 p34-38, 38-39, 41, 42-45.
      Headway Maths   Book 4 p66-67, 71-73. Book 5 p10-15, 30-34.
      Mathematics for Life   Book B3 p6-7. Book C1 p26-27. Book C2 p2-5, 6-7, 10-15, 24-27, 32. Book C3 p30-31.
      Maths (Holt)   4th Year p60-61, 64, 67.
                   5th Year p16-17, 20-21, 56-57, 91-93.
                   5th Year Workbook p2.
      Maths Matters   Book 2 p4-5, 10-11.
      Mathsworks   Book 1 p11, 14-15, 30-31. Tryouts 1 p39, 40.
                  Book 2 p42, 43, 46, 47. Tryouts 2 p24.
      Maths You Need   p9-11, 26-30, 31-33, 34-35, 54-55, 84-86.
      On Our Own Two Feet   Book 2 p1-15, 19-22.
                       Book 5 p5-12, 15-17, 22-23.
      Understanding Money   Book 1 p19-36, 46-47, 48-49, 49-52, 54-55.
                    Book 2 p1-6, 15-18, 62-68, 77-80.

SM   *Check it Again*   Book 3 p17-18.
       Problems   Third Problems p58, 60.

Place Value

Contents

Introduction to place value. Grouping experiences and number bases with two digits. PV1

Idea of place value of two digit numbers through experience grouping, exchanging and positioning everyday materials: e.g. 8 eggs ———→1 box and 2 eggs i.e. 12 in base 6.

Number bases with two digits and their notation.

Note that understanding of place value depends on left, right discrimination (See Sh4).

See also M10   Foreign currency.
           PV2   Place value base 10 to 99.
           PV3   Number bases with more than two digits.
           N12(2) Introduction to division.
           N14   Multibase arithmetic.
           VR8, L9   Use of varied scales.
           S3   Subsets. The complement of the set.
           T6   Seconds, minutes, etc. Grouping in 60's.
           T8   The calendar. Grouping in 7's.
           Imp.   Imperial units. Grouping in 12's, etc.

P   *Basic Mathematics*   Book 1 p20. Book 2 p55-56. Book 3 p33, 34. Book 5 p10-11.
     Hey Mathematics   Mod 1. Book 5 p7-25.
                       Mod 2. Book 2 p40. Book 5 p26-28.
     Key Maths   Level 1. Book 5 p5-8.
     Making Sure of Maths   Book 3 p72-73.
     Mathematics for Schools   Level 2 (1st ed.). Book 5 p1-2. Book 6 p64.
     Maths Adventure   1. Pupil's Book p14-15, 17. Activity Book p14-15.
     Nuffield Maths 5-11   2. Worksheets N8 2·1-2·4.
                         3. Pupils' Book p10-14.
     Our First School Maths   Book 6 p5-7.
     Oxford Middle School Mathematics   Book 1 p58, 60.
     Towards Mathematics   Core Unit 3 p11-14. Core Unit 7 p1.

S   *Focus Mathematics*   Book 9 p7-9.
     Maths (Holt)   Book 3 p19.

Books for teachers
    Mathematics: the first 3 years   p90, 119-121.
    Mathematics: the later Primary years   p1.
    Nuffield Maths 5-11   2. Teachers' Handbook p12-20.
                         3. Teachers' Handbook Chapter 3.

Place value to 100. PV2

Experience grouping in tens leading to an extension of the number line with meaningful symbols to 100.

Ordering numbers to 100 by size. Dot-to-dot pictures, etc.

The word form of numeral.

Approximations: rounding off numbers to the nearest ten or five.

Note that understanding of place value depends on left, right discrimination (See Sh4).

See also M2,4   Counting money to £1.
           PV1   Number bases with 2 digits.
           PV5   Tenths as decimals. Grouping in 10's.
           N12(2) Introduction to division.
           N13   Patterns and sequences to 100.
           VR1,2,3,4,8   Representing, comparing and ordering quantities to 100.
           VR8, L9   Use of scales 1:10.
           S3   Subsets. The complement of the set.
           Sh13, CV3,5,6, A3,4,6, L3,4, W3,5, T3,6,9, Temp, Imp.   Measuring and ordering quantity in arbitrary
                and standard units (to 100).
           L5,6   Converting millimetres to centimetres and vice versa.
           T7,10   Telling the time.
           T8   The calendar.
           Temp   The thermometer number line.

PV3 Number bases with more than two digits. Alternative number systems.

1. Number bases with more than two digits.

Idea of place value of three and more digit numbers through experience grouping, exchanging and positioning everyday materials and structured apparatus in different bases.

Notation of multibase numbers.

Conversion from one number base to another.

See also M10 Foreign currency.
    PV1 Number bases with 2 digits.
    PV4,7 Place Value base 10 over 99.
    N14 Multibase arithmetic.
    S3 Subsets. The complement of the set.

S   *A World of Mathematics*   Book 4 p57-59, 60.
       Focus Mathematics   Book 9 p10-17.
       Impact Maths   Pupil's Book 1 p28.
       Maths (Holt)   Workbook 2 p13. Book 3 p16-17, 27. Workbook 3 p11, 14.
                 4th Year p72-73. 5th Year p64-66.

SM   *Mathematics and Metric Measuring*   Book 4 p41-43.

Books for teachers
      Mathematics: the later Primary years   p1-2.

2. Alternative number systems.

Historical and foreign methods of counting and recording numbers: Roman, Babylonian, Egyptian, etc.

See also   T7   Clocks using Roman numerals.

P   *Basic Mathematics*   Book 1 p1, 52-53. Book 2 p10, 31, 53, 54. Book 3 p18, 19, 77, 78, 80.
                             Book 4 p4, 5, 101. Book 5 p9.
       Mathematics for Schools   Level 2 (2nd ed.) Book 1 p2-4.
       Maths Adventure   2. Pupil's Book p5. Activity Book p11.
                    4. Pupil's Book p85.

S   *A World of Mathematics*   Book 1 p14-16.
       Focus Mathematics   Book 3 p7-29.

SM   *Check it Again*   Book 5 p30-32.
       Four a Day series   Book 6 p14-15. Book 7 p35-36. Book 8 p30. Book 9 p17-18. Book 10 p17.
       Mathematics and Metric Measuring   Book 4 p3.
       Problems   Third Problems p56-57.

Books for teachers
      Mathematics: the first 3 years   p102.

Place value to 1,000.   PV4

Experience grouping in tens and hundreds, leading to an extension of the number line with meaningful symbols to 1,000.

Ordering numbers to 1,000 by size.

The word form of numeral.

Approximations: rounding off numbers to the nearest ten, fifty or hundred.

See also   M4   Counting money (over £1) without decimal notation.
           M6   Notation of pound. Grouping in 100's.
           PV3   Number bases with 3 digits.
           PV6   Hundredths as decimals. Grouping in 100's.
           VR8   Representing, comparing and ordering quantities to 1,000.
           VR8, L9   Use of scale 1:100.
           S3   Subsets. The complement of the set.
           Sh 13, CV5, L5, W5,10, T6   Measuring and ordering quantities in standard units to 1,000.
           CV7,8, A8, L5,6,12, W10   Converting measurements from one unit to another when exchange point is 100.
           T9   Centuries.

P   *Alpha (new ed.)*   Alpha 1 p47, 85.
       Beta (new ed.)   Beta 2 p27, 28. Beta 3 p4.
       Basic Mathematics   Book 1 p26-29, 30, 31, 34. Book 2 p2-3, 23, 64. Book 3 p1.
       Hey Mathematics   Mod 2. Book 1 p11, 17, 21. Book 2 p2, 25. Book 3 p32. Book 4 p38.
                       Mod 3. Book 1 p18, 21, 34. Book 2 p14.
                       Mod 5. Book 1 p5.
                       Mod 6. Book 2 p11.
       Key Maths   Level 2. Book 1 p6-14. Book 3 p3-6.
       Making Sure of Maths   Introductory Book p51-53.
                          Book 1 p10-13.
       Mathematics for Schools   Level 2 (1st ed.). Book 3 p7-11.
       Maths Adventure   1. Pupil's Book p83.
                    2. Pupil's Book p6, 8, 9. Activity Book p13.
                    3. Pupil's Book p8. Activity Book p5.
       Primary Mathematics (SPMG)   Stage 2. Workbook 1 p17-20.
       Towards Mathematics   Core Unit 3 p16.

S *Headway Maths* Book 2 p2.
Impact Maths Pupil's Book 1 p27.
Inner Ring Maths Book 1 p11, 12.
Maths (Holt) Workbook 1 p2-3.

SM *Check it Again* Book 3 p14-16. Book 4 p4-5.
Four a Day series Book 6 p9-14. Book 7 p15-16, 18. Book 8 p7-8. Book 9 p8.
Number Workbook Addition p12.
Problems Second Problems p16, 45.

PV5 Tenths as decimals.

Experience grouping everyday materials, structured apparatus, etc. leading to an understanding of the first decimal place.

Ordering numbers, expressed as decimals, by size.

Halves, tenths and fifths as decimals.

Understanding readings from stop watches, cyclometers, mileometers, etc.

Approximations: rounding off decimals to nearest whole number or point five.

See also   PV2   Place value to 100. Grouping in 10's.
  F2,3 Fractions. Equivalent fractions.
  S3   Subsets. The complement of of the set.
  L5,6 Converting millimetres to centimetres and vice versa using decimal notation. Measuring and ordering lengths expressed as decimals.

P   *Alpha (new ed.)* Alpha 1 p87-88. Alpha 2 p4-6.
Beta (new ed.) Beta 3 p49, 50.
Basic Mathematics Book 3 p7, 8.
Hey Mathematics Mod 3. Book 1 p3. Book 5 p7.
  Mod 4. Book 3 p12-14.
  Mod 6. Book 1 p15.
Key Maths Level 2. Book 5 p6-8. Book 6 p48.
Making Sure of Maths Book 1 p62-63. Book 2 p33-34. Book 3 p20.
Mathematics for Schools Level 2 (1st ed.) Book 4 p56-61. Book 6 p39.
Maths Adventure 2. Pupil's Book p65-66.
  3. Activity Book p50.
Oxford Middle School Mathematics Book 2 p48-49.
Primary Mathematics (SPMG) Stage 3 Textbook p81-82. Workbook p27.
  Stage 4 Textbook p28.
  Stage 5 Textbook p101.
Towards Mathematics Core Unit 9 p10, 11, 12, 13. Core Unit 13 p4.

S   *Headway Maths* Book 2 p66-67. Book 3 p39.
Impact Maths Pupil's Book 1 p48-49.
Mathematics for Life Book B1 p20-21.
Maths (Holt) Book 2 p85. Book 3 p38, 39.
Maths Matters Book 2 p13.

SM   *Four a Day series* Book 9 p46-48.
Number Workbook Decimals p4-5, 6, 8.

Books for teachers
  Mathematics: the later Primary years p127-135.

PV6 Hundredths as decimals.

Experience grouping structured apparatus and metric units of measurement leading to an understanding of the second decimal place.

Ordering numbers, expressed as decimals, by size.

The relationships between fractions and decimals of this order.

Understanding readings from meters.

Approximations: rounding off decimals to the nearest whole number, point five or point one.

See also   M6   Decimal notation of the pound.
            PV4   Place value to 1,000. Grouping in 100's.
            N24   Percentages.
            F2,3   Fractions. Equivalent fractions.
            S3   Subsets. The complement of the set.
            CV7,8, A8, L5,6,12, W10   Converting measurements from one unit to another using decimal notation when exchange point is 100. Measuring and ordering quantities expressed as decimals.

P   *Alpha (new ed.)*   Alpha 2 p68, 69, 70. Alpha 3 p4, 42.
      Beta (new ed.)   Beta 3 p71, 72. Beta 4 p6. Beta 6 p28, 29.
      Hey Mathematics   Mod 4. Book 1 p27-39. Book 2 p17-19. Book 3 p15-16. Book 4 p8-9.
                            Mod 6. Book 1 p16, 28. Book 2 p11.
      Key Maths   Level 2. Book 5 p11-13. Book 6 p49.
      Making Sure of Maths   Book 2 p40. Book 3 p21. Book 5 p26, 28.
      Mathematics for Schools   Level 2 (1st ed.). Book 6 p40-43.
      Maths Adventure   3. Pupil's Book p52.
                       4. Pupil's Book p32, 57.
                       5. Pupil's Book p32-33.
      Oxford Middle School Mathematics   Book 2 p58-59.
      Primary Mathematics (SPMG)   Stage 4 Textbook p29-32. Workbook p7. Card 26.
                                    Stage 5 Textbook p36, 48, 101.
      Towards Mathematics   Core Unit 14 p5, 6.

S   *A World of Mathematics*   Book 2 p17-19.
      Focus Mathematics   Book 4 p78-87.
      Headway Maths   Book 3 p40. Book 4 p28.
      Maths (Holt)   Book 3 p76. Workbook 3 p34.
      Maths Matters   Book 1 p28-29. Book 2 p12.
      Mathsworks   Tryouts 1 p9.
      Maths You Need   p45-46.

SM   *Four a Day series*   Book 9 p48-50, 51.
      Number Workbook   Decimals p10-13, 16, 18.
      Problems   Second Problems p46, 48.

Books for teachers
    Mathematics: the later Primary years   p85-89, 127-135.
    Mathematics: from Primary to Secondary   p23-24.

Thousands, millions, etc.   **PV7**

Experience grouping in hundreds and later thousands, leading to an understanding of place value of four and later more digit numbers.

Ordering numbers by size.

The word form of numeral.

Populations.

Reading and understanding meters (e.g. electricity).

Approximations: rounding off numbers to the nearest thousand, ten thousand, hundred thousand or million.

See also   M13   Cost of house, flat, etc.
            PV3   Number bases with 4 and more digits.
            PV8   Third and further decimal places. Grouping in 1,000's etc.
            N26   Expressing large numbers using powers.
            VR8   Representing, comparing and ordering quantities over 1,000.
            VR8, L9   Use of scale 1:1,000 etc.
            S3   Subsets. The complement of the set.
            CV7,8, A8, L5,6,12, W6,7,10   Converting measurements from one unit to another when exchange point is 1,000 or more.
            L12, T13   World and space distances.
            T9   Dates in history.

P   *Alpha (new ed.)*   Alpha 1 p85. Alpha 2 p4. Alpha 3 p5. Alpha 4 p4.
      Beta (new ed.)   Beta 3 p25, 26. Beta 4 p4-5. Beta 5 p1. Beta 6 p1-2, 85.
      Basic Mathematics   Book 2 p4-5, 8-9, 11, 36, 95. Book 3 p2, 3, 4, 5, 6, 9. Book 4 p1, 2, 3, 6, 7. Book 5 p3, 4, 5, 6.
      Hey Mathematics   Mod 3. Book 1 p15-16, 20, 24, 26. Book 2 p3, 10, 21. Book 3 p2, 3, 6, 8, 10, 23.
                            Book 4 p6, 7, 10, 13, 18, 21, 30, 31, 33.
                    Mod 4. Book 1 p2-6.
                    Mod 5. Book 1 p1, 5-6.
                    Mod 6. Book 2 p11.

Key Maths Level 2. Book 2 p1-3. Book 3 p7-12. Book 4 p1-3. Book 5 p1-5. Book 6 p1-8, 25.
Making Sure of Maths Book 2 p5-6.
Mathematics for Schools Level 2 (1st ed.) Book 5 p13-14. Book 9 p49.
Maths Adventure 2. Pupil's Book p7. Activity Book p15.
                  3. Activity Book p8, 20-21.
                  4. Pupil's Book p13.
Primary Mathematics (SPMG) Stage 2. Workbook 4 p21-23 Card 4.
                  Stage 3. Textbook p1.
                  Stage 4. Textbook p2-3.
                  Stage 5. Textbook p101.
Towards Mathematics Core Unit 7 p5.

S *A World of Mathematics* Book 1 p16-17, 25-28.
Impact Maths Pupil's Book 1 p26.
Inner Ring Maths Book 2 p6.
Maths (Holt) Book 1 p55. Book 2 p85.
Maths Matters Book 1 p30, 31. Book 2 p2-3.
Maths You Need p76, 81.

SM *Check it Again* Book 4 p5-6. Book 5 p3-5.
Four a Day series Book 7 p18-22. Book 8 p8-13, 14-15. Book 9 p9-17. Book 10 p8-14.
Mathematics and Metric Measuring Book 4 p8-10.
Problems Second Problems p17. Third Problems p4, 7.

Books for teachers
Mathematics: the later Primary years p168-173.

PV8 Third and further decimal places.

Experience grouping structured apparatus and metric units of measurement leading to the understanding of the third and later further decimal places.

Ordering numbers, expressed as decimals, by size.

The relationships between fractions and decimals of these orders. Recurring decimals e.g. $\frac{1}{3}$ as equivalent to $0 \cdot 33\overset{..}{3}$...

Approximations: rounding off decimals to the second or third decimal place.

See also PV7 Thousands, millions, etc. Grouping in 1,000's, etc.
F2,3 Fractions. Equivalent fractions.
S3 Subsets. The complement of the set.
CV7,8, A8, L5,6,12, W6,7,10 Converting measurements from one unit to another using decimal notation when exchange point is 1,000 or more. Measuring and ordering quantities expressed as decimals.

P *Alpha (new ed.)* Alpha 3 p42-44, 79. Alpha 4 p5.
Beta (new ed.) Beta 4 p35, 36. Beta 5 p1, 2, 33, 50, 87. Beta 6 p62.
Basic Mathematics Book 4 p40, 41, 66. Book 5 p40, 41, 42.
Hey Mathematics Mod 4. Book 4 p25-26.
                  Mod 6. Book 1 p16. Book 3 p1.
Key Maths Level 2. Book 5 p73. Book 6 p52-54.
Making Sure of Maths Book 4 p15.
Mathematics for Schools Level 2 (1st ed.). Book 7 p7-9. Book 8 p20-21. Book 9 p49, 50.
Maths Adventure 4. Pupil's Book p56, 59.
                  5. Pupil's Book p36.
Oxford Middle School Mathematics Book 3 p74.
Primary Mathematics (SPMG) Stage 5. Textbook p45, 101. Card 22.

S *A World of Mathematics* Book 3 p56. Book 5 p25, 27.
Headway Maths Book 3 p48.
Mathsworks Tryouts 1 p18, 19, 56.

SM *Check it Again* Book 5 p24-25.
Four a Day Series Book 9 p66-67. Book 10 p42-45, 48.
Number Workbook Decimals p24-25, 28, 29, 30, 31.

Books for teachers
Mathematics: from Primary to Secondary p24-26.

Number. Operations on number.

Contents

N20 Addition over 100.
 1. Exploration of patterns and methods.
 2. Practice.

N21 Subtraction over 100.
 1. Exploration of patterns and methods.
 2. Practice.

Addition and subtraction over 100. Applications, problems and mixed practice.

N22 Addition and subtraction of decimals.

N23 Introduction to ratio, rate and proportion.

N24 Percentages.

N25 Further number sequences and patterns.

N26 Powers idea and index notation.

N27 Introduction to directed numbers.

N28 The distributive law for multiplication.

N29 Multiplication of numbers over 100 by single digit numbers and 10.
 1. Exploration of patterns and methods.
 2. Practice.

N30 Division of numbers over 100 by single digit numbers and 10.
 1. Exploration of patterns and methods.
 2. Practice.

Multiplication and division over 100. Applications and problems.

Addition, subtraction, multiplication and division over 100. Mixed applications and problems.

N31 Multiplication of decimals.

N32 Division of decimals.

N33 Multiplication of two and more digit numbers by two and more digit numbers.
 1. Exploration of patterns and methods.
 2. Practice.

N34 Division of two and more digit numbers by two and more digit numbers.
 1. Exploration of patterns and methods.
 2. Practice.

N35 Operations on directed numbers.

N36 Statistics I Surveys and generalisations.

N37 Statistics II Average, mode and median.

N38 Statistics III Probability.
 1. Permutations and combinations.
 2. Investigating probability.

Topics with a sequence of development extending over considerable time.

28

One-to-one correspondence.

Comparison of the numbers of elements in two and later more sets, by matching each element in one set with an element in another.

Equivalent and non-equivalent sets.

Discussion, developing vocabulary: more, less, few, too many, enough, not enough, difference, as many as, the same number, etc.

Recording the number of elements in a set temporarily using counters, etc. (See VR1) and more permanently using pictures of the elements (See VR2), shapes of uniform size (See VR3) and tally marks.

See also N3   Numerals 0-9.
          N4,5   'More', 'less', 'same number' using number symbols.
          N7   'Difference' aspect of subtraction.
          S2   Relations between sets. The equivalent relation.
          L8   Plans and maps with one-to-one scale.

P   *Come and Count* Book 1 p1-9.
    Hey Mathematics Mod 1. Book 1 p1-6, 15-16, 19-21, 33-34. Book 2 p37. Book 3 p1, 37. Book 5 p5-6.
    Key Maths Level 1. Book 2 p19-29, 35-37. Book 3 p1-2.
    Making Sure of Maths Pink Book p2-3.
    Mathematics for Schools Level 1 (2nd ed.). Book 1 p47-60. Book 3 p4.
                         Level 2 (2nd ed.). Book 1 p1.
    Maths Adventure Kites 1 p9-23.
                  1. Activity Book p4.
    Nuffield Maths 5-11 Bronto Books Set A, Comparing with Bronto. Set B, Greedy Pig. Set C,
                My Dad's Garage. Set D, Bird has three eggs. Bronto at the fair.
                1. Worksheets N1. 1·1-1·4. N2. 1·1-1·2, 2·1-2·8, 3·1-3·2.
                3. Pupils' Book p11.
    Numbers and Words Book 1 p6-11, 28-29.
    Our First School Maths Book 1 p8-17.

SM *Four a Day series* Book 4 p1-5, 10.

Books for teachers
    Early Mathematical Experiences 'Water. Raw Materials'.
                         'Towards Number. Apparatus, Toys and Games' esp. p6-8.
                         'The Passage of Time. Rhymes and Stories' esp. p13-22.
                         'Home Corner. The Family'.
                         'Outdoor Activities. The Environment'.
                         'Space and Shape. Comparisons' esp. p22.
    Mathematics: the first 3 years p22-23, 24.
    Nuffield Maths 5-11 Notes at end of listed Bronto Books.
                1. Teachers' Handbook p14-25.

Oral counting 0-10.

Counting rhymes and number games e.g. Three little piggies went to market.

See also N1   One-to-one correspondence.
          VR1,2,3 Counting quantity represented visually.
          S1,3   Sorting and classifying.

P   *Hey Mathematics* Mod 1. Book 5 p1.
    Nuffield Maths 5-11 Bronto Books. Set B, Bronto joins the circus. Set D, Bird, Frog and Bronto.
                Bronto at the zoo.

Books for teachers
    Early Mathematical Experiences particularly — 'Towards Number. Apparatus, Toys and Games' p8-9.
                                      'The Passage of Time. Rhymes and Stories' p13-22.
                                        'Home Corner. The Family'.
                                        'Outdoor Activities. The Environment'.
    Mathematics: the first 3 years p35.
    Nuffield Maths 5-11 1. Teachers' Handbook p26-28.

N3 Numerals 0-9.

Recognition of the numerals 0, 1, 2, 3, 4, 5, 6, 7, 8 and 9, and use of these symbols for recording and labelling sets.

The word form of numeral.

See also M2 Recognition of coins.
N1 One-to-one correspondence.
N4,5 Conservation. Cardinal and ordinal number.
VR1,2,3 Counting quantity represented visually.
S1,3 Sorting and classifying. The empty set.

P *Ready for Alpha and Beta (new ed.)* p1-3.
Beta (new ed.) Beta 1 p4.
Come and Count Book 1 p16-24. Book 2 p2-5, 8, 22-24. Book 3 p2-9, 23.
Hey Mathematics Mod 1. Book 1 p22-25, 27, 35-40. Book 2 p11, 13-15, 29, 31, 38.
    Book 3 p31. Book 5 p3-4.
Key Maths Level 1. Book 2 p38-44. Book 3 p3-26. Book 4 p1-2. Book 5 p1-2.
Making Sure of Maths Pink Book p7-9, 12-15. Green Book p2-5, 8-9, 11-14. Yellow Book p2.
    Introductory Book p7-8.
Mathematics for Schools Level 1 (2nd ed.) Book 2. Book 3 p1-2, 5-6.
Maths Adventure Kites 2 p3-8, 15-16, 23.
Nuffield Maths 5-11 Bronto Books. Set A, Counting with Bronto. Counting Backwards.
    1. Worksheets N3 2·1-2·2, 2·4-2·11. 3·1-3·4, 4·1-4·4, S1. 1·4.
Numbers and Words Book 1 p14, 16-19, 22-27. Book 2 p1. Book 3 p6-8, 9-11, 14-17, 22. Book 4 p24.
Our First School Maths Book 1 p19-21, 23, 31-32. Book 2 p20-21.
Towards Mathematics Core Unit 1 p7.

SM *Check it Again* Book 1 p2.
Four a Day series Book 4 p6-9, 11, 14, 34. Book 5 p5-6.

Books for teachers
Mathematics: the first 3 years p35.
Nuffield Maths 5-11 1. Teachers' Handbook p28-37.

N4 Cardinal number. Conservation.

Cardinal number refers to an abstract concept of number e.g. the 'fiveness' of any set of five elements. Prior to this stage, five is only meaningful when describing a particular set of five elements.

Conservation of number (or invariance) refers to the understanding that number is independent of other attributes — shape, space, size i.e. the number of elements in a set does not change when they are spread or rearranged.

Extensive experience of equivalent sets may be necessary for the acquisition of these crucial concepts.

See also M2 Equivalent amounts.
N1 One-to-one correspondence — 'same number'.
N3 Numerals 0-9.
N10 Number bonds.
VR1,2,3,4. Visual representation of quantity.
S1,3 Sorting and classifying. The empty set.
S2 The equivalent relation.
Sh1,2 2D shapes; 'threeness' of sides of triangle, etc.
CV4, A5, L2, W4 Conservation.

P *Ready for Alpha and Beta (new ed.)* p3.
Come and Count Book 1 p10-13, 18-22. Book 2 p6-11. Book 3 p23, 24. Book 5 p2-3.
Hey Mathematics Mod 1. Book 1 p13-14, 32-33.
Key Maths Level 1. Book 2 p39, 41. Book 3 p2, 4, 7, 9, 10, 13, 15, 16, 18, 19, 21, 22.
Making Sure of Maths Pink Book p10-11. Green Book p6-7.
Mathematics for Schools Level 1 (2nd ed.) Book 2.
Maths Adventure Kites 2 p3-5.
Nuffield Maths 5-11 1. Worksheets N3. 2·3, 5·1-5·4. N4. 4·1.
Numbers and Words Book 1 p12-19, 21, 22, 26. Book 3 p6-8, 14-17. Book 4 p24.

SM *Four a Day series* Book 4 p10, 34. Book 5 p7.

Books for teachers
Early Mathematical Experiences 'Towards Number. Apparatus, Toys and Games' esp. p3, 9.
Mathematics: the first 3 years p23-24, 35-36, 38.
Nuffield Maths 5-11 1. Teachers' Handbook p38-40.

Ordinal number.

Ordinal number refers to the ordering and sequencing of numbers.

It has two aspects:
1. The idea of position — first, second, third . . . last;
2. The idea of position in relation to other numbers:
    e.g. 4 comes after 3 and before 5,
        7 is more than 4,
        3 is less than 5.

$>$ $<$ notation.

Number line 0-10 and later to 20. Counting forward and back on the number line.

Dot-to-dot exercises.

See also M2   Relationships between coins.
       N1   One-to-one correspondence — 'more than', 'less than', etc.
       N3   Numerals 0-9.
       N7   'Difference' aspect of subtraction.
       N8,9   Addition and subtraction on number line.
       AR1,2 Open sentences involving $>$ or $<$ relation.
       VR1,2,3,4   Ordering quantities represented visually.
       VR6, T1 Flow charts; sequencing events.
       S2   Relations between sets.
       Sh10, CV2, A2, L2, W2, T2   Ordering quantity without measuring units (e.g. 1st, 2nd, etc.).
       Sh12   Order of rotational symmetry.
       CV3,5, A3,6, L3,4, W3,5, T3,9   Comparing and ordering quantities using arbitrary or a single standard unit.
       T4   Observing movement of clock hands.
       T5,8   Days, months and the calendar.

P   *Alpha (new ed.)* Alpha 1 p4.
    Beta (new ed.) Beta 1 p13.
    Basic Mathematics Book 1 p2.
    Come and Count Book 2 p12-15, 18-21. Book 3 p10-22. Book 4 p14-17, 18-19.
    Hey Mathematics Mod 1. Book 1 p20-21, 26, 31. Book 2 p12, 16, 25, 33-35. Book 3 p9, 15, 32. Book 5 p2.
    Key Maths Level 1. Book 2 p12. Book 3 p27, 32-44. Book 4 p3.
    Making Sure of Maths Green Book p10, 15. Yellow Book p13.
    Mathematics for Schools Level 1 (2nd ed.) Book 2 p19-21, 41, 47, 60. Book 3 p3, 5-6.
                                Book 6 p15. Book 7 p30, 33, 35-38, 43.
    Maths Adventure Kites 2 p9-14, 17-22.
          1. Pupil's Book p5. Activity Book p4-5.
    Nuffield Maths 5-11 Bronto Books. Set A, Counting backwards. Set C, 3 buses. Set D, Bronto at the zoo.
          1. Worksheets N4 $1 \cdot 1$-$1 \cdot 2$, $2 \cdot 1$-$2 \cdot 6$, $3 \cdot 1$-$3 \cdot 4$, $4 \cdot 1$-$4 \cdot 4$.
          2. Worksheets N7. $2 \cdot 1$.
    Numbers and Words Book 1 p30-32. Book 2 p2, 27. Book 3 p9, 11-13, 18-19. Book 4 p11-12, 25. Book 8 p26.
    Our First School Maths Book 1 p18, 30-31. Book 2 p3. Book 4 p2-4. Book 5 p12-13.
    Towards Mathematics Core Unit 1 p1, 2, 5, 14, 15.

S   *Headway Maths* Book 1 p2-3.
    Mathematics for Life Book A1 p2-3.
    Maths (Holt) Book 2 p10. Workbook 3 p3.

SM *Check it Again* Book 1 p3-4, 27-28.
    Four a Day series Book 4 p12-13, 15-21. Book 5 p7-9.

Books for teachers
    Early Mathematical Experiences 'The Passage of Time. Rhymes and Stories' esp. p13-22.
                                       'Outdoor Activities. The Environment'.
                                     'Space and Shape. Comparisons'.
    Mathematics: the first 3 years p36-38.
    Nuffield Maths 5-11 1. Teachers' Handbook p42-55.

Introduction to addition.

Introduction to addition as the union (or combining) of two or more disjoint sets.

Discussion developing vocabulary: altogether, together makes, all, add on, etc.

Recording concrete examples using arrows and later the addition and equal signs.

See also N8   Addition to 20.
           F2   Adding simple fractions represented visually.
           VR1,2,3,4   Adding quantities represented visually.
           S2   Relations between sets; use of arrows and the equivalent relation (equals).
           S3   Disjoint subsets.

P   *Come and Count*   Book 4 p6-8. Book 5 p4.
    Hey Mathematics   Mod 1. Book 1 p28-30. Book 2 p1-2, 21, 23-24, 30, 32.
    Key Maths   Level 1. Book 3 p50, 56, 57. Book 4 p4-7, 12.
    Making Sure of Maths   Yellow Book p3-4, 7-8. Blue Book p2, 5. Introductory Book p5, 9-10.
    Mathematics for Schools   Level 1 (2nd ed.). Book 3 p10-11, 24-25, 37. Book 4 p9.
    Maths Adventure   Kites 3 p3-22.
    Nuffield Maths 5-11   1. Worksheets N5 $2 \cdot 1$-$2 \cdot 2$. N6 $4 \cdot 1$-$4 \cdot 2$. $5 \cdot 1$.
    Numbers and Words   Book 2 p3-4, 7-8. Book 3 p23, 25.
    Our First School Maths   Book 1 p24-25. Book 2 p2, 4-7, 10, 12, 30-31.

SM   *Four a Day series*   Book 5 p10-12.

Books for teachers
    Mathematics: the first 3 years   p41-42.
    Nuffield Maths 5-11   1. Teachers' Handbook p63-65, 69-74, 82-83.
                    2. Teachers' Handbook p2-3, 5-8.

N7   Introduction to subtraction.

Introduction to subtraction as
        1. the 'difference' between two numbers, and
        2. the partitioning of the universal set i.e. 'taking away'.

Discussion developing vocabulary: more than, less than, difference between, take away, left, etc.

Recording concrete examples using arrows and later the subtraction and equal signs.

See also N1   One-to-one correspondence; idea of 'difference'.
           N5   Ordinal number.
           N9   Subtraction to 20.
           F2   Subtracting simple fractions from 'whole', represented visually.
           VR1,2,3,4   Comparing and subtracting quantities represented visually.
           S2   Relations between sets; use of arrows and the equivalent relation (equals).
           S3   Partitioning the universal set into subsets.

P   *Come and Count*   Book 4 p9-11. Book 5 p5.
    Hey Mathematics   Mod 1. Book 3 p12-14, 16, 20.
    Key Maths   Level 1. Book 3 p57. Book 4 p29, 30, 32-33. Book 7 p1.
    Making Sure of Maths   Yellow Book p5, 9, 11-12. Blue Book p3-4. Introductory Book p6, 11-12.
    Mathematics for Schools   Level 1 (2nd ed.). Book 4 p14-18, 24-25.
    Maths Adventure   Kites 4 p3-14.
    Nuffield Maths 5-11   2. Worksheets N7 $1 \cdot 1$-$1 \cdot 4$, $3 \cdot 1$-$3 \cdot 2$, $4 \cdot 3$-$4 \cdot 4$. N10 $1 \cdot 1$-$1 \cdot 4$, $3 \cdot 1$-$3 \cdot 3$, $4 \cdot 1$-$4 \cdot 4$.
    Numbers and Words   Book 2 p15-16, 18-19, 26. Book 3 p27-29.
    Our First School Maths   Book 1 p24-25. Book 2 p2, 14-15.

S   *Maths (Holt)*   Workbook 1 p8-9.

SM   *Four a Day series*   Book 4 p43. Book 5 p15-17.

Books for teachers
    Mathematics: the first 3 years   p48-49.
    Nuffield Maths 5-11   2. Teachers' Handbook Chapter 4, and p42, 44-45.

N8   Addition to 20.

Abstract examples of addition to 10 and later 20. Use of abacus, counters, etc. to aid operations.

Recording by mapping (arrows), use of the addition and equals signs and the vertical form:

$$\text{e.g.} \quad (3,4) \xrightarrow{\text{add}} 7$$
$$3 + 4 \qquad\qquad = 7$$

$$\begin{array}{r} 3 \\ +\,4 \\ \hline 7 \\ \hline \end{array}$$

Addition by counting forward on the number line. Use of the equaliser.

The addition square with totals up to 20.

See also   p36   Applications, problems and mixed practice in addition and subtraction to 20.
             M3   Vertical form of addition in bills.
             PV2   Place value to 20.
             N5   Introduction to number line.
             N6   Introduction to addition.
             N11   Multiplication as repeated addition.
             VR1,2,3,4   Adding quantities represented visually.
             VR7   Coordinates — relates to use of addition square.
             S2   Relations between sets; use of arrows and the equivalent relation (equals).

P   *Alpha (new ed.)* Alpha 3 p7.
          Beta (new ed.) Beta 1 p6. Beta 2 p8.
          Basic Mathematics Book 1 p5, 8, 25, 48.
          Come and Count Book 4 p20-21, 24. Book 5 p22.
          Hey Mathematics Mod 1. Book 2, p6, 9-10, 18, 20, 22, 28. Book 3 p2, 6-7, 22, 33, 35, 38-39.
                             Book 4 p1, 10, 32. Book 5 p27.
                     Mod 2. Book 1 p2, 7, 8. Book 2 p2, 5, 8, 11, 15, 16, 19, 21, 26, 32. Book 3 p9, 14, 21, 23, 29.
                             Book 4 p37. Book 5 p12.
                     Mod 4. Book 1 p7-8.
          Key Maths Level 1. Book 3 p51-52, 54, 55. Book 4 p8-11, 13, 15, 22-23, 25, 31.
                             Book 6 p1, 3, 23-25, 31, 38, 39, 44. Book 7 p6.
                     Level 2. Book 1 p15, 25. Book 5 p17.
          Making Sure of Maths Introductory Book p18, 25.
                             Book 1 p5, 6.
          Mathematics for Schools Level 1 (2nd ed.) Book 3 p7-9, 12-14, 29, 40, 56-60. Book 4 p10-11, 13.
                             Book 5 p11-22, 33-34. Book 6 p13-14. Book 7 p54.
                     Level 2 (2nd ed.) Book 1 p5, 10.
          Maths Adventure Kites 3 p23. Kites 5 p16. Kites 7 p3, 8.
                             1. Pupil's Book p6-7, 13, 46-47. Activity Book p8-9, 13, 37.
          Nuffield Maths 5-11 1. Worksheets N5 3·1-3·2. N6 2·1-2·2, 3·3, 3·4, 5·2-5·4, 6·1.
                             2. Worksheets N8 3·3, 3·7, 3·8, 3·10. N9 1·5-1·6, 2·1, 3·1-3·4.
                             3. Pupils' Book p2, 3.
          Numbers and Words Book 2 p5, 9, 13. Book 3 p24, 26. Book 4 p2, 13, 30. Book 5 p24-26, 31.
                             Book 6 p9, 14. Book 7 p3, 5, 31-32. Book 8 p29.
          Our First School Maths Book 2 p13, 23-26, 28, 31. Book 3 p2-3, 10-11, 16. Book 4 p29.
          Primary Mathematics (SPMG) Stage 1. Workbook 1 p9, 12, 29, Card 1a, 2a, 2b.
                             Workbook 2 Card 1a, 1b.
                     Stage 2. Workbook 1 p2.
          Towards Mathematics Core Unit 1 p11, 14, 15.

S   *Headway Maths* Book 1 p4-5.
          Impact Maths Pupil's Book 1 p12-13.
          Inner Ring Maths Book 1 p10, 18, 19, 20. Book 3 p5.
          Maths (Holt) Book 1 p7, 29, 71. Workbook 1 p6.

SM   *Blackie's Practice Workbooks* Book 1 p1-2, 5-6, 13.
          Check it Again Book 1 p4-7, 13-14. Book 2 p5-7, 8, 13, 14. Book 3 p2.
          Four a Day series Book 4 p22-29, 35, 38-39, 41-42. Book 5 p13-15. Book 6 p15-16.
          Number Workbook Addition p8.

Books for teachers
          Mathematics: the first 3 years p46.
          Nuffield Maths 5-11 1. Teachers' Handbook p65-67, 75-79, 80-82, 83-85.
                             2. Teachers' Handbook p33-39.

Subtraction to 20.   N9

Abstract examples of subtraction from numbers not exceeding 10 and later 20. Use of abacus, counters, etc. to aid operations.

Recording by mapping (arrows), use of the subtraction and equals signs, and the vertical form:

$$\text{e.g.} \quad (7, 4) \xrightarrow{\text{difference}} 3$$

$$7 - 4 \qquad = 3$$

$$\begin{array}{r} 7 \\ -4 \\ \hline 3 \end{array}$$

Subtraction by counting back on the number line.

N10   Number bonds to 20. Patterns and relationships in addition and subtraction.

Partitioning equivalent sets in different ways

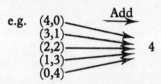

Number bonds to 10 and later 20.

Recognition of the commutative law for addition
e.g. $3 + 5 = 5 + 3$

the associative law for addition
e.g. $2 + 1 + 3 = 1 + 3 + 2$

the complementary nature of addition and subtraction
e.g. $3 + 5 = 8.$ So $8 - 5 = 3$ and $8 - 3 = 5.$

Patterns in addition and subtraction to 20 e.g. adding two odd numbers.

Introduction to box arithmetic (early algebraic relations)
e.g. $3 + \square = 5$
       $\square - 2 = 7$

See also M2   Different ways of making up a sum of money (to 20p).
         PV2   Place value to 20.
         PV1,2, N12   Grouping experiences.
         N4   Cardinal number and conservation.
         N8,9 Addition and subtraction to 20.
         N19   Complementary nature of multiplication and division. Commutativity and associativity of multiplication.
         AR1   Open sentences with one place holder.
         AR2   Open sentences with two place holders. Patterns.
         S2   Relations between sets; use of arrows and the equivalent relation.
         S3   Partitioning the universal set into subsets.

P   *Ready for Alpha and Beta (new ed.)* p5, 7, 12-14.
         Alpha (new ed.) Alpha 1 p6, 7.
         Beta (new ed.) Beta 1 p5, 6, 16, 17.
         Basic Mathematics Book 1 p6, 7, 10, 11, 12, 13, 17, 35, 62, 91. Book 2 p16.
         Come and Count Book 4 p12-13. Book 5 p7-8, 10-15. Book 6 p2.
         Hey Mathematics Mod 1. Book 2 p3-5, 7-8, 16-17, 19, 25. Book 3 p8, 24-29, 30, 32, 34, 36.
                           Book 4 p20. Book 5 p38.
                   Mod 2. Book 1 p4, 6, 16, 23-25, 26, 34-35. Book 2 p3, 6, 27, 28, 36, 37-38.
                           Book 3 p14, 27, 30, 32, 33. Book 4 p6, 15.
         Key Maths Level 1. Book 3 p48-49. Book 4 p14, 16-21, 24, 36, 38, 41. Book 5 p3.
                           Book 6 p12-13, 15-18, 21, 33, 36-37, 40-42, 44.
                   Level 2. Book 1 p16, 18, 23. Book 5 p20.
         Making Sure of Maths Blue Book p6-11, 16. Introductory Book p17, 20-21, 30.
                           Book 1 p8. Book 2 p9.
         Mathematics for Schools Level 1 (2nd ed.) Book 2 p55, 58. Book 3 p26-28, 38-39, 41-42, 54-55.
                           Book 4 p13, 19-23, 32-36. Book 5 p21-22, 43-45.
                           Book 6 p16-17, 18, 19-21, 22-23, 28-29. Book 7 p5-6, 13, 23, 46-49.
                   Level 2 (2nd ed.) Book 1 p7-9, 11, 13-14.
                   Level 2 (1st ed.) Book 9 p4.
         Maths Adventure Kites 4 p15-19. Kites 5 p22-23. Kites 7 p4-8, 12-13.
                   1. Pupil's Book p10-11, 27, 31-32, 37, 47, 62. Activity Book p10-11, 25-29, 35-37.
                   2. Pupil's Book p4. Activity Book p1-2, 8.
         Nuffield Maths 5-11 1. Worksheets N5 1·1-1·8. N6 1·1-1·8, 3·1-3·2, 3·3, 6·2.
                   2. Worksheets N9 1·1-1·4, 2·2-2·3, 2·4-2·5.
                   3. Pupils' Book p1, 2, 3, 4-5, 32, 33, 66.
         Numbers and Words Book 2 p11-12, 29-30. Book 3 p2-4. Book 4 p4-10, 18-19, 26, 29.
                           Book 6 p5-8, 13, 16-21, 22. Book 7 p8-10, 12-15, 18-22. Book 8 p6-7, 12-14.
         Our First School Maths Book 2 p11. Book 3 p12, 24.
         Oxford Middle School Mathematics Book 1 p10-11.
         Primary Mathematics (SPMG) Stage 1. Workbook 1 p2-3, 6, 12, 25-28, 30. Workbook 2 p19.
                           Stage 2. Workbook 1 p2, 5.
                           Stage 4. Card 13.
         Towards Mathematics Core Unit 1 p12. Core Unit 2 p11. Core Unit 8 p15.

S   *A World of Mathematics* Book 1 p32, 33.
         Impact Maths Pupil's Book 1 p8-9, 22, 40, 41, 61.
         Inner Ring Maths Book 1 p14, 29.
         Maths (Holt) Book 1 p8. Workbook 1 p5, 15-18. Book 2 p14. Book 3 p67.

SM   *Blackie's Practice Workbooks* Book 1 p11, 13, 15, 16, 21. Book 2 p1-2.
         Check it Again Book 1 p9-11. Book 2 p10-11.
         Four a Day series Book 4 p30-33, 36, 40. Book 5 p14, 22-24. Book 6 p18-19. Book 7 p22-23, 25.
         Number Workbook Addition p4. Subtraction p4, 7.
         Problems First Problems p13.

Books for teachers
         Mathematics: the first 3 years p46-47, 49-50, 118-119.
         Mathematics: the later Primary years p53.
         Nuffield Maths 5-11 1. Teachers' Handbook p57-62, 69-74, 80, 85-87.
                   2. Teachers' Handbook p29-33.
                   3. Teachers' Handbook Chapter 1.

Addition and subtraction to 20. Applications, problems and mixed practice.

1. *Applications and problems.*

See also   M2   Counting money to 20p. Different ways of making up a sum of money.
           M3   Shopping to 20p. Change. Bills.
           AR3   Introduction to, and use of 'variables'.
           VR1,2,3,4   Addition and subtraction arising from visual representation of quantities.
           CV3,5,6, A3,4,6, L3,4, W3,5, T3   Estimating quantity, measuring using arbitrary or a single standard unit and recording error.
           L7   Calculating perimeters, and lengths given the perimeter and other dimensions.
           T7,10,11   Simple calculations related to telling the time.
           T8   Simple problems related to the calendar.
           T9   Comparing children's ages, etc.
           T14   Calculating o'clock times in other countries given time differences. BST and GMT.

P   *Ready for Alpha and Beta (new ed.)*   p6, 15.
      Alpha (new ed.)   Alpha 1 p6.
      Beta (new ed.)   Beta 1 p6, 7, 61.
      Hey Mathematics   Mod 1. Book 3 p4-5, 12-13
                         Mod 2. Book 3 p9.
      Key Maths   Level 1. Book 6 p26, 29-30, 45.
                Level 2. Book 1 p20.
      Making Sure of Maths   Book 1 p9.
      Maths Adventure   1. Pupil's Book p48, 76, 77.
      Numbers and Words   Book 8 p28.
      Primary Mathematics (SPMG)   Stage 1. Workbook 1 Card 3a, 3b. Workbook 2 Card 3a, 3b.

S   *Headway Maths*   Book 1 p6, 15.
      Mathematics for Life   Book A1 p8-9. Book A2 p2-7.
      Maths (Holt)   Book 1 p6.

SM   *Blackie's Practice Workbooks*   Book 1 p9-10, 27. Book 2 p9-10.
      Check it Again   Book 1 p12, 15. Book 2 p11-12.
      Problems   First Problems p1-2, 4-7.

2. *Mixed practice in addition and subtraction. Estimating answers and approximations.*

P   *Ready for Alpha and Beta (new ed.)*   p4-5.
      Alpha (new ed.)   Alpha 1 p6. Alpha 2 p12. Alpha 4 p8.
      Beta (new ed.)   Beta 1 p8, 12, 61.
      Hey Mathematics   Mod 1. Book 3 p21, 24. Book 4 p2, 8, 19, 20, 21. Book 5 p28, 29.
                         Mod 2. Book 2 p19. Book 3 p31. Book 4 p7.
      Key Maths   Level 1. Book 4 p37, 39, 40, 41. Book 6 p22, 34, 50.
                Level 2. Book 1 p21.
      Making Sure of Maths   Yellow Book p15-16. Blue Book p15.
                         Introductory Book p13, 16, 17, 26, 33.
      Mathematics for Schools   Level 1 (2nd ed.) Book 7 p31-34.
                         Level 2 (2nd ed.) Book 1 p6.
      Maths Adventure   Kites 5 p20-21.
                1. Pupil's Book p33.
      Nuffield Maths 5-11   3. Pupils' Book p36.
      Numbers and Words   Book 2 p20, 31. Book 3 p32. Book 5 p1. Book 6 p1, 26. Book 7 p7, 27. Book 8 p4-5.
      Primary Mathematics (SPMG)   Stage 1. Workbook 1 p11.
      Towards Mathematics   Core Unit 13 p13.

S   *Maths Matters*   Book 3 p14.

SM   *Blackie's Practice Workbooks*   Book 2 p15-16.
       Four a Day series   Book 4 p37. Book 6 p20.

Introduction to multiplication as repeated addition leading to the idea of 'sets of':
  e.g. bicycles: 5 sets of 2 wheels make 10 wheels altogether.

Repeated addition using the number line.

Recording concrete and number line examples by mapping number pairs and use of the multiplication and equals signs:
  e.g. $5(2) \longrightarrow 10$
    $5 \times 2 \qquad = 10$

See also M3,8 Calculating price of several identical items by repeated addition.
    N8   Addition to 20. Use of number line.
    N13   Patterns and sequences to 100.
    N17   Multiplication of single digit numbers.
    S2   Relations between sets; use of arrows and the equivalent relation (equals).

P *Beta (new ed.)* Beta 1 p34, 44, 53, 64.
  Basic Mathematics Book 1 p41-42, 44.
  Come and Count Book 6 p14-19.
  Hey Mathematics Mod 1. Book 3 p10-11, 18.
      Mod 2. Book 3 p6, 13, 16, 38-40. Book 4 p12, 24. Book 5 p6.
  Key Maths Level 1. Book 7 p32-41.
      Level 2. Book 2 p10-12. Book 3 p33, 34.
  Making Sure of Maths Blue Book p14.
      Introductory Book p31-32.
  Mathematics for Schools Level 1 (2nd ed.) Book 5 p46-54. Book 6 p32-34.
      Level 2 (2nd ed.) Book 1 p37.
  Maths Adventure Kites 6 p3-15. Kites 7 p14-17, 21-23.
      1. Pupil's Book p19, 64-68, 90. Activity Book p42, 44.
  Nuffield Maths 5-11 1. Worksheets N6 2·3-2·4.
      2. Worksheets N9 2·6. N11 1·1-1·2, 2·1-2·6.
      3. Pupils' Book p42-43.
  Numbers and Words Book 4 p31, 32. Book 7 p29, 30. Book 8 p18-19.
  Our First School Maths Book 4 p22-23. Book 6 p23.
  Oxford Middle School Mathematics Book 1 p16-17.
  Primary Mathematics (SPMG) Stage 1. Workbook 2 p2-4. Workbook 4 p2-5, 8.
      Stage 2. Workbook 2 p2-3.

S *A World of Mathematics* Book 2 p9.
  Headway Maths Book 1 p14, 20, 38-39.

SM *Four a Day series* Book 5 p47-51. Book 6 p23. Book 7 p29, 30.
  Book 8 p21-22. Book 9 p24-26.

Books for teachers
  Mathematics: the first 3 years p50-51, 90, 113.
  Nuffield Maths 5-11 2. Teachers' Handbook p49-54.
      3. Teachers' Handbook p57-59.

1. *Equal sharing* i.e. number of subsets known.

Sharing the members of a set equally between a known number of subsets.

Recording concrete examples by mapping, the fractional form and the division and equals signs:
  e.g. Share 6 sweets equally between 2 children.

  $\dfrac{6}{2} \longrightarrow 3$

  $6 \div 2 \qquad = 3$

See also N18 Division to 100.
    F1,2 Fractions and fraction notation. Finding a simple fraction of a whole number.
    S2   Relations between sets; use of arrows and the equivalent relation (equals).
    S3   Partitioning the universal set into subsets.

P   *Come and Count* Book 6 p20-23.
       Hey Mathematics Mod 2. Book 1 p19. Book 5 p22-24
                          Mod 3. Book 1 p31.
                          Mod 4. Book 2 p31-32.
       Key Maths Level 1 Book 7 p48.
                  Level 2 Book 2 p22.
       Mathematics for Schools Level 1 (2nd ed.) Book 6 p1-5. Book 7 p9-12, 15.
                              Level 2 (2nd ed.) Book 1 p52.
                              Level 2 (1st ed.) Book 4 p29.
       Maths Adventure Kites 6 p16-23. Kites 7 p18-19.
                        1. Pupil's Book p92.
       Nuffield Maths 5-11 2. Worksheets N11 1·2. N12 1·1, 1·3.
                        3. Pupils' Book p54-55.
       Numbers and Words Book 4 p31. Book 7 p29. Book 8 p22-23.
       Oxford Middle School Mathematics Book 1 p25, 26.
       Primary Mathematics (SPMG) Stage 2. Workbook 3 p8.
       Towards Mathematics Core Unit 2 p12.

S   *Headway Maths* Book 1 p14, 20, 21.

Books for teachers
     Mathematics: the first 3 years p89-90.
     Mathematics: the later Primary years p81.
     Nuffield Maths 5-11 2. Teachers' Handbook p62-65.
                        3. Teachers' Handbook Chapter 12.

2. *Grouping to find factors* i.e. size of subset known.

Partitioning a set into subsets of known size.

Recording concrete examples using arrows, the fractional form and the division and equals signs:
     e.g. I have 6 sweets. How many children can have 2 each?

$$\frac{6}{2} \longrightarrow 3$$

$$6 \div 2 \qquad = 3$$

Division as repeated subtraction. Use of number line to divide.

See also PV1,2 Grouping experiences.
           N9   Subtraction to 20. Use of number line.
           N13   Patterns and sequences to 100
           and topics listed for N12(1).

P   *Basic Mathematics* Book 1 p40.
       Come and Count Book 5 p18-20. Book 6 p23.
       Hey Mathematics Mod 2. Book 5 p26-28, 30.
       Key Maths Level 1 Book 5 p4. Book 7 p30-31.
       Mathematics for Schools Level 1 (2nd ed.) Book 5 p6-10. Book 7 p7-8.
                              Level 2 (2nd ed.) Book 1 p54.
       Nuffield Maths 5-11 2. Worksheets N10 2·1-2·2. N12 1·2, 2·1-2·4.
                        3. Pupils' Book p55, 56-57.
       Numbers and Words Book 4 p32. Book 7 p30. Book 8 p20-21.
       Our First School Maths Book 4 p21. Book 6 p5-7, 22.
       Oxford Middle School Mathematics Book 1 p24, 25, 26.
       Primary Mathematics (SPMG) Stage 2. Workbook 3 p7.
       Towards Mathematics Core Unit 2 p10, 12.

S   *Headway Maths* Book 1 p16, 20.
       Impact Maths Pupil's Book 1 p53.

SM   *Four a Day series* Book 5 p52-53.

Books for teachers
     Hey Mathematics Mod 3. Teachers' Book p26-27.
     Mathematics: the first 3 years p90.
     Mathematics: the later Primary years p81.
     Nuffield Maths 5-11 2. Teachers' Handbook p62-63, 65-68.
                        3. Teachers' Handbook Chapter 12.

Patterns and sequences to 100.

Exploration of sequences, patterns and relationships using the 100 number square and number line:
e.g.   odd and even numbers,
       finding numbers that end in 4,
       finding numbers in the third row of number square,
       patterns of fives, tens etc.
       finding the next number in a series.

Arrays using counters, etc.
       square numbers: 1, 4, 9, 16, etc.
       rectangular numbers i.e. all except 1 and prime numbers.
       triangular numbers: 1, 3, 6, 10, etc.

Introduction to permutations (see also N38(1)).

See also   PV2   Place value to 100.
       N8,9,15,16   Addition and subtraction to 100. Patterns.
       N11,12   Multiplication as repeated addition. Division as repeated subtraction.
       N19(3)   Patterns in multiplication and division.
       N26   Square numbers; powers idea and index notation.
       VR7   Coordinates — relates to use of number square.
       Sh2   Square, rectangle and triangle.
       Sh17   Similarity, enlargement and reduction.

P   *Ready for Alpha and Beta (new ed.)*   p19, 26.
    Beta (new ed.)   Beta 1 p36. Beta 2 p5.
    Basic Mathematics   Book 1 p3-4, 18-19. Book 2 p38. Book 4 p85-90.
    Come and Count   Book 4 p18. Book 6 p1.
    Hey Mathematics   Mod 1. Book 2 p36. Book 4 p8-10, 24.
            Mod 2. Book 1 p2, 4, 8. Book 3 p20. Book 5 p1.
            Mod 3. Book 5 p15, 20.
            Mod 5. Book 5 p13, 15-16, 22.
    Key Maths   Level 1 Book 5 p51-52. Book 6 p14. Book 7 p5, 28-29.
    Making Sure of Maths   Book 1 p88, 90. Book 2 p22-23. Book 3 p74-76.
    Mathematics for Schools   Level 1 (2nd ed.) Book 2 p22-30, 35, 46. Book 4 p59.
                        Book 5 p9-11, 23-25. Book 6 p49.
            Level 2 (2nd ed.) Book 1 p12.
            Level 2 (1st ed.) Book 3 p59-62. Book 6 p35-38, 55. Book 7 p58-59, 60. Book 8 p27.
    Maths Adventure   1. Pupil's Book p7, 19, 45, 63, 89. Activity Book p54.
            2. Pupil's Book p22, 32, 73 Card 23.
            4. Pupil's Book p16, 63. Activity Book p20-21.
    Nuffield Maths 5-11   3. Pupils' Book p78.
    Numbers and Words   Book 7 p2. Book 8 p31-32.
    Our First School Maths   Book 3 p18-19, 32. Book 4 p9-10. Book 6 p8, 10, 32.
    Oxford Middle School Mathematics   Book 1 p42-43. Book 2 p8-9, 88-89. Book 3 p5.
    Primary Mathematics (SPMG)   Stage 2. Workbook 2 p20, Card 3a, 3b.
                        Stage 3. Card 36, 37.
    Towards Mathematics   Core Unit 1 p8. Core Unit 2 p1-3.
                 Core Unit 12 p12-16.

S   *A World of Mathematics*   Book 1 p40-41. Book 2 p14, 40-41.
    Focus Mathematics   Book 1 p26-29. Book 4 p7-13.
    Headway Maths   Book 1 p16, 45.
    Mathematics for Life   Book A1 p2-3.
    Maths (Holt)   Book 1 p86, 89. Workbook 1 p46. Book 2 p7, 92. Book 3 p10-11.
            Workbook 3 p16. 4th Year p28-29. 5th Year Workbook p45.
    Mathsworks   Book 1 p32-33.

SM   *Check it Again*   Book 4 p14-15. Book 5 p8-9.
    Four a Day series   Book 9 p34.
    Problems   Second Problems p3, 61.

Books for teachers
    Mathematics: the first 3 years   p55-59, 112-113, 115-117.
    Mathematics: the later Primary years   p77-80, 83-84.
    Nuffield Maths 5-11   3. Teachers' Handbook p104.

N14 Multibase arithmetic.

Operations on numbers expressed in bases other than base ten. Exploration of addition, subtraction, multiplication and division involving two and later more digit numbers, when the place value of these numbers is understood.

Experience of operations in bases other than base ten may promote a deeper understanding of operations in base ten, and could usefully take place alongside N15, 16, 17, 18, 20, 21, 22, 29, 30, 31, 32, 33 and 34.

See also   M10   Foreign currency.
           PV1,3   Number bases.
           T6,7,10,11,12   Operations in base 60.
           T8   The calendar. Operations in base 7.
           Imp.   Operations using imperial units.

P   *Mathematics for Schools*   Level 2 (1st ed.) Book 5 p3-6.
      Maths Adventure   3. Pupil's Book p45, 56.
                          4. Activity Book p18-19.
                          5. Pupil's Book p47-48.
      Oxford Middle School Mathematics   Book 1 p70-72, 80-82.
      Towards Mathematics   Core Unit 7 p6. Core Unit 11 p2-5, 8-9.
                              Core Unit 16 p5.

S.   *A World of Mathematics*   Book 4 p59.
      Focus Mathematics   Book 9 p17-26.
      Maths (Holt)   Book 3 p28.

SM   *Mathematics and Metric Measuring*   Book 4 p44-47.

Books for teachers
      Mathematics: the later Primary years   p2-4.

N15 Addition to 100.

1. *Exploration of patterns in addition and methods of adding numbers.*

Construction and use of addition square.

Patterns in addition explored:
         Number bonds to 100. Magic squares.
         Adding 10 and multiples of 10 to a number.
         Adding 9 as equivalent to adding 10 and subtracting 1.
         Adding 11 as equivalent to adding 10 and adding 1.
         Adding odd/even numbers.
         4 + 8, 14 + 8, 24 + 8 etc., and similar patterns.

Methods of adding numbers investigated.
         Initially numbers counted on using a number square, abacus, etc. but gradually more efficient methods investigated:

e.g.   26 + 45   20 + 6
                    40 + 5
                    $\overline{60 + 11}$ = 71

Use of the addition square and a calculator allows patterns and methods to be investigated without the interference of routine manipulations.

See also   M4   Different ways of making up a sum of money (to £1).
           PV2   Place value to 100.
           N8   Addition to 20.
           N10   Number bonds to 20. Commutativity and associativity.
           N13   Sequences, patterns and relationships to 100.
           N14   Multibase arithmetic.
           N20   Addition over 100.
           AR1,2   Open sentences with one or two place-holders. Patterns.
           VR7   Coordinates — relate to use of addition square.

P   *Ready for Alpha and Beta (new ed.)*   p20.
      Alpha (new ed.)   Alpha 1 p18.
      Beta (new ed.)   Beta 2 p10.
      Basic Mathematics   Book 1 p50, 54.
      Come and Count   Book 6 p3, 8.

Hey Mathematics   Mod 1. Book 4 p13-17, 22, 25-27, 33-34, 36-40.
                     Mod 2. Book 1 p5. Book 3 p1, 3, 25, 36-37. Book 4 p2, 3, 5, 21, 25, 28.
                     Mod 3. Book 1 p28, 30.
                     Mod 5. Book 5 p4-6.
Key Maths   Level 1. Book 5 p36, 39, 46. Book 6 p10. Book 7 p7-8, 12, 14-17, 21.
               Level 2. Book 1 p26, 33-34, 42-45. Book 2 p6. Book 3 p16, 17.
Making Sure of Maths   Introductory Book p54-55.
                         Book 1 p14, 15, 20. Book 2 p7, 19.
Mathematics for Schools   Level 1 (2nd ed.) Book 4 p58-59. Book 6 p50-53.
                            Level 2 (2nd ed.) Book 1 p24-31.
                            Level 2 (1st ed.) Book 3 p6, 59.
Maths Adventure   Kites 5 p13-15.
                     1. Pupil's Book p49-51, 86. Activity Book p38.
                     2. Pupil's Book p12-13. Activity Book p9.
                     3. Activity Book p1.
Nuffield Maths 5-11   3. Pupils' Book p20-23.
Our First School Maths   Book 4 p30. Book 5 p2, 4-5. Book 6 p3.
Oxford Middle School Mathematics   Book 1 p50-51, 75.
Primary Mathematics (SPMG)   Stage 1. Workbook 2 p15-16, 18, 20, Card 4, 6a, 6b.
                               Stage 2. Workbook 1. Card 6a. Workbook 4, Card 3.
                               Stage 4. Card 14.
Towards Mathematics   Core Unit 1 p13. Core Unit 2 p14-15.

S   *A World of Mathematics*   Book 1 p34.
         Focus Mathematics   Book 1 p20-24.
         Headway Maths   Book 1 p26, 28.
         Impact Maths   Pupil's Book 1 p7, 10-11, 14, 15, 16, 62.
         Inner Ring Maths   Book 3 p3.
         Maths (Holt)   Book 1 p14, 18, 24, 39, 90. Workbook 1 p18,39. Workbook 2 p18.
                          Workbook 3 p23. 4th Year p79, 82-83.

SM   *Check it Again*   Book 4 p6-7.
          Four a Day series   Book 5 p39, 43-44. Book 8 p16. Book 10 p21.
          Number Workbook   Addition p16, 17.

Books for teachers
     Hey Mathematics   Mod 3 Teachers's Book p7-8, 9-12.
     Mathematics: the first 3 years   p114-117.
     Mathematics: the later Primary years   p4-6, 24-26, 53-58.
     Nuffield Maths 5-11   3. Teachers' Handbook Chapter 5.

2.   Practice in addition. Estimating answers and approximations.

See also   p43   Applications, problems and mixed practice in addition and subtraction to 100.
            p49   Mixed applications and problems in addition, subtraction, multiplication and division to 100.

P   *Alpha (new ed.)*   Alpha 1 p19, 25. Alpha 3 p7.
         Beta (new ed.)   Beta 1 p70, 71, 95. Beta 2 p15. Beta 3 p5.
         Basic Mathematics   Book 1 p73.
         Hey Mathematics   Mod 1. Book 4 p35.
                             Mod 2. Book 1 p10, 15, 30, 31, 32. Book 2 p24.
                                    Book 3 p5, 7, 17, 34, 35. Book 4 p7, 30, 33.
                             Mod 3. Book 1 p38.
                             Mod 4. Book 1 p9.
                             Mod 5. Book 3 p21.
         Key Maths   Level 1. Book 7 p22, 26.
                       Level 2. Book 1 p36, 46. Book 3 p16, 17.
         Making Sure of Maths   Book 1 p17.
         Mathematics for Schools   Level 1 (2nd ed.) Book 4 p60.
         Nuffield Maths 5-11   3. Pupils' Book p24.
         Oxford Middle School Mathematics   Book 1 p65-66.
         Primary Mathematics (SPMG)   Stage 1. Workbook 2 p17, 21, Card 7a, 7b. Workbook 3 p7.

S   *Headway Maths*   Book 1 p27, 29, 47.
         Impact Maths   Pupil's Book 1 p14.
         Maths (Holt)   Workbook 1 p19.

SM   *Blackie's Practice Workbooks*   Book 1 p12, 17. Book 2 p11, 12, 17-18, 27-28. Book 3 p2, 3. Book 5 p20.
         Check it Again   Book 3 p4.
         Four a Day series   Book 6 p9, 22. Book 7 p13.
         Number Workbook   Addition p6-7, 9-11.

N16 Subtraction to 100.

1. Exploration of patterns in subtraction and methods of subtracting numbers.

Construction and use of subtraction square. Use of the addition square to subtract.

Patterns in subtraction explored:
Subtracting 10 and multiples of 10 from a number.
Subtracting 9 as equivalent to subtracting 10 and adding 1.
Subtracting 11 as equivalent to subtracting 10 and subtracting 1.
64 – 5, 54 – 5, 44 – 5, etc. and similar patterns.

Methods of subtracting numbers investigated.
Initially numbers counted back using a number square, abacus, etc., but gradually more efficient methods investigated:

e.g. (a) Complementary addition i.e. adding to the smaller number till the bigger number is reached:

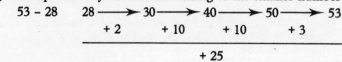

53 – 28

So 53 – 28 = 25

(b) Decomposition

$$53 - 28 \quad \begin{array}{r} 50 + 3 \\ - 20 + 8 \\ \hline \end{array} \longrightarrow \begin{array}{r} 40 + 13 \\ - 20 + 8 \\ \hline 20 + 5 \\ \hline \end{array}$$

So 53 – 28 = 25

(c) Equal addition

$$53 - 28 \quad \begin{array}{r} 53 + 2 \\ - 28 + 2 \\ \hline \end{array} \longrightarrow \begin{array}{r} 55 \\ - 30 \\ \hline 25 \\ \hline \end{array}$$

So 53 – 28 = 25

Use of the subtraction square and a calculator allows patterns and methods to be investigated without the interference of routine manipulations.

See also PV2 Place value to 100.
N9 Subtraction to 20.
N10 Number bonds to 20. Complementary nature of addition and subtraction.
N13 Sequences, patterns and relationships to 100.
N14 Multibase arithmetic.
N15(1) Number bonds to 100. Addition square.
N21 Subtraction over 100.
AR1,2 Open sentences with one or two place-holders. Patterns.
VR7 Coordinates: relate to use of addition and subtraction squares.

P   *Alpha (new ed.)*   Alpha 1 p18.
Beta (new ed.)   Beta 1 p72, 73. Beta 2 p10.
Basic Mathematics   Book 1 p51.
Hey Mathematics   Mod 1. Book 4 p15, 16, 22, 25.
Mod 2. Book 1 p6. Book 4 p22, 30.
Mod 3. Book 5 p3.
Key Maths   Level 1. Book 5 p37-38, 40. Book 7 p9-10, 13, 14, 16, 17, 19, 20.
Level 2. Book 1 p35, 47, 48. Book 2 p7, 9. Book 3 p22.
Mathematics for Schools   Level 2 (2nd ed.) Book 2 p5-13.
Level 2 (1st ed.) Book 3 p26.
Maths Adventure   Kites 5 p19.
1. Pupil's Book p78-79, 87.
2. Pupil's Book p13.
Nuffield Maths 5-11   3. Pupils' Book p35, 67-70.
Primary Mathematics (SPMG)   Stage 1. Workbook 2 p15-16, Card 6a, 6b. Workbook 3 p3-5.
Stage 2. Workbook 1 p7, Card 3a, 3b. Workbook 4, Card 2a.
Towards Mathematics   Core Unit 12 p5, 6, 7, 8. Core Unit 19 p5.

S   *A World of Mathematics*   Book 3 p34.
Headway Maths   Book 1 p31-32.
Impact Maths   Pupil's Book 1 p18, 20-21.
Maths (Holt)   Book 1 p15. Workbook 1 p18, 39.

SM *Check it Again* Book 4 p7-8.
Four a Day series Book 5 p40, 44-45.
Number Workbook Subtraction p11-12, 20, 21.

Books for teachers
Hey Mathematics Mod 3. Teachers' Book p13-15, 16-17.
Mathematics: the later Primary years p60-63.
Nuffield Maths 5-11 3. Teachers' Handbook Chapter 15.

2. Practice in subtraction. Estimating answers and approximations.

See also p43 Applications, problems and mixed practice in addition and subtraction to 100.
p49 Mixed applications and problems in addition, subtraction, multiplication and division to 100.

P *Ready for Alpha and Beta (new ed.)* p20.
Alpha (new ed.) Alpha 1 p20, 25. Alpha 3 p8.
Beta (new ed.) Beta 1 p72, 73, 95. Beta 2 p15. Beta 4 p12.
Basic Mathematics Book 1 p49, 55, 73.
Hey Mathematics Mod 2. Book 1 p10, 29, 33. Book 3 p10, 34. Book 4 p31.
Mod 3. Book 1 p34. Book 2 p12.
Mod 5. Book 1 p15.
Key Maths Level 1. Book 7 p23.
Level 2. Book 1 p36, 49. Book 2 p8.
Making Sure of Maths Book 1 p19.
Maths Adventure 1. Pupil's Book p33, 35.
3. Pupil's Book p10.
Primary Mathematics (SPMG) Stage 1. Workbook 3, Card 1a, 1b, 2a, 2b.

S *A World of Mathematics* Book 1 p46, 47.
Headway Maths Book 1 p30, 33, 47. Book 2 p3.
Impact Maths Pupil's Book 1 p19, 24.

SM *Blackie's Practice Workbooks* Book 1 p18. Book 2 p11, 12, 19-20, 23-26. Book 3 p4-5. Book 5 p20.
Check it Again Book 3 p4.
Four a Day series Book 6 p22. Book 7 p25.
Number Workbook Subtraction p2, 5-6, 8-10.

Addition and subtraction to 100. Applications, problems and mixed practice. **N15**

1. Applications and problems.

See also p49 Mixed applications and problems in addition, subtraction, multiplication and division to 100.
M4 Counting money to £1. Different ways of making up a sum of money.
M5 Shopping to £1. Change. Bills.
N24 Addition and subtraction of percentages.
AR3 Introduction to and use of 'variables'.
AR8 Algebraic solution of simple equations.
VR1,2,3,4,8 Addition and subtraction arising from visual representation of quantities.
CV3,5,6, A3,4,6, L3,4, W3,5, T3,6 Estimating quantity, measuring using arbitrary or a single standard
unit and recording error.
CV7, A8, L5, W6, T6 Addition and subtraction of metric units.
CV10, A10, L10, W8, T12, Temp. Problems and applications relating to measurement.
L7 Calculating perimeters, and lengths given the perimeter and other dimensions.
W7 Weighing liquids.
W8 Net and gross. Wet and dry weights.
W9 Weighing objects in water and air.
T7,10,11 Calculations relating to telling the time, timetables, etc.
T8 Problems relating to the calendar.
T9 Problems relating to ages of children and adults.

P *Alpha (new ed.)* Alpha 1 p26.
Beta (new ed.) Beta 2 p16.
Basic Mathematics Book 1 p76.
Hey Mathematics Mod 2. Book 1 p30. Book 2 p17.
　　　　　　　　Mod 3. Book 2 p22. Book 5 p13.
Key Maths Level 2. Book 1 p22, 37, 50-51.
Making Sure of Maths Book 1 p9, 18-19.
Mathematics for Schools Level 2 (1st ed.) Book 3 p6.
Maths Adventure 1. Pupil's Book p77.
Nuffield Maths 5-11 3. Pupils' Book p71.
Oxford Middle School Mathematics Book 1 p67.
Primary Mathematics (SPMG) Stage 1. Workbook 2 Card 5a, 5b, 8a, 8b, 9a.
　　　　　　　　　　　　　　　Workbook 3 p6, Card 3a, 3b, 4a.
　　　　　　　　　　Stage 2. Workbook 1 p8-9, Card 1a, 1b, 5.

S *A World of Mathematics* Book 6 p48.
Headway Maths Book 1 p6, 34, 46.
Mathematics for Life Book A1 p8-9. Book A2 p24, 26. Book B1 p4, 8.
Maths (Holt) Book 2 p8. Workbook 2 p2.
Maths Matters Book 1 p16-17.
Maths You Need p94-95.
On Our Own Two Feet Book 3 p5-6, 15, 16.

SM *Blackie's Practice Workbooks* Book 1 p19-20, 28. Book 2 p21-22. Book 3 p7.
Check it Again Book 4 p9-10.
Four a Day series Book 5 p42-43.
Problems First Problems p7-10, 17.

2. *Mixed practice in addition and subtraction. Estimating answers and approximations.*

P *Beta (new ed.)* Beta 2 p10.
Hey Mathematics Mod 1. Book 4 p39.
　　　　　　　　Mod 2. Book 1 p36. Book 2 p34-35. Book 3 p33.
Key Maths Level 1. Book 5 p40. Book 6 p10, 11. Book 7 p19-20.
　　　　　Level 2. Book 2 p8. Book 4 p7.
Maths Adventure 1. Pupil's Book p33, 35.
Oxford Middle School Mathematics Book 1 p64.

S *Inner Ring Maths* Book 3 p7.

SM *Blackie's Practice Workbooks* Book 2 p11-14, 15, 16. Book 3 p1, 6. Book 5 p20.
Check it Again Book 3 p4. Book 4 p2.
Four a Day series Book 6 p20. Book 7 p12, 13-14.

N17 Multiplication of single digit numbers.

Abstract examples of multiplication of single digit numbers. Use of everyday materials, number line, number squares, abacus, structured apparatus, etc. to aid operations.

Recording by mapping number pairs, use of the multiplication and equals signs, and the vertical form.

Finding products.

The Cartesian Cross Product ('partnering'). This is a special operation on two sets such that each member of the first set is matched to each member of the second set.
　　e.g. If there are 2 members of a set of teeshirts and 3 members of a set of trousers, how many different sets each containing a teeshirt and a pair of trousers can there be? Examples of this operation in the references below are indicated (CP).

See also p49　　Applications and problems in multiplication and division to 100.
　　　　　p49　　Mixed applications and problems in addition, subtraction, multiplication and division to 100.
　　　　　PV2　　Place value to 100.
　　　　　N11　　Introduction to multiplication.
　　　　　N14　　Multibase arithmetic.
　　　　　N19　　Patterns and relationships in multiplication and division.
　　　　　N29,33　Multiplication of higher numbers.
　　　　　N38(1)　Combinations.

P *Alpha (new ed.)*   Alpha 2 p25. Alpha 3 p13.
   Beta (new ed.)   Beta 1 p78. Beta 2 p72. Beta 3 p8. Beta 4 p15.
   Basic Mathematics   Book 1 p43.
   Hey Mathematics   Mod 2. Book 3 p6, 12, 20, 21, 23. Book 4 p1, 6, 11, 13, 15, 21, 29, 33, 34, 37.
        Book 5 p6, 10, 36-39(CP).
      Mod 3. Book 1 p6, 8, 12, 22, 37. Book 2 p1, 9, 12, 31, 36. Book 3 p3, 21. Book 4 p4, 12, 15, 34.
      Mod 4. Book 2 p1, 3-4(CP), 5.
      Mod 6. Book 1 p10. Book 2 p10.
   Key Maths   Level 2. Book 2 p14, 17, 18. Book 5 p24.
   Making Sure of Maths   Introductory Book p36.
   Mathematics for Schools   Level 1 (2nd ed.) Book 5 p55. Book 6 p59. Book 7 p56-58.
        Level 2 (2nd ed.) Book 1 p41-42. Book 2 p19-20(CP), 25.
        Level 2 (1st ed.) Book 3 p39-40(CP), 41, 45.
   Maths Adventure   Kites 7 p20.
      1. Pupil's Book p69, 91. Activity Book p57-59.
      2. Pupil's Book p18(CP), 53(CP). Activity Book p51, 59-61.
      3. Pupil's Book p18(CP). Activity Book p51.
      4. Pupil's Book p7.
      5. Pupil's Book p1-2(CP). Activity Book p22(CP).
   Nuffield Maths 5-11   2. Worksheets N11 4·3-4·4.
        3. Pupils' Book p43, 80.
   Primary Mathematics (SPMG)   Stage 1. Workbook 4 p19.
        Stage 2. Workbook 4 p15.
        Stage 3. Textbook p3.
   Towards Mathematics   Core Unit 2 p8. Core Unit 6 p8, 9, 10.

S *A World of Mathematics*   Book 2 p10.
   Headway Maths   Book 2 p46. Book 3 p4. Book 4 p4. Book 5 p5.
   Impact Maths   Pupil's Book 1 p32-33, 36-38, 40.
   Inner Ring Maths   Book 3 p12.
   Maths (Holt)   Book 1 p79. Workbook 1 p24.
      Book 2 p65(CP), 69(CP). Workbook 2 p16, 29.
   Maths Matters   Book 2 p32.

SM *Blackie's Practice Workbooks*   Book 3 p8, 17, 19, 21. Book 4 p1, 11, 17.
   Check it Again   Book 3 p13.
   Four a Day series   Book 6 p23-24.
   Number Workbook   Multiplication p4, 9.

Books for teachers
   Mathematics: the later Primary years   p63-65.
   Nuffield Maths 5-11   2. Teachers' Handbook p56(CP).

Division of numbers to 100 by a single digit number.   N18

Abstract examples of division of numbers below 100 by a single digit number. Use of everyday materials, number line, number square, abacus, structured apparatus, etc. to aid operations.

Recording by mapping, the fractional form, the division and equals signs and the traditional algorithmic form:

e.g. $5\underline{|25}$ or $5\overline{)25}$

Division with remainders.

For exploration of regrouping and other methods for dividing numbers below 100 (see N30(1)).

See also p49   Applications and problems in multiplication and division to 100.
    p49   Mixed applications and problems in addition, subtraction, multiplication and division to 100.
    PV1,2   Grouping experiences. Place value to 100.
    N12   Introduction to division.
    N14   Multibase arithmetic.
    N19   Patterns and relationships in multiplication and division.
    N30,34   Division of higher numbers.
    F1,2,4   Fraction notation. Finding a fraction of a whole number.

P *Alpha (new ed.)*   Alpha 1 p74, 82. Alpha 2 p25. Alpha 3 p14.
   Beta (new ed.)   Beta 1 p35, 45, 46, 54, 55, 66, 78, 85, 86. Beta 2 p72. Beta 3 p8, 23. Beta 4 p16.
   Basic Mathematics   Book 1 p45, 99.
   Come and Count   Book 6 p24.

Hey Mathematics　　Mod 1. Book 4 p30.
　　　　　　　　　　Mod 2. Book 1 p20.
　　　　　　　　　　Mod 3. Book 1 p22. Book 2 p9, 10, 20, 23, 32. Book 3 p3, 22, 23. Book 4 p6, 27, 30.
　　　　　　　　　　Mod 4. Book 3 p29.
　　　　　　　　　　Mod 5. Book 2 p34-35. Book 4 p26.
　　　　　　　　　　Mod 6. Book 2 p1, 30.
Key Maths　　Level 2. Book 2 p23, 30-31.
Making Sure of Maths　　Book 1 p27, 33, 42, 77.
Mathematics for Schools　　Level 1 (2nd ed.) Book 7 p59.
　　　　　　　　　　　　Level 2 (2nd ed.) Book 1 p55. Book 2 p35-39.
Maths Adventure　　1. Pupil's Book p93. Activity Book p55.
　　　　　　　　　　2. Pupil's Book p19-20, 61-62.
　　　　　　　　　　3. Pupil's Book p71.
Nuffield Maths 5-11　　2. Worksheets. N12 4·1-4·2.
　　　　　　　　　　　3. Pupils' Book p99-100.
Primary Mathematics (SPMG)　　Stage 2. Workbook 3 p9-11, 14-15, Card 1.
　　　　　　　　　　　　　　　Stage 3. Textbook p24, 26, 28, 30.
Towards Mathematics　　Core Unit 7 p13, 14, 15, 16.

S　A World of Mathematics　　Book 2 p23-25.
Headway Maths　　Book 1 p42-44, 50, 59, 64, 79. Book 2 p47.
　　　　　　　　Book 3 p5. Book 4 p4.
Impact Maths　　Pupil's Book 1 p39, 51, 52, 54, 55.
Maths (Holt)　　Book 1 p56. Book 2 p74.

SM　Blackie's Practice Workbooks　　Book 3 p10, 14, 16, 17, 23, 25. Book 4 p2.
Four a Day series　　Book 5 p54-55. Book 6 p28-29, 31.
Number Workbook　　Division p4, 5, 6, 10.

Books for teachers
Mathematics: the later Primary years　　p82-83.
Mathematics: from Primary to Secondary　　p46-48.
Nuffield Maths 5-11　　2. Teachers' Handbook p70-71.
　　　　　　　　　　　3. Teachers' Handbook p130-132.

N19　Multiplication and division to 10 × 10. Patterns and relationships.

1.　Division as the inverse of multiplication.

e.g.　$6 \times 2 = 12$. So $\dfrac{12}{2} = 6$ and $\dfrac{12}{6} = 2$

Use of the multiplication square to divide.

Box arithmetic (early algebraic relations):

e.g.　$\square \times 2 = 12$

e.g.　$12 \div \square = 6$

See also　N10　　Subtraction as the inverse of addition.
　　　　　N11,12,17,18　　Multiplication and division to 100.
　　　　　AR1　　Open sentences with one place holder.
　　　　　AR2　　Open sentences with two place holders. Patterns.
　　　　　AR8　　Solution of equations by inverse operation.

P　Ready for Alpha and Beta (new ed.)　p24-25.
Alpha (new ed.)　　Alpha 1 p32, 33, 43, 58, 60.
Beta (new ed.)　　Beta 1 p35, 45, 46, 54, 55, 65, 66.
Basic Mathematics　　Book 1 p46, 98. Book 2 p21, 30.
Hey Mathematics　　Mod 2. Book 4 p29. Book 5 p29, 31.
　　　　　　　　　　Mod 3. Book 1 p9, 11, 19, 39. Book 2 p31, 32. Book 3 p30.
　　　　　　　　　　Mod 4. Book 2 p30-31. Book 3 p20.
　　　　　　　　　　Mod 6. Book 1 p1-3, 4, 5, 6.
Key Maths　　Level 2. Book 2 p25. Book 3 p38-40. Book 4 p21. Book 5 p32.
Making Sure of Maths　　Book 1 p44-45. Book 2 p20.
Mathematics for Schools　　Level 1 (2nd ed.) Book 7 p13-14 (See also under N12).
　　　　　　　　　　　　Level 2 (2nd ed.) Book 1 p43, 53. Book 2 p40.
　　　　　　　　　　　　Level 2 (1st ed.) Book 4 p30, 31, 32.

Maths Adventure 2. Pupil's Book p20.
                3. Pupil's Book p32.
                5. Pupil's Book p43.
Nuffield Maths 5-11 2. Worksheets N12. 3·1-3·2 (See also under N12).
                3. Pupils' Book p43, 45, 96-98.
Towards Mathematics Core Unit 2 p13. Core Unit 7 p12.
                Core Unit 8 p16. Core Unit 12 p9.

S *Headway Maths* Book 2 p5, 7, 19, 21, 27, 35, 37, 43, 45. Book 4 p5.
    Impact Maths Pupil's Book 1 p42, 43, 54.
    Maths (Holt) Book 1 p57, 59, 66.

SM *Blackie's Practice Workbooks* Book 3 p9, 11, 22, 24. Book 4 p3, 4, 13-14, 16.
     Four a Day series Book 5 p53. Book 6 p25.
     Number Workbook Multiplication p4, 9.

Books for teachers
    Hey Mathematics Mod 3 Teachers' Book p28.
    Nuffield Maths 5-11 2. Teachers' Handbook p68-69.
                3. Teachers' Handbook p128-130.

2. Commutativity and Associativity.

Recognition that multiplication is:
1. commutative
     e.g. $5 \times 3 = 3 \times 5$
The investigation of numbers in rectangular array may promote understanding:
    e.g.

$2 \times 3 = 6$ $3 \times 2 = 6$

2. associative
     e.g. $5 \times 3 \times 2 = 3 \times 5 \times 2 = 2 \times 3 \times 5$

Recognition that division is not commutative

     e.g. $12 \div 3 \neq 3 \div 12$

See also N10 Commutativity and associativity of addition.
       N11, 12, 17, 18 Multiplication and division to 100.
       N13 Square and rectangular numbers.

P *Beta (new ed.)* Beta 1 p34, 44, 53, 64.
    Basic Mathematics Book 2 p34. Book 3 p36. Book 4 p9. Book 5 p17.
    Hey Mathematics Mod 2. Book 3 p4, 15. Book 4 p14. Book 5 p2-3, 5, 12.
                Mod 3. Book 1 p2.
                Mod 4. Book 2 p1.
                Mod 6. Book 1 p8.
    Key Maths Level 2. Book 2 p13, 14, 15, 17. Book 3 p34. Book 6 p17.
    Making Sure of Maths Introductory Book p34-35, 37. Book 1 p25-26. Book 6 p11-15.
    Mathematics for Schools Level 1 (2nd ed.) Book 5 p56-58. Book 7 p14. (See also under N12).
                Level 2 (2nd ed.) Book 1 p38-40. Book 2 p24.
                Level 2 (1st ed.) Book 9, p1, 3. Book 10 p4.
    Maths Adventure 2. Pupil's Book p4, 26, 75.
                3. Pupil's Book p23.
                4. Pupil's Book p79.
    Nuffield Maths 5-11 2. Worksheets N11. 3·1-3·4.
                3. Pupils' Book p44, 46, 77.
    Our First School Maths Book 5 p9.
    Oxford Middle School Mathematics Book 1 p52-53.
    Towards Mathematics Core Unit 2 p5, 8, 9.

S *Impact Maths* Pupil's Book 1 p42, 43.

SM *Four a Day series* Book 5 p51. Book 6 p23. Book 7 p31-32.
                Book 8 p22-23, 24. Book 9 p26-27.

Books for teachers
    Hey Mathematics Mod 3. Teachers' Book p18-19.
    Mathematics: the later Primary years p66-67, 68.
    Nuffield Maths 5-11 2. Teachers' Handbook p54-55.
                3. Teachers' Handbook p60, 102-103.

3. Patterns in multiplication and division.

Construction and use of the multiplication square (up to 10 × 10). The multiplication square and calculators allow patterns and relationships to be investigated without the interference of routine manipulations.

Multiplying and dividing by 0, 1, 10.

Multiplying and dividing odd numbers, odd number by an even number etc.

Multiples of 2, 3, 4, etc. Divisors.

Tables, when understood, may be learned.

Later: common multiples and divisors investigated:

        e.g.   12, 24 etc. are common multiples of 4 and 6.

      Idea of lowest common multiple.

      Factors. Prime numbers i.e. numbers with only two factors: one and the number itself.

      Introduction to Sieve of Eratosthenes.

      Digital roots.

See also   PV2   Place value to 100. Counting in 10's.
            N11,12,17,18   Multiplication and division to 100.
            N13   Patterns and sequences to 100.
            N23   Ratio, rate and proportion.
            F3   Equivalent and lowest term fractions.
            AR2   Patterns and graphs associated with multiples etc.
            VR7   Co-ordinates: relate to use of multiplication square.
            S4,5   Intersection of two and more sets.
            T7   Telling the time, counting in 5's.
            T8   The calendar, counting in 7's.

P   *Alpha (new ed.)*   Alpha 1 p32-33, 43, 58, 60, 72. Alpha 2 p36.
     Beta (new ed.)   Beta 1 p34, 35, 36, 44, 45, 53-55, 64-66, 78.
                  Beta 2 p19, 38, 39, 46, 47, 54, 55, 62, 63, 72, 73. Beta 3 p9. Beta 5 p4, 34, 35.
     Basic Mathematics   Book 1 p43. Book 2 p21, 30, 32, 43, 61-63.
                  Book 3 p41-42. Book 4 p16, 17, 26-27, 92.
                  Book 5 p23-24, 25-28.
     Hey Mathematics   Mod 2. Book 3 p28. Book 4 p19. Book 5 p17, 20-21.
                  Mod 3. Book 1 p40. Book 4 p22, 29.
                  Mod 6. Book 1 p8.
     Key Maths   Level 2. Book 2 p16, 24. Book 3 p35, 46. Book 4 p21-22. Book 5 p24. Book 6 p20, 27, 86.
     Making Sure of Maths   Introductory Book p43-44, 46-47.
                  Book 1 p32, 41, 42, 43-45, 50-53, 66-69, 77, 83, 84. Book 2 p20. Book 3 p69-71, 75-76.
                  Book 5 p11-13.
     Mathematics for Schools   Level 1 (2nd ed.) Book 7 p56.
                  Level 2 (2nd ed.) Book 2 p21-23, 24, 26.
                  Level 2 (1st ed.) Book 3 p38, 46. Book 7 p60, 61.
     Maths Adventure   1. Activity Book p43.
                  2. Pupil's Book p21, 26-29, 36-37, 42, 43-45, 48, 49, 60, 63. Activity Book p42-43.
                  3. Pupil's Book p12-13, 22, 41, 59, 68, 80. Activity Book p3, 5, 14-15, 37, 48-49.
                  4. Pupil's Book p6, 10-11. Activity Book p9, 12-16.
                  5. Pupil's Book p3-4, 58-59. Activity Book p15, 20, 33.
     Nuffield Maths 5-11   2. Worksheets N11. 4·1-4·2.
                  3. Pupils' Book p45, 46, 78-79.
     Our First School Maths   Book 6 p8-11.
     Oxford Middle School Mathematics   Book 1 p56. Book 3 p16, 30-31, 48-49. Book 4 p5.
     Primary Mathematics (SPMG)   Stage 1. Workbook 4 p6-9, 12-16, Card 1a, 2a, 3a, 4a.
                  Stage 2. Workbook 1 p6. Workbook 2 p4, 11, 14, 17, 20.
                          Workbook 4 p3, 5, 7-8, 10-11, 13, 17, Card 1.
                  Stage 3. Textbook p23, 25, 27, 29. Workbook p5-7. Card 3.
                  Stage 4. Workbook p2-3. Card 1, 2, 11, 12.
     Towards Mathematics   Core Unit 2 p3, 4, 6, 7, 9. Core Unit 6 p3, 4, 5, 6, 7, 9, 11, 12. Core Unit 8 p7. Core Unit 11 p15. Core Unit 12 p15, 16. Core Unit 16 p9. Core Unit 23 p3, 4, 5, 9, 10, 11, 13.

S   *A World of Mathematics*   Book 2 p40-41. Book 5 p12.
     Focus Mathematics   Book 1 p27-28. Book 4 p16-17.
     Headway Maths   Book 2 p4-7, 18-21, 26-27, 34-37, 42-45, 84.
     Impact Maths   Pupil's Book 1 p34-35, 55, 64.
     Maths (Holt)   Book 1 p50, 59. Book 2 p62. 5th Year Workbook p6-7
     Maths Matters   Book 2 p16-17.
     Mathsworks   Tryouts 1 p10, 16, 46.

SM   *Check it Again*   Book 1 p16-17, 19, 21-22. Book 2 p15-17, 18-20. Book 3 p5, 6-12, 16-17, 19.

Books for teachers
Hey Mathematics   Mod 3. Teachers' Book p20-21, 23-24, 27-28.
Mathematics: the first 3 years   p113.
Mathematics: the later Primary years   p67-71, 76, 83-85, 86.
Nuffield Maths 5-11   2. Teachers' Handbook p57-60.
                       3. Teachers' Handbook p58, 59, 104-106.

Multiplication and division to 10 × 10. Applications and problems.

N17 18, 19 (cont.)

See also   p49   Mixed applications and problems in addition, subtraction, multiplication and division to 100.
           M8   Unit pricing and best buys (to £1).
           N23   Ratio, rate and proportion.
           N38   Probability.
           AR3   Introduction to and use of variables.
           AR8   Algebraic solution of simple equations.
           VR8, L9   Using and interpreting scales.
           Sh21   Bisecting angles (to 100).
           CV9   Volume of cube and cuboid.
           CV10, A10, L10,12, W8,10, T12   Problems and applications relating to measurement, e.g. measuring in
                 bulk to find fractional amounts.
           CV12   Volume of triangular prism etc.
           A7   Area of square and rectangle.
           A11   Area of cross section of cube and cuboid.
           A12   Area of triangle, parallelogram etc.
           L7   Perimeter of square.

P   *Alpha (new ed.)*   Alpha 1 p45, 62.
    Beta (new ed.)   Beta 1 p46, 55. Beta 2 p73.
    Hey Mathematics   Mod 2. Book 3 p23, 24.
                        Mod 3. Book 1 p13. Book 2 p18, 33, 35.
    Key Maths   Level 2. Book 2 p19, 32. Book 3 p42.
    Making Sure of Maths   Book 1 p28, 33, 67, 69.
    Mathematics for Schools   Level 2 (2nd ed.) Book 1 p44-45.
    Maths Adventure   1. Pupil's Book p91.
                        2. Pupil's Book p92.
                        3. Pupil's Book p23.
    Nuffield Maths 5-11   3. Pupils' Book p58.
    Oxford Middle School Mathematics   Book 1 p25-26, 84-85.
    Primary Mathematics (SPMG)   Stage 1. Workbook 4 p11, 18.
                                   Stage 2. Workbook 3 p11, Card 3a. Workbook 4 p16.

S   *A World of Mathematics*   Book 5 p13, 37-38.
    Headway Maths   Book 3 p71, 82. Book 4 p9, 42.
    Impact Maths   Pupil's Book 1 p55.
    Inner Ring Maths   Book 3 p6, 19.
    Maths (Holt)   Book 1 p62, 65.

SM *Blackie's Practice Workbooks*   Book 3 p12, 20, 28. Book 4 p9-10, 22-23.
    Check it Again   Book 1 p20, 23. Book 2 p20.
                       Book 3 p17-18. Book 4 p12-14.
    Four a Day series   Book 5 p55-56.

Addition, subtraction, multiplication and division to 100. Mixed applications and problems.

N15 16, 17, 18, 19 (cont.)

Problems requiring the selection of the appropriate operation from these four.

Problems requiring the use of more than one of these operations.

See also   p43   Applications and problems in addition and subtraction to 100.
           p49   Applications and problems in multiplication and division to 100.
           N37   Averages (addition and division).
           AR3   Introduction to and use of 'variables'.

AR8   Algebraic solution of simple equations.
Sh23   Pythagoras' theorem.
A7,12 Area of composite shapes involving squares, rectangles, triangles, etc. (multiplication and addition).
A11,12 Surface area of cubes, cuboids, triangular prisms, etc. (multiplication and addition).

P   *Basic Mathematics* Book 1 p78.
       Hey Mathematics   Mod 3. Book 1 p32.
       Mathematics for Schools   Level 1 (2nd ed.) Book 6 p60.
                                 Level 2 (2nd ed.) Book 2 p46.
                                 Level 2 (1st ed.) Book 3 p63-64.
       Maths Adventure   2. Pupil's Book p91.
                       3. Pupil's Book p31.
       Oxford Middle School Mathematics   Book 1 p28-29, 46.

S   *Headway Maths*   Book 2 p8.
       Mathematics for Life   Book A1 p16-17. Book A2 p2-5. Book B1 p8-9.
       Maths (Holt)   Book 2 p75.
       On Our Own Two Feet   Book 3 p7-10.

SM   *Check it Again*   Book 2 p17-18. Book 4 p33-35.
       Problems   First Problems p14-17, 21-22.
                  Second Problems p20, 27, 34.

N20 Addition of numbers with totals exceeding 100.

1. *Exploration of patterns in addition and methods of adding numbers.*

Patterns and methods of adding numbers with totals below 1,000 explored as in N15, ensuring that any technique eventually used is fully understood.

Gradual extension to the addition of numbers with totals over 1,000 when place value of such numbers is fully understood.

Use of a calculator allows patterns and methods to be investigated without the interference of routine manipulations.

See also   PV2,4,7 Place value of whole numbers.
           N14   Multibase arithmetic.
           N15(1) Addition to 100; patterns and methods.

P   *Basic Mathematics*   Book 1 p74. Book 3 p35.
       Hey Mathematics   Mod 2. Book 1 p7. Book 3 p24. Book 4 p38.
                         Mod 3. Book 1 p1, 12, 21. Book 2 p17. Book 3 p6, 12, 22. Book 4 p7, 21.
                         Mod 5. Book 5 p6.
       Key Maths   Level 2. Book 3 p15, 18.
       Making Sure of Maths   Book 1 p14, 15.
       Mathematics for Schools   Level 2 (1st ed.) Book 3 p12-15. Book 5 p15.
       Primary Mathematics (SPMG)   Stage 2. Workbook 1 p21. Workbook 4 p24.
                                     Stage 4. Card 48, 49.
       Towards Mathematics   Core Unit 7 p7-8. Core Unit 11 p1.

S   *A World of Mathematics*   Book 3 p6-7.

SM   *Four a Day series*   Book 7 p23-24.
       Mathematics and Metric Measurement   Book 4 p19-22.

Books for teachers
       Hey Mathematics   Mod 3 Teachers' Book p7-12.
       Mathematics: the later Primary years   p55-56.

2. *Practice in addition. Estimating answers and approximations.*

See also   p52   Applications, problems and mixed practice in addition and subtraction over 100.
          p60   Mixed applications and problems in addition, subtraction, multiplication and division over 100.

P   *Alpha (new ed.)*   Alpha 1 p51. Alpha 2 p17.
         Beta (new ed.)   Beta 2 p33. Beta 4 p11.
         Basic Mathematics   Book 1 p75.
         Hey Mathematics   Mod 3. Book 1 p5, 21, 28. Book 2 p1, 13, 21. Book 3 p1, 4, 7, 25. Book 4 p4, 13.
                            Mod 4. Book 1 p10-16.
                            Mod 6. Book 2 p12, 13.
         Key Maths   Level 2. Book 3 p15-17. Book 4 p8, 9. Book 5 p18, 19. Book 6 p9, 10.
         Making Sure of Maths   Book 2 p8.
         Primary Mathematics (SPMG)   Stage 2. Workbook 1 p22, 23, Card 6b, 7a, 7b. Workbook 4 Card 5.

S   *A World of Mathematics*   Book 3 p8-10.
         Focus Mathematics   Book 1 p52-53.
         Headway Maths   Book 1 p54, 55. Book 2 p3, 10. Book 3 p2. Book 4 p2.
         Maths Matters   Book 2 p12.

SM   *Blackie's Practice Workbooks*   Book 4 p24, 26. Book 5 p1, 5.
         Four a Day series   Book 7 p16. Book 8 p16-17. Book 9 p19. Book 10 p15.
         Number Workbook   Addition p13-15, 18-23.

Subtraction from numbers over 100.   **N21**

1. *Exploration of patterns in subtraction and methods of subtracting numbers.*

Patterns and methods of subtracting from numbers below 1,000 explored as in N16, ensuring that any technique eventually used is fully understood.

Gradual extension to subtraction from numbers over 1,000 when place value of such numbers is fully understood.

Use of a calculator allows patterns and methods to be investigated without the interference of routine manipulations.

See also   PV2,4,7   Place value of whole numbers.
           N14   Multibase arithmetic.
           N15(1) Number bonds to 100.
           N16(1) Subtraction to 100; patterns and methods.

P   *Basic Mathematics*   Book 1 p74. Book 3 p5.
         Hey Mathematics   Mod 2. Book 3 p24.
                            Mod 3. Book 1 p4, 8, 29. Book 2 p19. Book 3 p6, 23. Book 4 p7, 24.
         Key Maths   Level 2. Book 4 p10, 11.
         Mathematics for Schools   Level 2 (1st ed.) Book 3 p27-30. Book 5 p17-18.
         Primary Mathematics (SPMG)   Stage 2. Workbook 2 p21-24. Workbook 4 p25.
         Towards Mathematics   Core Unit 12 p5. Core Unit 19 p5.

SM   *Mathematics and Metric Measuring*   Book 4 p23-24.

Books for teachers
         Hey Mathematics   Mod 3. Teachers' Book p13-17.

2. *Practice in subtraction. Estimating answers and approximations.*

See also   p52   Applications, problems and mixed practice in addition and subtraction over 100.
           p60   Mixed applications and problems in addition, subtraction, multiplication and division over 100.

P   *Alpha (new ed.)*   Alpha 1 p52. Alpha 2 p18.
         Beta (new ed.)   Beta 2 p34.
         Hey Mathematics   Mod 3. Book 1 p.18. Book 2 p17, 18, 20. Book 3 p20. Book 4 p5.
                            Mod 4. Book 1 p24-26.
                            Mod 6. Book 2 p12, 13.
         Key Maths   Level 2. Book 3 p23, 58. Book 4 p8, 11. Book 5 p21, 22. Book 6 p11, 12.
         Making Sure of Maths   Book 1 p16, 18. Book 2 p8.

S   *Headway Maths*   Book 1 p54, 55, 72-73. Book 3 p3. Book 4 p3.
         Maths Matters   Book 2 p13.

SM   *Blackie's Practice Workbooks*   Book 4 p25, 27. Book 5 p2, 6.
         Four a Day series   Book 7 p16. Book 8 p17-18. Book 9 p20.
         Number Workbook   Subtraction p3, 13-19, 22-23.

Addition and subtraction over 100. Applications, problems and mixed practice.

1. Applications and problems.

See also
	p60	Mixed applications and problems in addition, subtraction, multiplication and division over 100.
	AR3	Introduction to and use of 'variables'.
	AR8	Algebraic solution of simple equations.
	VR8	Addition and subtraction arising from visual representation of quantities.
	Sh13,CV5, L4, W5, T6	Estimating quantity, measuring using a single standard unit and recording error.
	Sh13,14,15,16	Calculations related to angle-sum-properties round a point, on one side of a straight line, of a triangle, quadrilateral and polygon.
	Sh19	Calculations related to corresponding, alternate and vertically opposite angles.
	CV7, A8, L5, W6, T6	Addition and subtraction of standard units.
	CV10, A10, L10, W8, T12	Problems and applications relating to measurement.
	L7	Calculating perimeters, and lengths given perimeter and other dimensions.
	W7	Weighing liquids.
	W8	Net and gross. Wet and dry weights.
	W9	Weighing objects in water and air.
	T9	Calculations relating to historical dates.
	T10,11	Calculations relating to 12 and 24 hour clocks, timetables, etc.

P   *Alpha (new ed.)*   Alpha 1 p53. Alpha 2 p19.
Beta (new ed.)   Beta 2 p34.
Basic Mathematics   Book 3 p40. Book 4 p19.
Hey Mathematics   Mod 3. Book 2 p2, 11, 16. Book 3 p18-19, 25, 31. Book 4 p5, 16.
        Mod 4. Book 1 p13-16, 23, 25-26.
Key Maths   Level 2. Book 3 p27, 29. Book 4 p12. Book 5 p19, 23. Book 6 p13.
Making Sure of Maths   Book 1 p86-87. Book 2 p8. Book 3 p7.
Mathematics for Schools   Level 2 (1st ed.). Book 3 p30-31. Book 5 p16, 17, 18, 19.
Maths Adventure   2. Pupil's Book p85.
        3. Pupil's Book p9.
Oxford Middle School Mathematics   Book 1 p73, 83. Book 2 p16, 44, 72-73.
Primary Mathematics (SPMG)   Stage 2. Workbook 1 p22, 23. Workbook 4 p26. Card 5.
        Stage 3. Textbook p2. Card 2.
        Stage 5. Card 2, 3.
Towards Mathematics   Core Unit 19 p8.

S   *A World of Mathematics*   Book 3 p8, 35. Book 4 p24-27.
Headway Maths   Book 1 p70. Book 2 p22-23, 76. Book 3 p61. Book 5 p3, 43.
Inner Ring Maths   Book 2 p17.
Mathematics for Life   Book A2 p24-27. Book B1 p10-11, 30-32. Book B2 p26-29.
Maths (Holt)   Book 2 p8.
Maths Matters   Book 1 p30-31. Book 3 p10.
Maths Works   Book 1 p4-5.
Maths you Need   p112-113.
On Our Own Two Feet   Book 4 p5-6,11.

SM   *Blackie's Practice Workbooks*   Book 5 p7-8.
Check it Again   Book 4 p8.
Four a Day series   Book 7 p27-28. Book 9 p21. Book 10 p16.
Problems   Second Problems p4-5, 17, 24.
        Third Problems p42.

2. Mixed practice in addition and subtraction. Estimating answers and approximations.

P   *Alpha (new ed.)*   Alpha 1 p53.
Hey Mathematics   Mod 3. Book 4 p11, 12, 13.
Maths Adventure   3. Pupil's Book p10.
Primary Mathematics (SPMG)   Stage 3. Textbook p2. Card 1.

SM   *Check it Again*   Book 5 p5.
Four a Day series   Book 7 p17. Book 8 p13. Book 10 p15-16.

Addition and subtraction of decimals.

Addition and subtraction of decimals to 2 and later more decimal places, focusing on applications.

Exploration of methods of adding and subtracting decimals as in N15, 16, 20, 21 ensuring that any technique eventually used is fully understood.

See also
M7   Shopping over £1. Bills. Addition and subtraction of money.
M9   Simple money management.
M11   Budgeting for self or household. Household bills, invoices, etc.
M12   Pay, payslips, take-home pay, etc.
M13   Calculating profit. Bank accounts and bank statements. Buying outright as opposed to renting.
PV5,6,8   Place value. Decimal notation.
N8,9,15,16,20,21   Addition and subtraction of whole numbers.
N14   Multibase arithmetic.
N24   Addition and subtraction of percentages.
N37   Averages (addition and division).
F2,5   Addition and subtraction of fractions.
CV7, A8, L5, W6   Addition and subtraction of measurements expressed as decimals.
CV8, L6, W7   Estimating quantity, measuring using decimals and recording error.
CV10, A10, L10, W8   Problems and applications relating to measurement.
L7   Calculating perimeters.
W7   Weighing liquids.
W8   Net and gross. Wet and dry wieights.
W9   Weighing objects in water and air.

P   *Alpha (new ed.)*   Alpha 1 p51, 52. Alpha 2 p6, 17, 18, 78. Alpha 3 p7, 8. Alpha 4 p8.
Beta (new ed.)   Beta 2 p42.
Basic Mathematics   Book 2 p29, 58, 59. Book 3 p51. Book 4 p43, 44, 57. Book 5 p43.
Hey Mathematics   Mod 4. Book 2 p19-29. Book 4 p3-7, 8.
                Mod 5. Book 1 p23.
                Mod. 6. Book 1 p25.
Key Maths   Level 2. Book 3 p21, 24. Book 4 p8. Book 5 p9, 10, 14. Book 6 p50-51.
Making Sure of Maths   Book 2 p34-35, 36-37, 41. Book 3 p21-22. Book 4 p14. Book 5 p27.
Mathematics for Schools   Level 2 (1st ed.). Book 4 p62. Book 6 p44-45. Book 7 p6, 10-12.
Maths Adventure   3. Pupil's Book p81.
                4. Pupil's Book p58. Activity Book p51.
                5. Pupil's Book p35.
Oxford Middle School Mathematics   Book 2 p70-71. Book 3 p18-19.
Primary Mathematics (SPMG)   Stage 3. Textbook p83-85. Workbook p28-29.
                Stage 4. Textbook p33-36.
                Stage 5. Textbook p37.
Towards Mathematics   Core Unit 14 p6, 7, 8, 10. Core Unit 19 p6, 7.

S   *A World of Mathematics*   Book 3 p57-58. Book 6 p37-38, 46, 48-49.
Focus Mathematics   Book 4 p87-95.
Headway Maths   Book 2 p12-13, 66-68, 70. Book 3 p13, 39, 41. Book 4 p18, 29. Book 5 p41-42.
Mathematics for Life   Book B1 p20-23.
Maths (Holt)   Book 3 p37, 39, 40, 76.
Maths Matters   Book 3 p6-7, 24-25.

SM   *Number Workbook*   Addition p24-31. Subtraction p24-31.
                       Decimals p6, 9, 14-15, 17, 18, 19, 25.

Books for teachers
   Mathematics: from Primary to Secondary   p12-13.

Introduction to ratio, rate and proportion.

Comparison of two and later more numbers or quantities, expressed as ratios.

Dividing quantities in certain ratios.

Ratio as a fraction. Concept of constant ratio.

Concepts of direct proportion and equal rate.

Applications and problems based on constant ratio, direct proportion and equal rate.

See also
M8   Unit pricing and best buys.
M10   Foreign currency and currency conversion.
M11,12,13 Unit pricing in adult life.
N17,18,19,29,30,31,32,33,34 Multiplication and division.
N24, M9,11,12,13 Percentage as ratio of 100. Finding percentages.
N37   Average.
N38   Probability as a ratio. Betting odds.
F1-7   Fractions as ratios. Equivalent fractions and operations on fractions.
AR2,4,7,9 The linear relationship. Constant ratio, direct proportion and equal rate. Gradients.
VR5   Pie charts.
VR8, L8,9 Scales as ratios.
Sh17, L7,13 Similarity, enlargement and reduction.
CV7,10, A10, L10, W8, T12,13, Temp. Relating two forms of measurement.
CV10, L12, W10 Measuring in bulk to find fractional amounts.
L11   'pi' as a ratio.
L13   Hill gradients as ratios.
Imp.   Imperial/metric conversions.
Temp. Fahrenheit/Celsius conversions.

P   *Alpha (new ed.)* Alpha 3 p26. Alpha 4 p33.
Beta (new ed.) Beta 4 p44-45. Beta 5 p48-50. Beta 6 p31.
Basic Mathematics Book 4 p74-75, 76-77. Book 5 p52-56.
Key Maths Level 2. Book 6 p103-106.
Making Sure of Maths Book 4 p27. Book 5 p52-55, 103.
Mathematics for Schools Level 2 (1st ed.). Book 8 p40-43.
Maths Adventure 4. Pupil's Book p52-53.
                5. Pupil's Book p74-76.
Oxford Middle School Mathematics Book 3 p22.
Primary Mathematics (SPMG) Stage 4. Textbook p9.
                              Stage 5. Textbook p103-108 Card 47, 48.
Towards Mathematics Core Unit 17 p7-8, 11. Core Unit 19 p2, 3. Core Unit 22 p9.

S   *A World of Mathematics* Book 6 p12-14.
Focus Mathematics Book 8 p16-24.
Headway Maths Book 5 p20-21.
Maths (Holt) Book 2 p91, 93. Book 3 p85, 90. 4th Year p68, 74. 5th Year p10-11, 45-46.
Mathsworks Book 2 p33. Tryouts 2 p25.
Maths You Need p36-37, 108, 124-126.

SM *Check it Again* Book 5 p16-17.
Problems Third Problems p61.

N24 Percentages.

Percentage as a fraction of 100 and as a ratio with a denominator of 100.

Conversion of fractions or decimals into percentages and vice versa initially using real quantities, e.g. structured apparatus.

Addition and subtraction of percentages.

Finding a percentage of a quantity.

Problems and applications involving percentages.

See also
M9   Percentage discounts and increases. Inflation.
M11   VAT and percentage service charges.
M12   Income tax.
M13   Saving, borrowing and interest.
PV6   Hundredths as decimals.
N15   Addition to 100. Number bonds of 100.
N23   Ratio, rate and proportion.
N29,31,32,33,34 Multiplication and division.
N36   Surveys and generalisations.
F2,3   Fraction notation and simple addition. Equivalent fractions.
F4   Multiplication of fraction by whole number.
VR5   Pie charts.

P   *Alpha (new ed.)*   Alpha 3 p58-60. Alpha 4 p34, 35, 36.
    Beta (new ed.)   Beta 4 p72-75. Beta 5 p26-27, 49, 50. Beta 6 p29, 30, 31.
    Basic Mathematics   Book 3 p54, 55. Book 4 p51-54.
                Book 5 p49, 50, 51.
    Hey Mathematics   Mod 5. Book 3 p4-19. Book 4 p5, 27. Book 5 p21.
                Mod 6. Book 1 p27, 40. Book 2 p31-40. Book 3 p4, 33-43.
    Key Maths   Level 2. Book 6 p64-68.
    Making Sure of Maths   Book 4 p30-32. Book 5 p31-33.
                Book 6 p53-55.
    Mathematics for Schools   Level 2 (1st ed.). Book 7 p22-24.
    Maths Adventure   3. Pupil's Book p91.
                4. Pupil's Book p80-81.
                5. Pupil's Book p87-89.
    Oxford Middle School Mathematics   Book 3 p78-81. Book 4 p42-43.
    Primary Mathematics (SPMG)   Stage 5. Textbook p11-13, 16-17, 74-75, 77-78, 119.
                Workbook p2, 4. Card 10, 11, 29, 30.
    Towards Mathematics   Core Unit 22 p1-11.

S   *A World of Mathematics*   Book 5 p56-59.
    Focus Mathematics   Book 8 p7-16.
    Headway Maths   Book 4 p58-61.
    Inner Ring Maths   Book 3 p27, 28, 29, 30.
    Mathematics for Life   Book C2 p14-15.
    Maths (Holt)   Book 2 p82-83. Book 3 p36. 52, 87, 4th Year p76, 90, 92-93. 5th Year p29, 31, 71.
                5th Year Workbook p3, 18.
    Mathsworks   Book 1 p10, 78-79. Tryouts p1-2. Book 2 p19, 33, 42, 48-49, 50. Tryouts 2 p23.
    Maths You Need   p11, 38-39, 42-43.

SM   *Check it Again*   Book 4 p35-36. Book 5 p18-19.

Books for teachers
    Mathematics: from Primary to Secondary   p27.

Number sequences and patterns.

Extension of N13 to more complex sequences and patterns eg. Pascal's triangle and Fibonacci numbers.

See also   N13,19(3)   Number sequences and patterns.
          N23   Ratio.

P   *Basic Mathematics*   Book 3 p42.
    Mathematics for Schools   Level 2 (1st ed.). Book 3 p60. Book 10 p32-33.
    Maths Adventure   4. Activity Book p21.
    Oxford Middle School Mathematics   Book 4 p36-38, 68-69.
    Primary Mathematics (SPMG)   Stage 4. Card 50.
                Stage 5. Card 48.

S   *Maths (Holt)*   Book 3 p85-86. 5th Year Workbook p42-43.
    Mathsworks   Book 1 p32-35, 48-50. Tryouts 1 p61,62.
                Book 2 p7. Tryouts 2 p4.

Powers idea and index notation in denary system (base 10).

Extension of N13 to square numbers (e.g. 4^2), cubic numbers (e.g. 4^3) etc.

Geometric progressions e.g. growth of yeast, reproduction of mice.

Later operations on powers, and square roots.

See also   PV7   Thousands, millions, etc.
          N17,31,33   Multiplication of numbers by themselves.
          AR2,5   Curved graphs. The quadratic relation.
          AR3   Substituting numbers into algebraic expressions.
          Sh23   Pythagoras' theorem.

CV6,7,8 Notation of, and relationships between, metric volume units.
CV9   Volume of cube.
CV11 Relationship between dimensions of squares and their volumes.
CV12 Volume of cylinder.
A6,8   Notation of, and relationships, between, metric area units.
A7   Area of square.
A13   Circle area.

P   *Alpha (new ed.)*   Alpha 2 p36. Alpha 3 p15. Alpha 4 p7, 72.
    Beta (new ed.)   Beta 3 p9. Beta 4 p15. Beta 6 p32, 33, 77-78.
    Basic Mathematics   Book 4 p99, 100. Book 5 p7, 8.
    Hey Mathematics   Mod 6. Book 1 p37-40.
    Making Sure of Maths   Book 1 p88-89. Book 4 p49-52. Book 6 p56-61.
    Mathematics for Schools   Level 2 (1st ed.). Book 9 p8-10, 50, 51-53.
    Maths Adventure   4. Pupil's Book p24-26.
                  5. Pupil's Book p77-79. Activity Book p30-31.
    Oxford Middle School Mathematics   Book 4 p64-66, 77.

S   *A World of Mathematics*   Book 4 p38-41.
    Focus Mathematics   Book 4 p99-103. Book 5 p98-100.
    Headway Maths   Book 3 p66. Book 4 p25, 56-57, 82-83. Book 5 p38.
    Maths (Holt)   Book 3 p78.
    Mathsworks   Book 1 p20-21. Book 2 p8-11, 18.
              Tryouts 2 p5, 6, 7, 11.

SM   *Check it Again*   Book 4 p36.
    Four a Day series   Book 10 p88-89.
    Mathematics and Metric Measuring   Book 4 p12-15.

Books for teachers
    Mathematics: the later Primary years   p77-79, 174-177.

N27   Introduction to directed numbers (integers).

Number line extended to include positive and negative numbers.

Notation of directed numbers e.g. $^+2. \ ^-5.$

Ordering directed numbers.

Games involving forward and backward shifts on the number line.

Applications.

See also   M13   Profit and loss. Bank statements.
           N35,AR7   Operations on directed numbers.
           N37   Idea of 'above' and 'below' average.
           VR7   Co-ordinates using directed numbers.
           Sh19   Translation. Vectors.
           L10   Heights above and below sea level.
           T7   'To' and 'past' times. Fast and slow clocks.
           T9   Time lines of a life. BC and AD dates.
           T14   World time. International date line.
           Temp.   Temperature above and below zero.

P   *Alpha (new ed.)*   Alpha 2 p23. Alpha 3 p34. Alpha 4 p12.
    Beta (new ed.)   Beta 3 p79-80. Beta 4 p55.
    Hey Mathematics   Mod 5. Book 1 p1-15, 19, 20-22. Book 5 p1-2, 8-9, 12.
    Making Sure of Maths   Book 6 p17-18.
    Mathematics for Schools   Level 2 (1st ed.). Book 8 p1.
    Maths Adventure   2. Pupil's Book p84.
                  3. Pupil's Book p65, 78, 82.
                  4. Pupil's Book p65-66.
    Oxford Middle School Mathematics   Book 4 p60-62.
    Towards Mathematics   Core Unit 13 p13-16. Core Unit 25 p4, 7.

S   *A World of Mathematics*   Book 5 p21-23.

Books for teachers
    Mathematics: the later Primary years   p142-143, 154-155.

The distributive law for multiplication.

Recognition of the distributive law for multiplication.

e.g. $12 \times 6 = (10 + 2) \times 6 = (10 \times 6) + (2 \times 6)$
$19 \times 6 = (20 - 1) \times 6 = (20 \times 6) - (1 \times 6)$

This understanding is essential prior to investigating methods of multiplying high numbers. The traditional form of long multiplication depends on the distributive law.

See also   N29,30,31,32,33,34   Multiplication and division; regrouping methods.
                AR3   Generalisations expressed using 'variables'.

P   *Basic Mathematics*   Book 2 p34. Book 3 p37. Book 4 p9, 10, 20.
     Hey Mathematics   Mod 2. Book 4 p8, 10, 19, 25, 32, 35.
                      Mod 3. Book 4 p1-2. Book 5 p8.
                      Mod 4. Book 2 p2.
     Key Maths   Level 2. Book 3 p36-37.
     Making Sure of Maths   Book 6 p15-16.
     Mathematics for Schools   Level 2 (1st ed.). Book 3 p47-50. Book 4 p13. Book 9 p5.
     Maths Adventure   2. Pupil's Book p89.
     Primary Mathematics (SPMG)   Stage 2. Workbook 2 p6, 8, 13, 16, 18, 19. Workbook 4 p2, 6, 9, 12, 14.
     Towards Mathematics   Core Unit 6 p13.

S   *A World of Mathematics*   Book 4 p8-11.
     Focus Mathematics   Book 4 p103-104.
     Maths (Holt)   Book 1 p44. Book 2 p60-61. 5th year p83.

SM   *Four a Day series*   Book 7 p32. Book 9 p28, 34.

Books for teachers
     Hey Mathematics   Mod 3 Teachers' Book p22-23, 25.
     Mathematics: the later Primary years   p71-73.

Multiplication of increasingly large numbers (over 10) by a single digit number. Multiplication by 10.

1. Exploration of patterns in multiplication and methods of multiplying numbers.

Mulitiplication of single digit numbers by 10 and multiples of 10.

Multiplication of two and more digit numbers by 10.

43×2, 430×2, 4300×2 and similar patterns.

Exploration of methods of multiplying numbers using structured apparatus, etc.

Initially methods of multiplying numbers below 100 explored; later these principles extended to the multiplication of numbers over 100 by a single digit number.

e.g.   a.   Repeated addition   b.   Regrouping

$$
\begin{aligned}
\text{e.g.} \quad 3 \times 89 &= 89 + 89 + 89 \\
&= 267
\end{aligned}
\qquad
\begin{aligned}
\text{e.g.} \quad 3 \times 92 &= 3 \times (90 + 2) \\
&= (3 \times 90) + (3 \times 2) \\
&= 270 + 6 = 276
\end{aligned}
$$

$$
\begin{aligned}
\text{Also} \quad 3 \times 89 &= 3 \times (90 - 1) \\
&= (3 \times 90) - (3 \times 1) \\
&= 270 - 3 = 267
\end{aligned}
$$

Eventually more efficient methods based on these ideas may be understood and thereafter used.

Note that understanding depends on appreciation of the distributive law for multiplication (See N28).

Use of a calculator allows patterns and methods to be investigated without the interference of routine manipulations.

See also   PV2,4,7   Place value of whole numbers.
            N14   Multibase arithmetic.
            N15,16,20,21   Addition and subtraction. Number bonds.
            N17   Multiplication to 100.
            N19(2) Commutativity and associativity of multiplication.
            N19(3) Patterns in multiplication and division to 10×10.
            N31   Multiplication of decimals.
            N33   Multiplication by 2 and more digit numbers.

P   *Alpha (new ed.)*   Alpha 1 p86.
 Beta (new ed.)   Beta 2 p28, 77.
 Hey Mathematics   Mod 3. Book 2 p2, 13, 15. Book 3 p12. Book 4 p1, 2, 25. Book 5 p8.
  Mod 4. Book 2 p6.
  Mod 6. Book 1 p19-20. Book 2 p14.
 Key Maths   Level 2. Book 3 p47. Book 5 p26, 27. Book 6 p19.
 Making Sure of Maths   Introductory Book p55-56.
 Mathematics for Schools   Level 2 (1st ed.). Book 3 p49-50. Book 4 p14-15, 16, 19.
 Maths Adventure   2. Pupil's Book p88, 90.
  3. Pupil's Book p19, 66.
 Our First School Maths   Book 5 p10-11.
 Oxford Middle School Mathematics   Book 1 p86-87, 95. Book 2 p18-19, 46.
 Primary Mathematics (SPMG)   Stage 2. Workbook 2 p5-8, 12-13, 16, 18.
  Workbook 4 p6, 9, 12, 14. Card 2b.
  Stage 3. Textbook p23, 25, 27, 29, 31.
 Towards Mathematics   Core Unit 6 p14-15. Core Unit 11 p5-7, 11. Core Unit 16 p1, 2, 8. Core Unit 17 p12.

S   *Headway Maths*   Book 1 p40. Book 3 p11.
 Maths (Holt)   Book 2 p63-64. Workbook 3 p28-29.

SM   *Four a Day series*   Book 9 p29-30.
 Number Workbook   Multiplication p5-7, 10, 14, 16, 18, 20.

Books for teachers
 Mathematics: the later Primary years   p75.

2.   *Practice in multiplication. Estimating answers and approximations.*

See also   p60   Applications and problems in multiplication and division over 100.
  p60   Mixed applications and problems in addition, subtraction, multiplication and division over 100.

P   *Alpha (new ed.)*   Alpha 1 p75. Alpha 2 p31, 82.
 Beta (new ed.)   Beta 1 p84, 96. Beta 2 p23.
 Basic Mathematics   Book 2 p22, 32.
 Hey Mathematics   Mod 3. Book 3 p8, 21, 22. Book 4 p33, 35.
  Mod 4. Book 2 p14.
  Mod 6. Book 1 p8, 19-20.
 Key Maths   Level 2. Book 3 p48, 49, 50, 51, 59. Book 4 p13, 14, 15. Book 5 p25, 27.
  Book 6 p18.
 Making Sure of Maths   Book 1 p27, 33, 42, 77.
 Maths Adventure   3. Pupil's Book p83. Activity Book p58.
  5. Activity Book p42-43.
 Primary Mathematics (SPMG)   Stage 2. Workbook 2 p15, 16, 18. Workbook 4 p4, 6, 9, 12, 14, 17.

S   *Headway Maths*   Book 1 p41, 64, 82. Book 2 p48. Book 3 p10. Book 4 p8.
 Maths (Holt)   Book 1 p88.
 Maths Matters   Book 1 p10-11.

SM   *Blackie's Practice Workbooks*   Book 3 p13, 15. Book 4 p28. Book 5 p9, 11, 15, 21.
 Number Workbook   Multiplication p2, 8, 11-13, 15, 16.

N30   Division of increasingly large numbers by a single digit number. Division by 10.

1.   *Exploration of patterns in division and methods of dividing numbers.*

Division by 10.

$72 \div 6$, $720 \div 6$, $7200 \div 6$ and similar patterns.

Exploration of methods of dividing numbers using structured apparatus, etc.

Initially methods of dividing numbers below 100 explored; later these principles extended to the division of numbers over 100 by a single digit number.

e.g. (a) Repeated subtraction, progressing to subtracting in groups.

e.g. $68 \div 4$

$$
\begin{array}{r|r}
4 & 68 \\
- & 20 \quad 5 \times 4 \\
\hline
 & 48 \quad + \\
- & 20 \quad 5 \times 4 \\
\hline
 & 28 \quad + \\
- & 20 \quad 5 \times 4 \\
\hline
 & 8 \quad + \\
- & 8 \quad 2 \times 4 \\
\hline
 & 0 \quad 17 \times 4
\end{array}
$$

So $68 \div 4 = 17$

(b) Regrouping

e.g.
$$
\begin{aligned}
68 \div 4 &= (40 + 28) \div 4 \\
&= (40 \div 4) + (28 \div 4) \\
&= \quad 10 \quad + \quad 7 \\
&= \quad\quad 17
\end{aligned}
$$

Eventually more efficient methods based on these ideas may be understood and thereafter used.

Later division with remainders expressed as decimals.

Use of a calculator allows patterns and methods to be investigated without the interference of routine manipulations.

See also PV2,4,7 Place value of whole numbers.
         PV5,6,8 Place value. Decimal notation.
         N14 Multibase arithmetic.
         N15,16,20,21 Addition and subtraction. Number bonds.
         N18 Division to 100.
         N19(1) Division as the inverse of multiplication.
         N19(2) Non-commutative nature of division.
         N19(3) Patterns in multiplication and division to 10×10.
         N32 Division of decimals.
         N34 Division by 2 and more digit numbers.

P   *Alpha (new ed.)* Alpha 1 p86.
    Beta (new ed.) Beta 2 p28, 78.
    Hey Mathematics Mod 3. Book 4 p38.
                Mod 4. Book 3 p23, 30-31.
                Mod 6. Book 1 p14-15, 16-17.
    Key Maths Level 2. Book 3 p41. Book 4 p25-28.
    Mathematics for Schools Level 2 (1st ed.). Book 4 p30-31, 33. Book 6 p6-7, 8-9.
    Maths Adventure 2. Pupil's Book p88, 93.
                4. Pupil's Book p28.
    Oxford Middle School Mathematics Book 2 p35-37, 47-49.
    Primary Mathematics (SPMG) Stage 2. Workbook 3 p12-13, 16.
                         Stage 3. Textbook p32. Card 28, 29, 33, 35.
    Towards Mathematics Core Unit 12 p10-11. Core Unit 16 p10.

S   *Focus Mathematics* Book 6 p45.
    Maths (Holt) Book 1 p60. Book 2 p72-73.

SM *Four a Day series* Book 6 p25. Book 8 p25-26.

Books for teachers
    Hey Mathematics Mod 3 Teachers' Book p28-29.
    Mathematics: from Primary to Secondary p48-49.

2. Practice in division. Estimating answers and approximations.

See also N18 Practice in division to 100.
         p60 Applications and problems in multiplication and division over 100.
         p60 Mixed applications and problems in addition, subtraction, multiplication and division over 100.

P   *Alpha (new ed.)* Alpha 1 p76. Alpha 2 p32, 82. Alpha 3 p14.
    Basic Mathematics Book 2 p22, 32.
    Hey Mathematics Mod 4. Book 2 p33. Book 3 p24, 32. Book 4 p27.
                Mod 5. Book 1 p25. Book 2 p24.
                Mod 6. Book 1 p11-12. Book 2 p17. Book 3 p3.
    Key Maths Level 2. Book 4 p24. Book 5 p33. Book 6 p21.
    Making Sure of Maths Book 1 p28.
    Maths Adventure 5. Pupil's Book p46.
    Primary Mathematics (SPMG) Stage 2. Workbook 3 p17-18, Card 2, 3b.
                         Stage 3. Textbook p4, 5, 24, 26, 28, 30. Card 22-27.

S   *A World of Mathematics* Book 5 p36-37.
    Headway Maths Book 1 p87. Book 2 p48. Book 3 p18. Book 4 p26, 27.

SM *Blackie's Practice Workbooks* Book 4 p12, 17, 29. Book 5 p10, 12, 16, 19, 21.
     Number Workbook Division p7-9, 11-17.

N29, 30, 33, 34 (cont.) Multiplication and division over 100. Applications and problems.

See also
	p60	Mixed applications and problems in addition, subtraction, multiplication and division over 100.
	N23	Ratio, rate and proportion.
	N24	Finding percentages.
	N38	Probability.
	AR3	Introduction to and use of 'variables'.
	AR8	Algebraic solution of simple equations.
	VR8, L9	Using and interpreting scales.
	Sh21	Bisecting angles.
	CV9	Volume of cube and cuboid.
	CV10, A10, L10,12, W8,10, T12	Problems and applications relating to measurement e.g. measuring in bulk to find fractional amounts.
	CV12	Volume of triangular prism, etc.
	A7	Area of square and rectangle.
	A11	Area of cross section of cube and cuboid.
	A12	Area of triangle, parallelogram, etc.
	L7	Perimeter of square.

P   *Alpha (new ed.)*   Alpha 3 p53.
Beta (new ed.)   Beta 4 p51.
Hey Mathematics   Mod 3. Book 5 p20.
         Mod 5. Book 1 p24, 25.
Key Maths   Level 2. Book 4 p20, 32.
Making Sure of Maths   Book 1 p51, 53. Book 2 p12. Book 3 p13.
Mathematics for Schools   Level 2 (1st ed.). Book 3 p18. Book 7 p14.
Maths Adventure   5. Pupil's Book p46.
Oxford Middle School Mathematics   Book 1 p96. Book 3 p41, 42, 43.
Primary Mathematics (SPMG)   Stage 2. Workbook 2 p15. Workbook 3 p18.
         Stage 3. Textbook p6, 64. Card 4, 41, 43, 53, 54, 55, 56.
         Stage 4. Textbook p10, 11.
         Stage 5. Textbook p2. Card 4.
Towards Mathematics   Core Unit 6 p16. Core Unit 11 p10.
         Core Unit 12 p11. Core Unit 15 p4.

S   *A World of Mathematics*   Book 5 p13, 37-38. Book 6 p14.
Headway Maths   Book 1 p78. Book 3 p19, 71.
         Book 4 p9, 26-27, 42. Book 5 p5.
Maths (Holt)   Book 1 p92. Book 2 p81.
         4th Year p23.
Maths Matters   Book 2 p22-23. Book 3 p3, 11.
Maths You Need   p82.

SM   *Blackie's Practice Workbooks*   Book 5 p17-18.
Check it Again   Book 3 p19-20.
Four a Day series   Book 6 p30. Book 8 p19.
Problems   First Problems p25, 28, 29.

N20, 21, 29, 30, 33, & 34 (cont.) Addition, subtraction, multiplication and division over 100. Mixed applications and problems.

Problems requiring the selection of the appropriate operation from these four.

Problems requiring the use of more than one of these operations.

See also
	p52	Applications and problems in addition and subtraction over 100.
	p60	Applications and problems in multiplication and division over 100.
	N37	Averages (addition and division).
	AR3	Introduction to and use of 'variables'.
	AR8	Algebraic solution of simple equations.
	Sh23	Pythagoras' theorem.
	A7,12	Area of composite shapes involving squares, rectangles, triangles, etc. (multiplication and addition).
	A11,12	Surface area of cubes, cuboids, triangular prisms, etc. (multiplication and addition).

P   *Hey Mathematics*   Mod 3. Book 3 p11. Book 4 p28, 32.
         Mod 4. Book 2 p15-16. Book 3 p4.
Making Sure of Maths   Book 1 p86-87.
Maths Adventure   4. Pupil's Book p88-89.
Oxford Middle School Mathematics   Book 1 p94. Book 2 p17.
Primary Mathematics (SPMG)   Stage 4. Card 5, 6.

S *Focus Mathematics*   Book 1 p61-63, 96-97.
Inner Ring Maths   Book 3 p14.
Mathematics for Life   Book B1 p10-11.
Maths (Holt)   Workbook 2 p21.
On Our Own Two Feet   Book 3 p1-4.

SM *Check it Again*   Book 5 p15-16.
Problems   First Problems p23-24, 25, 27, 30.
Second Problems p28, 35, 39, 40-41.
Third Problems p21-22.

Multiplication of decimals by whole numbers and later by decimals.   N31

Multiplication of decimals by 10, 100, etc. and multiples of these numbers.

Exploration of methods of multiplying decimals as in N29, 33, ensuring that any technique eventually used is fully understood.

Applications.

See also   M8   Unit pricing. Multiplication of money.
M11   Household bills based on unit pricing.
M12   Pay; piecework and timework.
M13   Regular payments. HP, etc.
PV5,6,8   Place value. Decimal notation.
N14   Multibase arithmetic.
N17,19,29,33   Multiplication of whole numbers.
N23   Ratio, rate and proportion.
F4,6   Multiplication of fractions.
Sh23, CV9,12, A7,11,12 and L7 (as listed on p78 and p82)   Using formulae when measurements are expressed as decimals.
CV10, A10, L10, W8, T12   Problems and applications relating to measurement.
CV12   Volume of cylinder ('pi' as $3 \cdot 14$).
A13   Circle area ('pi' as $3 \cdot 14$).
L11   Circle circumference ('pi' as $3 \cdot 14$).

P *Alpha (new ed.)*   Alpha 1 p81. Alpha 2 p31, 82. Alpha 3 p50.
Beta (new ed.)   Beta 2 p84. Beta 4 p48. Beta 5 p30. Beta 6 p34-36.
Basic Mathematics   Book 3 p10. Book 4 p47, 48. Book 5 p44, 45.
Hey Mathematics   Mod 4. Book 3 p5-9. Book 4 p7, 10-17.
Mod 5. Book 1 p28-41. Book 2 p1-5, 7-8, 9-15, 40. Book 3 p26, 37. Book 5 p21.
Mod 6. Book 1 p26. Book 2 p26-27. Book 3 p2, 3.
Key Maths   Level 2. Book 4 p15, 20. Book 5 p40, 43, 44. Book 6 p23, 24, 55-57.
Making Sure of Maths   Book 3 p22-23. Book 4 p14-15. Book 5 p27.
Mathematics for Schools   Level 2 (1st ed.). Book 4 p21. Book 5 p48. Book 6 p46. Book 7 p36-40.
Maths Adventure   3. Activity Book p39.
4. Pupil's Book p31, 60-61. Activity Book p49.
5. Pupil's Book p34, 38.
Oxford Middle School Mathematics   Book 3 p22-23. Book 4 p22-23.
Primary Mathematics (SPMG)   Stage 3. Textbook p86. Workbook p30.
Stage 4. Textbook p65-67. Card 39, 40.
Stage 5. Textbook p38-42.
Towards Mathematics   Core Unit 10 p5. Core Unit 11 p12, 13, 14.
Core Unit 17 p12, 13, 14, 15. Core Unit 19 p14.
Core Unit 21 p11.

S *A World of Mathematics*   Book 3 p58. Book 5 p26, 28-29.
Focus Mathematics   Book 6 p33, 39-44.
Headway Maths   Book 2 p52. Book 3 p20, 42-43, 44. Book 4 p32, 46.
Maths (Holt)   5th Year p83.
Maths Matters   Book 2 p28-29.
Mathsworks   Book 1 p86-87.

SM *Check it Again*   Book 4 p25-26.
Four a Day series   Book 10 p49, 50-51.
Number Workbook   Multiplication p22-31. Decimals p19, 20, 22, 26.

Books for teachers
Mathematics: from Primary to Secondary   p50-53.

N32 Division of decimals by whole number and later by decimals.

Division of decimals by 10, 100, etc. and multiples of these numbers.

Exploration of methods of dividing decimals as in N30, 34 ensuring that any technique eventually used is fully understood.

Applications.

See also   M8   Unit pricing and value for money. Division of money.
           M9,11,12,13   Percentage operations on money.
           M12   Piecework and timework; checking payslip.
           PV5,6,8   Place value. Decimal notation.
           N14   Multibase arithmetic.
           N18,19,30,34   Division of whole numbers.
           N23   Ratio, rate and proportion.
           N24   Finding percentages.
           N37   Averages (addition and division).
           F7   Division of fractions.
           Sh23, CV9,12, A7,11,12 and L7 (as listed on p78 and p82)   Using formulae to calculate single dimensions by division when measurements are expressed as decimals.
           CV10, A10, L10,12, W8,10, T12   Problems and applications relating to measurement e.g. measuring in bulk to find fractional amounts.
           CV12, A13, L11   Finding one dimension given cylinder volume, circle area or circumference and other necessary dimensions. ('pi' as $3\cdot14$).

P   *Alpha (new ed.)*   Alpha 1 p82. Alpha 2 p32, 82. Alpha 3 p52.
     Beta (new ed.)   Beta 2 p85. Beta 5 p31, 32, 33.
                      Beta 6 p4, 63.
     Basic Mathematics   Book 3 p10, 52. Book 4 p49. Book 5 p46, 47.
     Hey Mathematics   Mod 4. Book 4 p18-22.
                      Mod 5. Book 1 p28-30. Book 2 p5-8, 25-29. Book 3 p22-26. Book 4 p1-3. Book 5 p17-20.
                      Mod 6. Book 1 p12-14, 17, 18, 33-35. Book 2 p17-19, 25, 26, 27, 28-29. Book 3 p2, 3, 4.
     Key Maths   Level 2. Book 5 p41. Book 6 p28, 58, 59-60.
     Making Sure of Maths   Book 3 p22-23. Book 4 p16-17. Book 5 p27-28.
     Mathematics for Schools   Level 2 (1st ed.). Book 7 p16-18. Book 8 p16-19.
     Maths Adventure   4. Pupil's Book p60-61, 62. Activity Book p49.
                      5. Pupil's Book p38.
     Oxford Middle School Mathematics   Book 3 p70-71. Book 4 p26-27.
     Primary Mathematics (SPMG)   Stage 3. Textbook p87-88. Workbook p31.
                      Stage 4. Textbook p68-70. Card 39, 40.
                      Stage 5. Textbook p49-52.
     Towards Mathematics   Core Unit 17 p16.

S   *A World of Mathematics*   Book 6 p25-28.
     Focus Mathematics   Book 6 p48-59.
     Headway Maths   Book 2 p72. Book 3 p21, 45, 46.
                      Book 4 p32, 47, 76-77.
     Maths Matters   Book 2 p28-29.
     Mathsworks   Book 1 p86-87.

SM   *Check it Again*   Book 4 p24-25, 27.
     Four a Day series   Book 10 p51.
     Number Workbook   Division p22-31. Decimals p21, 23, 27.

Books for teachers
     Mathematics: from Primary to Secondary   p53-54.

N33 Multiplication of two and later more digit numbers by two and later more digit numbers.

1. Exploration of patterns in multiplication and methods of multiplying numbers.

Multiplication by 10, 100, 1000, etc. and by multiples of these numbers.

Methods of multiplying investigated as in N29, ensuring that any technique eventually used is fully understood.

Note that understanding depends on appreciation of the distributive law for multiplication (See N28).

Use of a calculator allows patterns and methods to be investigated without the interference of routine manipulations.

See also PV2,4,7 Place value of whole numbers.

   N14 Multibase arithmetic.

   N15,16,20,21 Addition and subtraction. Number bonds.

   N19(2) Commutativity and associativity of multiplication.

   N19(3) Patterns in multiplication and division to 10 × 10.

   N29(1) Multiplication by single digit numbers; patterns and methods.

   N31 Multiplication of decimals.

P *Alpha (new ed.)* Alpha 3 p50.

 Beta (new ed.) Beta 3 p47. Beta 4 p48.

 Basic Mathematics Book 2 p52. Book 3 p12, 13. Book 4 p20, 21, 93-98, 100. Book 5 p17.

 Hey Mathematics Mod 4. Book 2 p7-9. Book 3 p1.

     Mod 6. Book 2 p14, 15.

 Key Maths Level 2. Book 4 p16, 17, 18, 19. Book 5 p28, 29. Book 6 p23, 24.

 Making Sure of Maths Book 2 p21. Book 3 p11.

 Mathematics for Schools Level 2 (1st ed.). Book 4 p15, 17-18. Book 5 p44-47, 49.

 Maths Adventure 3. Pupil's Book p42-43, 67, 85.

     4. Pupil's Book p27. Activity Book p33.

     5. Pupil's Book p6, 42, 78-79.

 Oxford Middle School Mathematics Book 3 p10-11, 67.

 Primary Mathematics (SPMG) Stage 3. Textbook p57-63. Card 44, 45, 46.

     Stage 4. Textbook p11. Card 9, 10.

 Towards Mathematics Core Unit 11 p16. Core Unit 16 p1, 2, 3.

S *A World of Mathematics* Book 5 p11.

 Focus Mathematics Book 4 p19-24. Book 6 p35-38.

 Headway Maths Book 2 p85. Book 3 p11, 12, 70. Book 4 p8, 9.

 Maths (Holt) Book 2 p60-61, 92.

SM *Check it Again* Book 4 p22-23. Book 5 p6.

 Four a Day series Book 9 p33-34. Book 10 p21-22.

 Number Workbook Multiplication p19, 20.

Books for teachers

 Mathematics: the later Primary years p75.

2. *Practice in multiplication. Estimating answers and approximations.*

See also p60 Applications and problems in multiplication and division over 100.

   p60 Mixed applications and problems in addition, subtraction, multiplication and division over 100.

P *Beta (new ed.)* Beta 6 p5.

 Hey Mathematics Mod 4. Book 3 p2, 3.

     Mod 6. Book 2 p15-16. Book 3 p3.

 Making Sure of Maths Book 3 p11

 Mathematics for Schools Level 2 (1st ed.). Book 4 p20.

 Maths Adventure 5. Pupil's Book p5. Activity Book p21.

 Primary Mathematics (SPMG) Stage 3. Textbook p64. Card 40, 42.

S *A World of Mathematics* Book 5 p12, 13.

 Focus Mathematics Book 6 p39.

 Headway Maths Book 3 p71, 82. Book 4 p9.

SM *Blackie's Practice Workbooks* Book 5 p26.

 Number Workbook Multiplication p3, 21.

Division of two and later more digit numbers by two and later more digit numbers.   N34

1. *Exploration of patterns in division and methods of dividing numbers.*

Division by 10, 100, 1000, etc. and multiples of these numbers.

Methods of dividing investigated as in N30, ensuring that any technique eventually used is fully understood.

Division with remainders expressed as decimals.

Use of a calculator allows patterns and methods to be investigated without the interference of routine manipulations.

See also PV2,4,7 Place value of whole numbers.
PV5,6,8 Place value. Decimal notation.
N14 Multibase arithmetic.
N15,16,20,21 Addition and subtraction. Number bonds.
N18 Division to 100.
N19(1) Division as the inverse of multiplication.
N19(2) Non-commutative nature of division.
N19(3) Patterns in multiplication and division to 10 × 10.
N24 Finding percentages.
N30(1) Division by single digit numbers; patterns and methods.
N32 Division of decimals.

P *Alpha (new ed.)* Alpha 3 p51-52.
Beta (new ed.) Beta 3 p48. Beta 4 p49-50.
Hey Mathematics Mod 4. Book 3 p21.
Mod 5. Book 3 p1-3, 19.
Mod 6. Book 1 p21-23.
Key Maths Level 2. Book 5 p36.
Making Sure of Maths Book 3 p13.
Mathematics for Schools Level 2 (1st ed.). Book 6 p10-11. Book 7 p13, 15.
Maths Adventure 3. Pupil's Book p25, 69.
4. Pupil's Book p29.
5. Pupil's Book p43.
Oxford Middle School Mathematics Book 3 p28-29. Book 4 p10-11.
Primary Mathematics (SPMG) Stage 4. Textbook p54-58, 97-98.

S *Focus Mathematics* Book 6 p46-47.
Headway Maths Book 2 p85. Book 3 p72-73.

SM *Check it Again* Book 4 p22-24.

Books for teachers
Mathematics: from Primary to Secondary p48-49.

2. *Practice in division. Estimating answers and approximations.*

See also p60 Applications and problems in multiplication and division over 100.
p60 Mixed applications and problems in addition, subtraction, multiplication and division over 100.

P *Basic Mathematics* Book 3 p14-15, 24-25.
Hey Mathematics Mod 4. Book 3 p24.
Mod 5. Book 5 p10-11.
Mod 6. Book 1 p24, 36. Book 2 p20.
Key Maths Level 2. Book 5 p34-35. Book 6 p22.
Making Sure of Maths Book 3 p11.
Mathematics for Schools Level 2 (1st ed.). Book 7 p14.
Maths Adventure 5. Pupil's Book p44-45, 46, 49.
Primary Mathematics (SPMG) Stage 4. Textbook p58, 96, 99. Workbook p16.
Stage 5. Card 5.

S *Focus Mathematics* Book 6 p48.
Headway Maths Book 3 p83. Book 4 p42.

SM *Blackie's Practice Workbooks* Book 5 p27-28.
Number Workbook Division p18-21.

N35 Operation on directed numbers.

Addition and subtraction of directed numbers, initially using the number line.

Investigation of patterns in addition and subtraction

e.g. (a) $^+4 + {^-3} = {^+1}$
$^+4 - {^+3} = {^+1}$
(b) $^+3 + {^+1} = {^+4}$
$^+3 - {^-1} = {^+4}$

The additive inverse.

Later multiplicaton of directed numbers.

Applications: temperature, bank accounts, etc.

See also   AR7   Open sentences involving directed numbers. Patterns and graphs.
            AR8   Identity and inverse elements,
            and topics listed for N27.

P   *Beta (new ed.)*   Beta 5 p13. Beta 6 p79-81.
         Hey Mathematics   Mod 5. Book 1 p16-18. Book 5 p12.
         Making Sure of Maths   Book 6 p18-22.
         Mathematics for Schools   Level 2 (1st ed.). Book 8 p2-6, 58-61. Book 9 p13-19. Book 10 p6, 7-12.
         Maths Adventure   3. Pupil's Book p78-79.
                             4. Pupil's Book p67. Activity Book p52.
                             5. Pupil's Book p25-26, 66-68, 69-70, 86. Activity Book p32.
         Oxford Middle School Mathematics   Book 4 p62-63, 90-91.
         Towards Mathematics   Core Unit 25 p1-3.

S   *A World of Mathematics*   Book 5 p23-25.
         Mathsworks   Book 2 p38-39. Tryouts 2 p18, 19, 20, 21.

SM   *Mathematics and Metric Measuring*   Book 4 p16-18.

Books for teachers
         Mathematics: the later Primary years   p143-157.
         Mathematics: from Primary to Secondary   p68-72.

Introduction to Statistics with an emphasis on the meaning and validity of descriptive and predictive statements made by the media, politicians, advertisers, etc.

e.g.   3 out of 4 cat owners feed their cats on 'Tiddles'.

The average man earns £100 per week.

15 year old children who smoke over 10 cigarettes a day are likely to . . .

Hiroshima atom-bomb survivors have a life expectancy nearly 2 years longer than other Japanese. Therefore atom bombs are good for you!

Statistics I.   Surveys and generalisations made from them.   N36

Importance of the sample: size, biased or random, etc.

See VR section for additional surveys and methods of recording frequency.

See also   M9   Advertising and trading stamps.
            N24   Percentages.
            AR4,5,6   Straight line, curved and scatter graphs. Generalisations.

P   *Hey Mathematics*   Mod 4. Book 5 p37.
                             Mod 5. Book 5 p28-32.
         Making Sure of Maths   Book 6 p84-88.
         Mathematics for Schools   Level 2 (1st ed.). Book 3 p1-4, 16-18. Book 5 p7-8, 64.
         Oxford Middle School Mathematics   Book 2 p86-87. Book 3 p60-61, 75.
         Primary Mathematics (SPMG)   Stage 3. Workbook p32-34.
                                         Stage 5. Textbook p53-55. Card 23, 24.
         Towards Mathematics   Core Unit 24 p1-5, 14-16.

S   *Focus Mathematics*   Book 5 p57-74.
         Maths (Holt)   5th Year p28-32, 42-43, 84-85.
         Mathsworks   Book 1 p29, 58-61, 76-80.
                        Tryouts 1 p12, 13, 35. Book 2 p76-77.
                        Tryouts 2 p37.
         Maths You Need   p95, 122-123.

Books for teachers
         Mathematics: from Primary to Secondary   p123-128.

N37 Statistics II.   Average (mean), mode and median.

Concept of average and experience finding averages using generalised formula, focusing on applications, e.g. height, weight.

The graph of normal distribution (See also AR5).

Idea of 'above' and 'below' average.

Applications: I.Q., reading ages, biscuit packet contents, etc.

The mode (i.e. the element that occurs most frequently) and the median (i.e. the middle element when the elements have been ordered by size).

See also   N8,15,18,20,30,34   Addition and division of whole numbers.
          N22,32 Addition and division of decimals.
          N23   Ratio, rate and proportion.
          N27,35   Directed numbers. Simple operations.
          AR3(1) Generalisations expressed using 'variables'.
          AR3(2) Substituting numbers into algebraic expressions.
          W8   Average weight.
          T13   Average speed.
          Temp. Average temperature.

P   *Alpha (new ed.)*   Alpha 2 p54. Alpha 3 p75.
      Beta (new ed.)   Beta 3 p62, 63. Beta 4 p9. Beta 5 p16-17.
                    Beta 6 p46-47, 87.
      Basic Mathematics   Book 3 p16, 17. Book 5 p21, 22.
      Hey Mathematics   Mod 5. Book 5 p40.
                    Mod 6. Book 4 p35-37.
      Key Maths   Level 2. Book 5 p45, 46. Book 6 p30-31, 116.
      Making Sure of Maths   Book 6 p86-88, 89-92.
      Mathematics for Schools   Level 2 (1st ed.). Book 5 p9-12. Book 7 p64. Book 8 p38. Book 9 p47, 48.
      Maths Adventure   3. Pupil's Book p51.
                    5. Pupil's Book p82-83.
      Oxford Middle School Mathematics   Book 1 p31. Book 3 p58-59, 70. Book 4 p11, 54-55.
      Primary Mathematics (SPMG)   Stage 3. Textbook p91-95, Card 49, 50.
                    Stage 4. Textbook p100-101.
                    Stage 5. Card 15.
      Towards Mathematics   Core Unit 14 p16. Core Unit 22 p12-16.

S   *A World of Mathematics*   Book 3 p19-22.
      Focus Mathematics   Book 5 p74-78, 168-169. Book 8 p39-50.
      Headway Maths   Book 3 p54-55, 83. Book 5 p65.
      Maths (Holt)   Book 3 p72-75, 80-81, 83. Workbook 3 p22.
                    4th Year p24-26, 36-39, 40-41, 76, 77, 80-81, 86. 4th Year Workbook p8.
                    5th Year p33, 36, 43, 62, 76. 5th Year Workbook p27.
      Mathsworks   Book 1 p17-19, 22, 26-29, 121-122, 123.
                    Tryouts 1 p12. Book 2 p74-75, 76, 77.
                    Tryouts 2 p37.
      Maths You Need   p120.

SM   *Check it Again*   Book 4 p17-18.
      Four a Day series   Book 8 p28-29. Book 9 p34-35. Book 10 p18-19.
      Mathematics and Metric Measuring   Book 2 p43-45.
      Problems   Third Problems p40-41, 42, 43.

Books for teachers
      Mathematics: from Primary to Secondary   p128-131.

N38 Statistics III.   Probability.

1. *Permutations and combinations.*

Permutations e.g. number of different ways of rearranging letters A B C D (introduced in N13).

Combinations e.g. number of possible combinations when throwing two dice (introduced in N17).

The meaning of betting odds.

Introduction to linear programming based on combinations within prescribed limits, e.g. pairs of items out of two sets that will together cost less than £5.

See also M13   Gambling.
         N23   Ratios.
         S4,5   Intersection of two and more sets.

P   *Basic Mathematics*   Book 1 p93. Book 2 p51.
       Key Maths   Level 2. Book 1 p61.
       Mathematics for Schools   Level 2 (1st ed.). Book 5 p35. Book 6 p27, 28. Book 7 p32, 33, 34, 35.
       Maths Adventure   3. Card 22.
                           4. Card 23.
                           5. Pupil's Book p1-2. Activity Book p22.
       Oxford Middle School Mathematics   Book 3 p69.
       Primary Mathematics (SPMG)   Stage 3. Workbook p35.

S   *Maths (Holt)*   Book 2 p78, 79. 4th Year p15, 33, 52, 56.
                         4th Year Workbook p29-30. 5th Year p57, 85.
       Mathsworks   Book 1 p36-37, 70-72. Tryouts 1 p14, 15, 32, 33, 47.
                      Book 2 p24-29, 70-71. Tryouts 2 p13-15, 35, 43.
       Maths You Need   p132-137.

SM *Mathematics and Metric Measuring*   Book 4 p29-33.

2.   Investigating probability.

Recording and discussing the frequency of occurence of events that are equally likely (e.g. outcome when tossing a coin or throwing one die) and not equally likely (e.g. totals when throwing two or more dice).

Idea of probability.

Using permutations or combinations to calculate theoretical probability.

Probability of event, S,
when possible outcomes $=$ $\dfrac{\text{number of ways S can happen}}{\text{number of possible outcomes}}$
are equally likely.

Expressing probability as a decimal or fraction.

Meaning of 0 and 1 as probabilities.

Comparison of theoretical probability with observed frequency.

Predictions based on probability.

Applications e.g. gambling.

See also M9   Advertising.
         M13   Gambling.
         PV5,6,8 Decimal notation.
         N23   Ratio.
         N30,34 Division with remainders expressed as decimals.
         F2,3   Fractions. Equivalent and lowest term fractions.
         AR6   Scatter graphs.

P   *Basic Mathematics*   Book 3 p56-57. Book 4 p72-73.
       Hey Mathematics   Mod 2. Book 5 p13.
       Key Maths   Level 2. Book 5 p114-116.
       Making Sure of Maths   Book 5 p92-94. Book 6 p78-83.
       Mathematics for Schools   Level 2 (1st ed.). Book 4 p34-37. Book 6 p25-27, 29.
                                   Book 7 p30-35. Book 10 p29-33.
       Oxford Middle School Mathematics   Book 1 p100-102. Book 3 p68. Book 4 p80-83.
       Towards Mathematics   Core Unit 24 p2-13.

S   *A World of Mathmatics*   Book 6 p52-55, 60-61.
       Focus Mathematics   Book 9 p81-100.
       Inner Ring Maths   Book 1 p28.
       Maths (Holt)   Book 1 p70-71. Book 3 p48, 57. Workbook 3 p30. 4th Year p34-35, 59-61.
                        4th Year Workbook p35. 5th Year p44, 77.
       Mathsworks   Book 1 p62-65, 68, 94-96, 124-126.
                      Tryouts 1 p28-31, 50-54. Book 2 p32, 72-73.
                      Tryouts 2 p36, 40, 45, 46.
       Maths You Need   p130-131.

SM *Mathematics and Metric Measuring*   Book 4 p34-40.

Books for teachers
       Mathematics: from Primary to Secondary   p131-141.

Fractions

Contents

Topics with a sequence of development extending over considerable time.

Half, quarter, whole one.

Introduction to half, quarter, whole one as they arise naturally in measuring, handling money, etc.

Notation of half and quarter.

Experience colouring in these fractions of a shape and cutting apples, etc. into halves and quarters.

Finding a half or a quarter of a small number.

See also   M2 $\frac{1}{2}$p coin.
            N12   Introduction to division.
            VR5   Pie charts.
            S3   Subsets. The complement of the set.
            Sh10   Idea of angle: $\frac{1}{2}$ turn, $\frac{1}{4}$ turn, etc.
            CV3, A3, L3, W3, T3   Use of arbitrary units for measurement.
            CV5, L4, W5   Use of standard units for measurement.
            A4,6   Area of compound and irregular shapes.
            T7   Telling the time.
            T9   Halves and quarters in ages of children.

P   *Ready for Alpha and Beta (new ed.)* p16, 17.
      Beta (new ed.) Beta 1 p24-25.
      Basic Mathematics Book 1 p56-57.
      Hey Mathematics Mod 1. Book 2 p40. Book 5 p39.
      Key Maths Level 1. Book 4 p42-43. Book 6 p46-47. Book 7 p45-46.
                  Level 2. Book 2 p26.
      Maths Adventure 1. Pupil's Book p70-71. Activity Book p45-46.
      Nuffield Maths 5-11 Bronto Books. Set A. Poor Bronto. Set B. Mini half-as-big.
                        1. Worksheets C1, 1·2.
                        2. Worksheets N12, 1·4.
      Numbers and Words Book 4 p28. Book 7 p23-24.
      Our First School Maths Book 5 p30-32.
      Primary Mathematics (SPMG) Stage 1. Workbook 3 p15-16, 19-20, Card 6, 7.
                                      Stage 2. Workbook 1 p13.

S   *Inner Ring Maths* Book 2 p18.

SM   *Four a Day series* Book 4 p50-51. Book 5 p33, 56-57.

Books for teachers
    Mathematics: the first 3 years p89.

Fractions and their notation.

Practical experience dividing 'whole' into equal parts to demonstrate $\frac{1}{3}$, $\frac{1}{5}$, $\frac{1}{6}$, $\frac{1}{10}$, etc.

Several of these parts combined (or added) to illustrate $\frac{2}{3}$, $\frac{3}{5}$, etc. (e.g. $\frac{2}{5} + \frac{1}{5} = \frac{3}{5}$) and later mixed numbers (e.g. $1\frac{3}{4}$) and improper fractions (e.g. $\frac{7}{4}$) introduced.

Understanding of the notation.

See also   M2,3,4,5,7   Addition and subtraction of $\frac{1}{2}$p's.
            PV5,6,8   Decimal fractions.
            N6   Introduction to addition.
             N12   Introduction to division. Fractional notation for division.
            N23   Ratio, rate and proportion.
            N24   Percentages.
            N38   Probability expressed as a fraction.
            VR5   Pie charts.
            S3   Subsets. The complement of the set.
            Sh10   Idea of angle: $\frac{3}{4}$ turn, etc.
            Sh13   Degree as $\frac{1}{360}$th of complete turn.
            A4,6   Area of compound and irregular shapes.
            T7   Telling the time.

P   *Alpha (new ed.)* Alpha 1 p12, 34, 59. Alpha 2 p37, 39.
                          Alpha 3 p24.
      Beta (new ed.) Beta 1 p56. Beta 2 p25, 26, 66, 67.
                      Beta 3 p13, 39. Beta 4 p23, Beta 5 p24, 25.
      Basic Mathematics Book 2 p39, 42. Book 3 p44, 45. Book 5 p32.

F3 Equivalent and lowest term fractions.

Ordering simple fractions (e.g. $\frac{1}{2} > \frac{1}{3} > \frac{1}{4}$) and later more complex fractions (e.g. $\frac{2}{3} > \frac{3}{8}$).

Equivalent fractions/fraction families (e.g. $\frac{1}{2}$ $\frac{2}{4}$ $\frac{3}{6}$ $\frac{4}{8}$ etc). This may be a difficult concept requiring concrete experience with varied units. Fraction diagrams may aid understanding

e.g.

demonstrates $\frac{3}{6}$ is equivalent to $\frac{1}{2}$.

Investigation of patterns in equivalent fractions (e.g. $\frac{1}{2}$ $\frac{2}{4}$ $\frac{3}{6}$ $\frac{4}{8}$ $\frac{5}{10}$ ...) leading to the idea of reducing any fraction to its lowest term fraction (e.g. $\frac{50}{100} \longrightarrow \frac{1}{2}$).

Finding common denominators for non-equivalent fractions by investigating the intersection of sets of multiples

    e.g.   multiples of 2 are 2, 4, 6, 8, 10, 12, etc.

           multiples of 3 are 3, 6, 9, 12, etc.

           common multiples of 2 and 3 are 6, 12, etc.

           So $\frac{1}{2}$, $\frac{2}{3}$ become $\frac{3}{6}$, $\frac{4}{6}$.

This understanding is assumed when adding fractions with different denominators (F5).

See also PV5,6,8   Decimal fractions.
          N19(3)   Multiples. Common multiples.
          N23   Ratio, rate and proportion.
          N24   Percentages.
          N38   Probability.
          AR2   Patterns and graphs from equivalent fractions.
          VR5   Pie charts.
          S2   Relations between sets. The equivalent relation.
          A2,5, L2   Ordering by area and length. Conservation.

P   *Alpha (new ed.)*   Alpha 1 p34, 35. Alpha 2 p55, 56, 57.
                   Alpha 3 p24. Alpha 4 p32.
    Beta (new ed.)   Beta 2 p68. Beta 3 p38, 39. Beta 4 p24.
                  Beta 5 p24, 25, 26. Beta 6 p27.
    Basic Mathematics   Book 3 p46, 47. Book 4 p28, 29, 30, 31, 32.
                    Book 5 p29, 30, 31.
    Hey Mathematics   Mod 5. Book 2 p31, 32, 37-38. Book 3 p32-37, 38-39.
                  Mod 6. Book 2 p1-9. Book 3 p5-11, 17-18, 20, 23-25.
    Key Maths   Level 2. Book 5 p53-56, 58, 60, 98, 99. Book 6 p33-35, 37-38.
    Making Sure of Maths   Book 2 p38, 39. Book 3 p24, 25, 26.
    Mathematics for Schools   Level 2 (1st ed.). Book 4 p42. Book 5 p21, 23. Book 7 p23.
    Maths Adventure   2. Pupil's Book p35, 51, 52.
                  3. Pupil's Book p49, 62. Activity Book p7, 54.
                  4. Pupil's Book p43-45. Activity Book p40-42.
                  5. Pupil's Book p16-18, 50. Activity Book p23, 25.
    Oxford Middle School Mathematics   Book 2 p30-31. Book 3 p38-39, 40.
    Primary Mathematics (SPMG)   Stage 3. Textbook p52-56. Workbook p15-16.
                             Stage 4. Textbook p23-25.
    Towards Mathematics   Core Unit 17 p1-11. Core Unit 21 p1.

S   *A World of Mathematics*   Book 2 p32. Book 3 p40, 41, 42, 43.
    Focus Mathematics   Book 4 p53-62.
    Headway Maths   Book 2 p56-57. Book 3 p28-29. Book 4 p20, 34.
    Impact Maths   Pupil's Book 1 p59, 60.
    Inner Ring Maths   Book 3 p18, 28.
    Maths (Holt)   Book 2 p24. Book 3 p87. Workbook 3 p31.
    Mathsworks   Tryouts 1 p7, 8.

SM   *Check it Again*   Book 5 p29.
    Four a Day series   Book 9 p38-39, 41, 43-44. Book 10 p27, 31-33.
    Number Workbook   Fractions p10-11, 12, 13, 14, 17.

Books for teachers
    Mathematics: from Primary to Secondary   p20-21.

Multiplication of fraction by whole number.   **F4**

Exploration of patterns and methods using structured apparatus, etc.

Progression from simple examples (e.g. $\frac{1}{3} \times 12$) to more complex ones (e.g. $\frac{3}{4} \times 8$ and later $\frac{2}{3} \times 8$).

Recognition of commutativity (e.g. $\frac{1}{3} \times 4 = 4 \times \frac{1}{3}$).

Applications.

See also   M8   Unit pricing e.g. $\frac{1}{2}$ kg at 24p a kg. 6 nails at $3\frac{1}{2}$p each.
          M9   Percentage discounts and increases in price. Inflation.
          M11,12,13   VAT, tax, interest, HP, etc.
          N19(2)   Commutativity of multiplication.
          N23   Ratio, rate and proportion.
          N24   Percentages.
          VR5   Pie charts.
          VR8, L9   Using and interpreting scales.
          Sh17   Similarity, enlargement and reduction.
          CV12, A13, L11   Circle circumference and area. Volume of cylinder ('pi' as $\frac{22}{7}$).
          A12   Area of triangle.
          T6,10,11 $\frac{1}{2}$ hour as 30 mins, etc.

P   *Alpha (new ed.)* Apha 1 p35, 59. Alpha 2 p38.
        Beta (new ed.) Beta 1 p57. Beta 2 p26, 66, 67, 68.
                Beta 3 p14.
        Basic Mathematics Book 1 p58. Book 2 p42. Book 4 p37.
                Book 5 p35.
        Hey Mathematics Mod 3. Book 2 p13, 20.
                Mod 4. Book 3 p34-35.
                Mod 5. Book 4 p27.
                Mod 6. Book 2 p30. Book 3 p16, 32.
        Key Maths Level 2. Book 2 p35. Book 4 p29. Book 5 p57, 61. Book 6 p41, 42.
        Making Sure of Maths Book 1 p59-61. Book 2 p32. Book 3 p27. Book 5 p14.
        Mathematics for Schools Level 2 (1st ed.). Book 5 p20, 50-53. Book 6 p18.
        Maths Adventure 2. Pupil's Book p50-51, 63.
                3. Pupil's Book p52.
                4. Pupil's Book p47.
                5. Pupil's Book p22.
        Nuffield Maths 5-11 3. Pupils' Book p88-90.
        Oxford Middle School Mathematics Book 2 p22, 23. Book 3 p57. Book 4 p39.
        Primary Mathematics (SPMG) Stage 1. Workbook 3 p21.
                Stage 2. Workbook 4 p27.
                Stage 5. Textbook p6-7. Card 8, 31.
        Towards Mathematics Core Unit 6 p1, 2. Core Unit 21 p8, 9, 10, 11, 12.

S   *A World of Mathematics* Book 1 p54. Book 5 p59.
        Focus Mathematics Book 4 p72-74.
        Headway Maths Book 1 p22-23, 37, 51.
                Book 4 p37.
        Impact Maths Pupil's Book 1 p39.
        Inner Ring Maths Book 2 p19. Book 3 p23, 24, 25, 26.
        Mathematics for Life Book B1 p4. Book C1 p10-11.
        Maths (Holt) Book 2 p36-37, 42-43, 71.
                Book 3 p40, 92.
        Mathsworks Book 2 p34.

SM   *Check it Again* Book 4 p30-33. Book 5 p30.
        Four a Day series Book 9 p42, 43. Book 10 p28-29.
        Number Workbook Fractions p22.

F5 Addition and subtraction of fractions.

Exploration of patterns and methods using structured apparatus, etc.

Progression from simple examples (e.g. $\frac{2}{5} + \frac{1}{5}$. See also F2) to more complex ones (e.g. $\frac{2}{8} + \frac{1}{4}$ and later $\frac{1}{7} + \frac{3}{9} + \frac{1}{2}$).

Addition and subtraction of mixed numbers.

Applications.

See also   N23   Ratio, rate and proportion.
            F3   Lowest term fraction.
            VR5   Pie charts.

P   *Alpha (new ed.)* Alpha 2 p57. Alpha 3 p25.
        Beta (new ed.) Beta 2 p66, 67. Beta 3 p40. Beta 4 p25.
                Beta 5 p27.
        Basic Mathematics Book 2 p40, 41. Book 3 p49. Book 4 p33.
                Book 5 p33, 34.
        Hey Mathematics Mod 5. Book 3 p30-31.
                Mod 6. Book 3 p10, 11-16, 19, 21-23, 27-32. Book 4 p32.
        Key Maths Level 2. Book 5 p63-66. Book 6 p39-40, 42, 43.
        Making Sure of Maths Book 2 p38. Book 3 p25-26.
        Mathematics for Schools Level 2 (1st ed.). Book 5 p24-26.
        Maths Adventure 3. Pupil's Book p63. Activity Book p55.
                4. Pupil's Book p46. Activity Book p43-44.
                5. Pupil's Book p19, 23. Activity Book p23.
        Oxford Middle School Mathematics Book 3 p56-57.
        Primary Mathematics (SPMG) Stage 2. Workbook 1 p11.
                Stage 4. Textbook p26-27, 91-95.
                Stage 5. Textbook p5.
        Towards Mathematics Core Unit 21 p2, 3, 4, 5, 6.

Multiplication of fraction by fraction.   **F6**

Exploration of patterns and methods using structured apparatus, etc.

Progression for examples where both numerators are one (e.g. $\frac{1}{4} \times \frac{1}{3}$) to examples where one fraction has a numerator greater than one (e.g. $\frac{1}{4} \times \frac{2}{3}$), finally considering examples where both fractions have numerators greater than one (e.g. $\frac{3}{4} \times \frac{2}{3}$).

Applications.

See also   N23   Ratio, rate and proportion.
          F7   Division of fractions; multiplying by inverse.

Division of fractions.   **F7**

Division of whole number by fraction and later division of fraction by fraction.

Exploration of patterns and methods using structured apparatus, etc.

With whole numbers, division can initially be undertaken as repeated subtraction. Later the discovery that dividing by a fraction is equivalent to multiplying by its reciprocal or inverse

e.g. $6 \div \frac{2}{3} = 6 \times \frac{3}{2} = \frac{18}{2} = 9$

and $\frac{3}{4} \div \frac{2}{3} = \frac{3}{4} \times \frac{3}{2} = \frac{9}{8} = 1\frac{1}{8}$.

Applications.

See also   N23   Ratio, rate and proportion.
          F4,6   Multiplication of fractions.
          AR8   Identity and inverse elements.

P   *Basic Mathematics*   Book 5 p39.
Making Sure of Maths   Book 3 p27-28.
Mathematics for Schools   Level 2 (1st ed.). Book 7 p24-29. Book 8 p7-11.
Maths Adventure   4. Pupil's Book p49-51.
                                    5. Pupil's Book p21.
Oxford Middle School Mathematics   Book 4 p74-76.
Primary Mathematics (SPMG)   Stage 5. Textbook p69-73. Workbook p3. Card 27, 28.
Towards Mathematics   Core Unit 21 p16.

S   *A World of Mathematics*   Book 6 p8-11.
Focus Mathematics   Book 7 p29-30.
Headway Maths   Book 5 p17.
Maths (Holt)   Book 2 p43.
Mathsworks   Book 2 p35-36.

SM   *Number Workbook*   Fractions p26-30.

Books for teachers
Mathematics: from Primary to Secondary   p49-50.

Algebraic Relations

Contents

Topics with a sequence of development extending over considerable time.

AR1 Open sentences with one place holder and their truth sets. Closed sentences.

Truth sets containing one item.

Non-numerical examples

e.g. ☐ had a little lamb.

The day after Wednesday is called ☐.

Numerical examples (See N10 and N19(1) for examples involving the four operations on number)

e.g. $\Box + 2 = 7$

$5 \times \Box = 15$.

Truth sets containing more than one item. Non-numerical and numerical examples

e.g. $\Box < 4$; if whole positive numbers are considered, the truth sets contains the numbers 1, 2 and 3.

An *open sentence* is a statement rendered incomplete by the presence of one or more *place holders*, shown as boxes in the above examples.
The *place holder* may be substituted for an item or items to make a *closed sentence* that may be *true* e.g. $\boxed{5} + 2 = 7$ or *false* e.g. $\boxed{3} + 2 = 7$.
The *truth set* of an open sentence with one place holder is the set containing the item or items which will make the sentence closed and true; e.g. for the open sentence $\Box + 2 = 7$, the truth set contains one item, 5.

See also   N5   Ordinal number.
            N10,19(1) Introduction to box arithmetic.
            S2   Relations between sets:
            and all other topics involving relationships.

P   *Basic Mathematics*   Book 2 p6.
        Come and Count   Book 6 p10-11.
        Mathematics for Schools   Level 1 (2nd ed.). Book 6 p11-17, 19-23. Book 7 p5-6, 23-24, 30-38, 44-45.
                            Level 2 (1st ed.). Book 8 p2.
        Maths Adventure   2. Pupil's Book p82, 86.
                            3. Pupil's Book p74.
                            5. Activity Book p28-29.
        Oxford Middle School Mathematics   Book 4 p12-13.
        Towards Mathematics   Core Unit 1 p12. Core Unit 7 p9-11.

S   *Focus Mathematics*   Book 1 p58.

Books for teachers
        Mathematics: the later Primary years   p49, 50.

AR2 Open sentences with two place holders and their truth sets. Patterns and graphs.

Non-numerical examples:

e.g.   ☐ coloured paint mixed with blue coloured paint together make △ coloured paint.

☐ has bigger feet than △ in this class.

Numerical examples using positive whole numbers:

e.g. $\Box + \triangle = 7$

$2 \times \Box = \triangle$

Truth sets of numerical examples involving the four operations on number consist of ordered pairs of numbers

e.g.   truth set of $\Box + \triangle = 7$ contains the following ordered pairs: (0,7) (1,6) (2,5) (3,4) (4,3) (5,2) (6,1) (7,0).

Patterns and relationships in ordered pairs investigated and discussed.

Later, by regarding the ordered pairs as the co-ordinators of points, they can be represented graphically. When the points are joined a graph of the open sentence is obtained.

Discussion of the graphs. The linear relationship shown in straight line graphs. Later, curved graphs discussed.

See also   N10,15   Number bonds to 20 and 100. Box arithmetic (addition and subtraction).
            N19(1)   Box arithmetic (multiplication and division).
            N19(3)   Patterns in multiplication and division, multiples, etc.
            N23   Ratio, rate and proportion.
            N26   Powers idea and index notation.
            F3   Equivalent fractions.
            AR4,5,6 Graphs using measurement data.
            VR7   Co-ordinates.
            S2   Relations between sets;
            and all other topics involving relationships.

P   *Alpha (new ed.)*   Alpha 4 p56-57.
        Beta (new ed.)   Beta 4 p70. Beta 5 p45. Beta 6 p48, 77, 78.
        Hey Mathematics   Mod 2. Book 2 p36.
                            Mod 3. Book 5 p35.
        Mathematics for Schools   Level 1 (2nd ed.). Book 6 p18, 35-38. Book 7 p44-49.
                                    Level 2 (1st ed.). Book 3 p53, 58-60. Book 5 p33-37. Book 6 p35-36, 48.
                                    Book 7 p46, 50, 51. Book 8 p27.
        Maths Adventure   2. Pupil's Book p83.
                            3. Pupil's Book p72, 73, 74.
                            4. Pupil's Book p68-71. Activity Book p53-55.
                            5. Pupil's Book p63-64, 65, 72-73, 84-85. Activity Book p26-27.
        Oxford Middle School Mathematics   Book 3 p8-9, 20-21, 48-49. Book 4 p28-29, 77.
        Primary Mathematics (SPMG)   Stage 4. Textbook p63. Card 23, 24.
                                       Stage 5. Card 31.
        Towards Mathematics   Core Unit 8 p9-14. Core Unit 12 p1-3.
                                Core Unit 13 p7-11. Core Unit 14 p14.

S   *A World of Mathematics*   Book 1 p22.
        Focus Mathematics   Book 1 p59, 60. Book 6 p106-108.
        Headway Maths   Book 4 p83.
        Maths (Holt)   Book 3 p44-47. Workbook 3 p12-13, 18-20, 37.
                         4th Year p8-9.
        Mathsworks   Book 1 p38-39, 105. Book 2 p66.

SM   *Problems*   Third Problems p52.

Books for teachers
        Mathematics: the later Primary years p49-52, 58-59, 61.
        Mathematics: from Primary to Secondary   p65-66.

The introduction to and use of 'variables'.

AR3

A variable (e.g. the letter x) is a symbol which denotes rather than holds a place for any member of a definite set (e.g. x + 4 = 10). Variables facilitate discussion about statements or equations.

1. Forming algebraic expressions.

Use of variables to make concise mathematical statements from verbal or written statements:

e.g.   (a)   John gets 50p pocket money a week; he spends 20p on sweets, 12p on a comic and saves the rest.

             20 + 12 + x = 50 where x represents the money he saves.

       (b)   Think of a number, double it and add seven.

             2x + 7 where x represents the number thought of.

Later simultaneous equations from problems:

e.g.   There were 24 dogs in two large kennels.

       There were 5 more in one kennel than the other.

       a + b = 24

       a + 5 = b where a and b represent the number of dogs in each kennel.

Using variables to express generalisations.

See also   N37,38, Sh23, CV9,12, A7,11,12,13, L7,11, T13 and other topics involving the discovery of generalised formulae;
            and all topics involving relationships between, and operations on number, and particularly problems and applications.

P *Beta (new ed.)* Beta 5 p68, 69. Beta 6 p15.
  Basic Mathematics Book 2 p7.
  Key Maths Level 2. Book 4 p30.
  Making Sure of Maths Book 2 p15, 16.
  Mathematics for Schools Level 2 (1st ed.). Book 10 p49-54.
  Maths Adventure 4. Pupil's Book p88-89.
  Oxford Middle School Mathematics Book 4 p12-14, 20-21, 28, 64.

S *Focus Mathematics* Book 4 p103, 105-106.
  Headway Maths Book 2 p86-87. Book 3 p59.
  Maths (Holt) Book 1 p21. Workbook 1 p13. 4th Year Workbook p25.
  Mathsworks Book 1 p33, 44, 66-67. 92, 93, 128.
    Tryouts 1 p36, 61-62. Book 2 p53, 86, 87.
    Tryouts 2 p38.

SM *Four a Day series* Book 9 p31.

Books for teachers
  Mathematics: from Primary to Secondary p66-67.

2. Substituting numbers into algebraic expressions.

  e.g. What is the value of 4x + 2 when x = 3?

See also N37 Averages.
     N38 Probability.
     Sh23 Pythagoras' theorem.
     CV9 Volume of cube and cuboid.
     CV12 Volume of cylinder and prism.
     A7 Area of square and rectangle.
     A11 Surface area of cube and cuboid.
     A12 Area of triangle.
     A13 Circle area.
     L7 Perimeters.
     L11 Circle circumference.
     T13 Speed.

P *Beta (new ed.)* Beta 5 p40, 41, 68, 91. Beta 6 p15, 87.
  Hey Mathematics Mod 4. Book 5 p28.
  Making Sure of Maths Book 6 p31.
  Mathematics for Schools Level 2 (1st ed.). Book 10 p50-54.

S *A World of Mathematics* Book 5 p39, 40, 41.
  Focus Mathematics Book 2 p30-33, 34-36. Book 4 p101-102, 103, 104-111.
  Headway Maths Book 3 p66, 67, 68. Book 4 p25.
    Book 5 p39, 40.
  Maths (Holt) 4th Year Workbook p25. 5th Year Workbook p17.
  Mathsworks Book 1 p33, 44, 45, 112. Tryouts 1 p36.
    Book 2 p55, 82. Tryouts 2 p26, 38.

SM *Check it Again* Book 5 p26-27.
  Four a Day series Book 9 p31. Book 10 p23.

3. Simplification of algebraic expressions.

  e.g. 3x + 2x + y - x

    becomes 4x + y.

Later simplification of expressions with brackets.

See also N10 Commutativity and associativity of addition. Non-commutativity of subtraction.
     N19(1) Commutativity and associativity of multiplication. Non-commutativity of division.
     A7,12 Area of composite shapes.
     A11,12,13 Surface areas.
     L7 Perimeter of square and rectangle.

P *Beta (new ed.)* Beta 5 p68. Beta 6 p42.
  Making Sure of Maths Book 6 p23.
  Oxford Middle School Mathematics Book 4 p67.

S *A World of Mathematics*   Book 4 p48-51. Book 5 p39.
　　Focus Mathematics   Book 4 p104. Book 5 p82-100.
　　Headway Maths   Book 3 p66, 67, 68, 69.
　　　　　　　　　Book 5 p39.
　　Mathsworks   Book 1 p108, 127. Tryouts 1 p49. Book 2 p51, 52, 55. Tryouts 2 p27, 41.

Patterns in measurement and shape: I Straight line graphs.   AR4

Constant ratio, direct proportion, equal rate.

　　e.g.　Conversion graphs:　currency conversion (see also M10), temperature Fahrenheit/Celsius (see also
　　　　　　　　　　　　Temp), imperial/metric measures (see also Imp), scales in block graphs, etc. and
　　　　　　　　　　　　maps (see also VR8 and L8,9).
　　　　　Unit pricing (See also M8).
　　　　　Weight/Volume of water (See also CV7).
　　　　　Perimeter of square/length of one side (See also L7).
　　　　　Diameter/circumference of circle (See also L11).
　　　　　Height of drop of rubber ball/height of first bounce.
　　　　　Weight or volume of water collected from dripping tap/time.
　　　　　Number of flashes of Belisha Beacon/time.
　　　　　Stretch of an extension spring/weight attached (See also W7).
　　　　　Distance/time at constant speed (See also T13).

Idea of the 'line of closest fit'. Data subject to error of measurement will tend not to give a perfect straight line.

Interpolation on the straight line graph i.e. using the graph to find things out:

　　e.g.　using the dollars/pounds graph to find the sterling equivalent of 7 dollars.

Relationships shown by the graphs discussed, and generalisations attempted.

See also　N23　Ratio, rate and proportion.
　　　　　N36　Surveys and generalisations.
　　　　　AR2　Straight line graphs arising from abstract operations.
　　　　　VR7　Co-ordinates.
　　　　　VR9　Line graphs for continuous data.
　　　　　CV10, A10, L10, W8, T12　Linear relationships between two forms of measurement.

P　*Alpha (new ed.)*　Alpha 3 p49, 85. Alpha 4 p13, 14.
　　Beta (new ed.)　Beta 4 p33, 34. Beta 5 p23, 65.
　　　　　　　　　Beta 6 p76.
　　Basic Mathematics　Book 3 p60-61, 97. Book 4 p56, 70-71.
　　　　　　　　　Book 5 p83-85.
　　Key Maths　Level 2. Book 6 p99, 120-122.
　　Making Sure of Maths　Book 4 p60. Book 5 p78-79.
　　Mathematics for Schools　Level 2 (1st ed.). Book 4 p46-49. Book 6 p51-53. Book 7 p45. Book 8 p30, 48-49.
　　　　　　　　　　　　Book 10 p38.
　　Maths Adventure　5. Pupil's Book p80-81. Activity Book p14.
　　Oxford Middle School Mathematics　Book 3 p72-73. Book 4 p94-96.
　　Primary Mathematics (SPMG)　Stage 4. Textbook p61-63, 113, 114. Card 35, 36, 37, 38.
　　　　　　　　　　　　Stage 5. Textbook p79-80. Card 31, 32.

S　*A World of Mathematics*　Book 4 p20-23. Book 5 p20.
　　Focus Mathematics　Book 4 p132-134. Book 8 p64-66.
　　Headway Maths　Book 3 p81.
　　Inner Ring Maths　Book 2 p27-28.
　　Maths (Holt)　Book 2 p12-13, 16. 5th Year p58-59.
　　　　　　　　　5th Year Workbook p20, 21, 31, 41.
　　Mathsworks　Book 1 p42, 57, 77, 104, 111.
　　　　　　　　　Tryouts 1 p11, 22, 23, 24, 39, 40.
　　　　　　　　　Book 2 p66, 67, 68, 69. Tryouts 2 p39.
　　Maths You Need　p101-105.

SM　*Check it Again*　Book 5 p44-45.
　　Four a Day series　Book 10 p79.
　　Mathematics and Metric Measuring　Book 1 p22-24, 32-33. Book 2 p8-10, 12-13.
　　　　　　　　　　　　Book 5 p15-19. Book 6 p18-19, 24-25, 27-29, 35-36.
　　Problems　Third Problems p51.

Books for teachers
　　Mathematics: from Primary to Secondary　p63-65.

AR5 Patterns in measurement and shape: II Curved graphs.

(a) Constant product group xy = c where x and y are variables and c is a constant.

These are hyperbola graphs:

    e.g.   Number of sides in a regular polygon/angle subtended at centre (See also Sh16).
            Number of sides in a regular polygon/interior angle (See also Sh16).
            Width of rectangle of constant area/its length (See also A9).

(b) $y = x^2$ group where y and x are variables.

These are parabola graphs.

    e.g.   Area of a square/length of one side (See also A9).
            Area of a circle/its radius (See also A13).
            Surface area of a cube/length of its edge (See also A11).
            Distance/time at constant acceleration (See also T13).
            Braking distance of a car/speed from Highway Code (See also T13).

(c) $y = x^3$ group where y and x are variables.

These are parabola graphs.

    e.g.   Volume of a cube/length of one edge (See also CV11).
            Volume of a sphere/its diameter (See also CV12).

(d) Graph of normal distribution (See also N37 Averages).

Idea of the 'line of closest fit' (See AR4).

Interpolation on the curved line i.e. using the graph to find things out,

    e.g.   using the graph of area of a square/length of one side to find the area of a square of given length.

Relationships shown by the graphs discussed, and generalisations attempted.

See also   N26   Powers idea and index notation.
               N36   Surveys and generalisations.
               AR2   Curved graphs arising from abstract operations.
               VR7   Co-ordinates.
               Sh8   The parabola, etc.

P   *Alpha (new ed.)*   Alpha 4 p14.
        Beta (new ed.)   Beta 5 p66-67. Beta 6 p76, 90.
        Mathematics for Schools   Level 2 (1st ed.). Book 6 p54-55. Book 7 p51-56. Book 8 p25-29. Book 10 p35, 37, 39.
        Maths Adventure   5. Pupil's Book p56, 76.
        Oxford Middle School Mathematics   Book 3 p83.
        Primary Mathematics (SPMG)   Stage 5. Card 49, 50, 51, 52, 53, 54, 55.

S   *A World of Mathematics*   Book 5 p14-15, 16.
        Focus Mathematics   Book 8 p70.
        Maths (Holt)   4th Year p20-21, 32.
                        5th Year Workbook p20-21, 41.
        Mathsworks   Book 1 p110. Tryouts 1 p27.

SM   *Mathematics and Metric Measuring*   Book 2 p35-36.
                                      Book 3 p7-8, 35-36, 39-40, 41-45.
                                      Book 5 p33-34. Book 6 p16-17, 21-22, 38-40.

Books for teachers
    Mathematics: from Primary to Secondary   p64-65.

AR6 Patterns in measurement and shape: III Scatter graphs.

Scatter graphs illustrate the degree of associaton between data that may be related, though not perfectly linearly or quadratically:

    e.g.   graph of span against height.
            graph of distance travelled against cost (See also L10, T12).
            graph of weight of coins against their value (See also W8).

Idea of association or correlation introduced

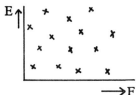
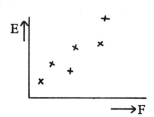

Random scatter:
no association.

Association:
F decreases as
E increases.

Association:
F increases as
E increases.

See also N36   Surveys and generalisations.
          N38   Probability.
          VR7   Co-ordinates.

P   *Hey Mathematics*   Mod 5. Book 5 p32.
        Mathematics for Schools   Level 2 (1st ed.). Book 8 p39.
        Oxford Middle School Mathematics   Book 3 p93-95.

S   *Maths (Holt)*   4th Year p46-49.
                         5th Year p84-85, 87.

Books for teachers
        Mathematics: from Primary to Secondary   p31-32.

Open sentences where the truth sets are ordered pairs of whole directed numbers. Patterns and graphs. AR7

Equality and inequality relationships (e.g. $\square < {}^+2$) and relationships involving operations on directed numbers
(e.g. $\square + \triangle = {}^+1$).

Ordered pairs plotted as co-ordinates, and graphs of the open sentences obtained.

Discussion of the graphs and generalisations attempted.

See also N23   Ratio, rate and proportion.
          N27   Introduction to directed numbers.
          N35   Operations on directed numbers.
          AR2   Open sentences with ordered pairs of positive numbers.
          VR7   Co-ordinates.
          Sh18,19,20   Reflection, Rotation and Translation.
          Temp.   Temperature.

P   *Beta (new ed.)*   Beta 6 p50, 79-81.
        Mathematics for Schools   Level 2 (1st ed.). Book 8 p2, 3, 6. Book 9 p13, 19. Book 10 p12, 16.
        Maths Adventure   4. Pupil's Book p65, 67.
                            5. Pupil's Book p71, 86.
        Oxford Middle School Mathematics   Book 4 p92-93.
        Towards Mathematics   Core Unit 25 p11-16.

Books for teachers
        Mathematics: the later Primary years   p163-176.

AR8   The algebraic solution of simple equations.

(a)   By carrying out the inverse operation i.e. undoing the operation

      e.g. $2x + 4 = 12$ equation to be solved.

$$4 \xleftarrow{\div 2} 8 \xleftarrow{-4} 12$$

      So $x = 4$

(b)   Use of identity and inverse elements.

Experience leading to concepts of identity and inverse elements.
Identity elements for real numbers using addition is 0 and using multiplication is 1 because

      $a + 0 = 0 + a = a$

and $a \times 1 = 1 \times a = a$

The inverse element is the number which, when added to or multiplied by a number, gives the identity element.

Equations can be solved by adding or multiplying the inverse to both sides of the equation.

      e.g. $2x + 4 = 12$ equation to be solved.

      Inverse of $^+4$ is $^-4$ for addition.

      So $2x + {}^+4 + {}^-4 = {}^+12 + {}^-4$.

$$2x = {}^+8$$
$$x = {}^+4$$

Also $\dfrac{x}{3} = 5$

      Inverse of $\frac{1}{3}$ is $\frac{3}{1}$ for multiplication.

      So $\dfrac{x}{^+3} \times \dfrac{^+3}{1} = {}^+5 \times \dfrac{^+3}{1}$

$$x = 15$$

(c)   Use of graphs to solve simple equations.

See also   N10   Complementary nature of addition and subtraction.
             N19(1) Complementary nature of multiplication and division.
             N27,35 Directed numbers. Operations using inverse element.
             F7   Division of fractions. Use of inverse element.
             AR1,2 Open sentences and truth sets.
             AR3   Introduction to and use of 'variables'.
             AR9   Further study of straight line graphs.
             Sh23, CV9,12, A7,11,12,13, L7,11, T13   Solution of equations based on generalised formulae.

P   *Beta (new ed.)*   Beta 6 p43.
      Hey Mathematics   Mod 6. Book 3 p44-46.
      Key Maths   Level 2. Book 3 p46. Book 4 p31. Book 5 p39.
      Making Sure of Maths   Book 2 p14. Book 3 p78. Book 4 p46-48.
                               Book 5 p47-49. Book 6 p24-30.
      Mathematics for Schools   Level 2 (1st ed.). Book 10 p6, 13, 53-54.
      Towards Mathematics   Core Unit 8 p15-16. Core Unit 21 p14, 15, 16.

S   *A World of Mathematics*   Book 6 p15-18.
      Headway Maths   Book 2 p88-89. Book 3 p59-60, 69. Book 4 p14-15.
      Mathsworks   Book 1 p90-91, 92, 93. Tryouts 1 p45.
                  Book 2 p52, 54, 60. Tryouts 2 p30-31.

Books for teachers
      Mathematics: the later Primary years   p138-141.
      Mathematics: from Primary to Secondary   p121-123, 158-167.

Further study of straight line graphs.

Study of factors determining steepness of slope, direction of slope, etc.

Graphs of two equations. Inequalities and intersections. Graphs that intersect at a single point. Graphs that do not intersect at all.

Gradients.

See also   N23   Ratio, rate and proportion.
          AR2,4   Straight line graphs.
          AR6   Scatter graphs. Association.
          AR8   Algebraic solution of simple equations.
          Sh17   Similarity enlargement and reduction.
          L11   Circle circumference; finding 'pi' from graph.
          L13   Inaccessible heights. Hill gradients.
          T13   Speed from distance/time graph.

P   *Beta (new ed.)*   Beta 6 p48, 49, 79, 80, 88.
      Basic Mathematics   Book 5 p84-85.
      Making Sure of Maths   Book 6 p37-41.
      Mathematics for Schools   Level 2 (1st ed.). Book 6 p49-50. Book 10 p4-6, 16.
      Towards Mathematics   Core Unit 13 p9, 11. Core Unit 25 p13-16.

S   *Focus Mathematics*   Book 6 p120-127.
      Mathsworks   Book 1 p40-41, 104. Tryouts 1 p22, 24, 39, 40.
                           Book 2 p40. Tryouts 2 p22, 39.

Books for teachers
      Mathematics: from Primary to Secondary   p67-68, 77-80, 120-123.

Visual Representation

Contents

ᚷ---Topics with a sequence of development extending over considerable time.

Using items themselves.

Using items themselves (e.g. children) and later counters, matchboxes, etc. for the temporary recording of comparisons.

    e.g.   boys/girls in a class; children with/without sisters.

See also   N1   One-to-one correspondence.
             N2,3,4,5, PV2   Counting and ordering to 100.
             N6,7,8,9,15,16   Addition and subtraction to 100.
             S1,3   Sorting and classifying. Venn diagrams, etc.
             S2   Relations between sets. Comparing and ordering quantity.
             L2   Ordering by length. Conservation.
             L3   Use of arbitrary units for measuring length.
             L8   Plans and maps with one-to-one scale.

P   *Primary Mathematics (SPMG)*   Stage 1. Workbook 1 p20.
      Towards Mathematics   Core Unit 3 p3.

SM   *Mathematics and Metric Measuring*   Book 1 p19.

Books for teachers
    Mathematics: the first 3 years   p23, 31-32.
    Nuffield Maths 5-11   1. Teachers' Handbook p23-24, 53-54.

Pictograms.

Permanent recording using pictogram. Each item of data is represented by a picture and the pictures arranged in orderly columns.

The need for a baseline and for units of uniform size.

Initially two columns only. Gradual increase in number of columns as the need arises e.g. pet ownership, birthday months.

See also   N36   Surveys and generalisations.
             Sh1   Idea of column and row.
             Sh7   Vertical and horizontal idea;
             and topics listed for VR1.

P   *Ready for Alpha and Beta (new ed.)*   p15.
      Alpha (new ed.)   Alpha 1 p21, 22.
      Beta (new ed.)   Beta 1 p28, 29.
      Basic Mathematics   Book 2 p12.
      Hey Mathematics   Mod 1. Book 5 p2.
      Key Maths   Level 1. Book 5 p59. Book 6 p29-30. Book 7 p3.
                   Level 2. Book 1 p40.
      Making Sure of Maths   Book 1 p22-23. Book 4 p60.
      Maths Adventure   1. Pupil's Book p20. Card 21.
      Nuffield Maths 5-11   Bronto Books. Set B. Left-Right.
                   1. Worksheets N4 4·1, 4·3, C1 5·2.
      Numbers and Words   Book 2 p2. Book 5 p22-23. Book 6 p11.
      Our First School Maths   Book 2 p19, 22, 29. Book 3 p27. Book 4 p5.
      Oxford Middle School Mathematics   Book 1 p8-9.
      Primary Mathematics (SPMG)   Stage 1. Workbook 1 p20-24. Workbook 4 Card 1b.
      Towards Mathematics   Core Unit 3 p4.

S   *Focus Mathematics*   Book 2 p93.

SM   *Check it Again*   Book 2 p33-34.
      Four a Day series   Book 7 p7-8, 11-12, 14-15, 27.

Books for teachers
    Mathematics: the first 3 years   p32-33.
    Nuffield Maths 5-11   1. Teachers' Handbook p53-55.

VR3 Block graphs.

Identity of individual items is lost as each item is represented by a shape of uniform size (e.g. sticky paper squares) placed or coloured in linear array from a baseline.

See also   N36   Surveys and generalisations.
             Sh1   Idea of column and row.
             Sh7   Vertical and horizontal idea;
             and topics listed for VR1.

P   *Alpha (new ed.)*   Alpha 1 p21, 22, 23.
       Beta (new ed.)   Beta 1 p29, 51-52, 90. Beta 2 p20-21.
       Basic Mathematics   Book 2 p15.
       Hey Mathematics   Mod 3. Book 5. p2.
                      Mod 4. Book 5 p36.
       Key Maths   Level 1. Book 3 p46-47. Book 7 p18, 24.
               Level 2. Book 1 p41. Book 2 p34-35, 43. Book 3 p13-14.
       Making Sure of Maths   Green book p13.
                      Book 1 p22-24, 105. Book 2 p25-26.
       Mathematics for Schools   Level 1 (2nd ed.). Book 4 p28-31.
                         Level 2 (2nd ed.). Book 1 p3-4.
       Maths Adventure   2. Pupil's Book p67.
                   3. Pupil's Book p64. Card 23.
       Nuffield Maths 5-11   1. Worksheets N4 4·4, C1 5·1.
                   2. Worksheets N10 1·4, W2 3·2, M2 1·2, C2 2·2, 2·4.
                   3. Pupils' Book p33.
       Our First School Maths   Book 5 p17-18. Book 6 p14, 25, 30-31.
       Primary Mathematics (SPMG)   Stage 1. Workbook 3 p11-14, Card 5. Workbook 4 p20, Card 5a.
                             Stage 2. Workbook 2 p9-10,11. Workbook 4 p7, 11.
                             Stage 3. Textbook p48, 91-93. Workbook p32-33. Card 5, 6.
                             Stage 5. Textbook p53-55.
       Towards Mathematics   Core Unit 3 p4, 5, 6, 7, 8. Core Unit 22 p12.
                     Core Unit 24 p3, 4, 6, 7, 11.

S   *Headway Maths*   Book 1 p67. Book 2 p82-83. Book 3 p17.
       Maths (Holt)   Book 1 p20, 25.
       Maths Matters   Book 3 p18-19.

SM   *Check it Again*   Book 1 p35-36. Book 2 p32-33.
       Four a Day series   Book 6 p21.
       Problems   Third Problems p29.

Books for teachers
       Mathematics: the first 3 years   p33-34. 39-40, 92-93.
       Nuffield Maths 5-11   1. Teachers' Handbook p53-55.

VR4 Column bar charts and bar line graphs.

More abstract representation; strips or lines rather than individual shapes are used to represent data. A numbered vertical axis becomes essential;

e.g.   Pets.

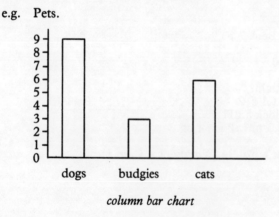

column bar chart

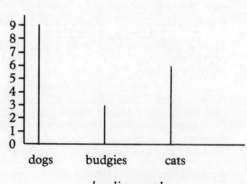

bar line graph

Later points can be joined making a line graph.

Ordered bar charts, bar line and line graphs i.e. when the order of the columns is important e.g. records of attendance on different days.

See also   N36   Surveys and generalisations.
AR2,4,5   Line graphs.
VR7   Co-ordinates.
VR9   Line graphs for continuous data.
Sh1   Idea of column and row.
Sh7   Vertical, horizontal and sloping ideas;
and topics listed for VR1.

P   *Alpha (new ed.)*   Alpha 1 p23. Alpha 2 p13-14.
Beta (new ed.)   Beta 1 p29. Beta 3 p24.
Basic Mathematics   Book 2 p44, 45, 77. Book 3 p23, 24.
Hey Mathematics   Mod 2. Book 5 p40.
Mod 3. Book 3 p39.
Mod 5. Book 5 p38-40.
Mathematics for Schools   Level 2 (1st ed.). Book 3 p1-4. Book 5 p12, 64.
Maths Adventure   3. Pupil's Book p65.
4. Pupil's Book p75.
Oxford Middle School Mathematics   Book 1 p30-31, 52-53. Book 3 p61.
Primary Mathematics (SPMG)   Stage 4. Textbook p59-61.

S   *A World of Mathematics*   Book 3 p48.
Focus Mathematics   Book 2 p98.
Mathematics for Life   Book B1 p2-3.
Maths (Holt)   Book 1 p30, 31, 83. Book 2 p93. 4th Year p89.
Maths Matters   Book 1 p18, 19.

SM   *Four a Day series*   Book 8 p20. Book 9 p22.
Mathematics and Metric Measuring   Book 1 p15-19.

Books for teachers
Mathematics: the first 3 years   p94-101.

Pie Charts.   VR5

A pie chart is a circle divided into sectors, so that the areas of the sectors represent the data.

Discussion of data represented in pie charts in newspapers, etc.

Construction of very simple pie charts. Only when angles and proportion are thoroughly understood should more complex pie charts be constructed.

The limitations of the pie chart.

See also   N23   Ratio, rate and proportion.
N24   Percentages.
N36   Surveys and generalisations.
F1,2,3   Fractions. Ordering fractions.
F4   Multiplication of fraction by whole number.
S3   Subsets. The complement of the set.
Sh8   Circle vocabulary.
Sh10,13   Angles and degrees.
Sh22   Circles. Construction techniques.
A5   Conservation of area.
A13   Circle area.

P   *Beta (new ed.)*   Beta 2 p83.
Basic Mathematics   Book 3 p22.
Hey Mathematics   Mod 5. Book 5 p36-37.
Mod 6. Book 4 p38.
Key Maths   Level 2. Book 5 p67. Book 6 p68.
Making Sure of Maths   Book 4 p62.
Mathematics for Schools   Level 2 (1st ed.). Book 8 p35-37.
Primary Mathematics (SPMG)   Stage 3. Card 7, 8. Stage 5. Card 29.

S   *A World of Mathematics*   Book 6 p5-7.
Focus Mathematics   Book 5 p70-74, 94, 167-168.
Book 6 p129.
Headway Maths   Book 4 p39.
Maths (Holt)   Book 3 p53-55. 5th year p38.
Maths Matters   Book 3 p30-31.
Mathsworks   Book 1 p74-75, 76, 123. Tryouts 1 p34, 35.
Book 2 p77-78. Tryouts 2 p41.
Maths You Need   p3.

SM   *Check it Again*   Book 1 p36-37. Book 2 p31-32.

VR6 Flow Charts.

See also N5   Ordinal number - 1st, 2nd, etc.
             S2   Relations between sets.
             T1   Ordering events in time.
             T4,7,10,11   Ordering events by clock times.
             T5   Continuous cycle of days of week and months of year.
             T8   Continuous cycle of seasons. The calendar.
             T9   Years. Life lines.
             T12   Realistic planning of a day, week, etc;
             and all topics involving a sequence of operations.

P   *Mathematics for Schools* Level 2 (1st ed.). Book 6 p1-5. Book 7 p57-61. Book 10 p18-21.
       Oxford Middle School Mathematics Book 1 p103. Book 2 p7, 11, 60, 94. Book 3 p63.
                           Book 4 p20, 24, 34-35, 38, 51, 64.

S   *Inner Ring Maths* Book 2 p29, 30, 31.
       Maths (Holt) Book 2 p92, 95. Book 3 p96. 4th Year p22, 40-41. 5th Year p60-61. 5th Year Workbook p30.

Books for teachers
    Mathematics: from Primary to Secondary p88-91.

VR7 Co-ordinates.

Plotting ordered pairs on lattice and grid and identifying the position of plotted points or spaces,

        e.g.   position of desk in classroom,
                game of battleships,
                grid references on maps.

Later plotting positive and negative numbers.

See also N8,13,15,16,19(3)   Use of number square and addition, subtraction and multiplication squares.
             N27   Introduction to directed numbers.
             AR2   Ordered pairs of numbers.
             AR2,4,5,6,7,9, VR9   Use of co-ordinates in graphs.
             S4   Intersection of two sets.
              Sh7   Vertical and horizontal idea.
             Sh17,18,19,20   Use of co-ordinates in transformations.
             L8,9   Plans and maps.
              L10   Distance tables.
              T8   The calendar.

P   *Alpha (new ed.)* Alpha 3 p72-73. Alpha 4 p58.
       Beta (new ed.) Beta 3 p75-76. Beta 4 p69, 71.
                          Beta 5 p44, 46-47. Beta 6 p51.
       Basic Mathematics Book 3 p58, 59. Book 5 p77, 78.
       Hey Mathematics Mod 3. Book 3 p40. Book 4 p36. Book 5 p28-30, 33-35.
                     Mod 5. Book 4 p28-39. Book 5 p23-24.
       Key Maths Level 2. Book 2 p36-38.
       Making Sure of Maths Book 4 p63-64. Book 6 p34-37.
       Mathematics for Schools Level 1 (2nd ed.). Book 4 p12.
                         Level 2 (2nd ed.). Book 2 p1-4.
                         Level 2 (1st ed.). Book 4 p45. Book 9 p63.
       Maths Adventure 2. Pupil's Book p95. Card 17.
                     3. Activity Book p29, 41.
                     4. Pupil's Book p17, 18-19. Activity Book p1.
                     5. Pupil's Book p25.
       Nuffield Maths 5-11 3. Pupils' Book p59-62.
       Oxford Middle School Mathematics Book 3 p34-35, 44-45.
       Primary Mathematics (SPMG) Stage 4. Textbook p12-15. Workbook p19. Card 15, 16, 17, 18.
       Towards Mathematics Core Unit 13 p1-6, Core Unit 25 p4-10, 14, 15, 16.

S   *A World of Mathematics* Book 1 p20-24.
       Focus Mathematics Book 6 p105-113.
       Headway Maths Book 2 p11. Book 3 p74-75.
       Maths (Holt) Book 1 p34-35. Book 3 p8-9, 68-70, 94.
                    Workbook 3 p25-27. 4th Year p14.
                    5th Year p18, 49, 50-51, 52-54.
                    5th Year Workbook p13, 15, 28.

SM *Check it Again* Book 5 p47-48.

Books for teachers
    Hey Mathematics Mod 3 Teachers' Book p47-49.
    Mathematics: the later Primary years p24-26, 45-49, 158-162.
    Nuffield Maths 5-11 3. Teachers' Handbook Chapter 13.

Pictograms, block graphs, column bar charts, bar line graphs and line graphs with varied scales.   VR8

The need for a scale arises naturally when the count is large

    e.g.   traffic census on a busy road.

Reading scales on dials: weighing machines, etc.

See also PV1   Grouping experiences. Number bases with two digits.
          PV2,4,7 Place value. Comparing and ordering whole numbers by size.
          N8,9,15,16,20,21 Addition and subtraction. Comparing and totalling data.
          N17,18,19,29,30 Multiplication and division.
          N23   Ratio, rate and proportion.
          N36   Surveys and generalisations.
          AR4   Straight line graphs: scale conversions.
          Sh17   Similarity, enlargement and reduction.
          CV3(2),8, L6,12, W7,10, Temp.   Reading the scales on varied measuring instruments.
          L8,9   Plans and maps with scales.
          T9   Time lines.

P   *Alpha (new ed.)*   Alpha 2 p43, 44. Alpha 3 p11-12, 48.
                     Alpha 4 p12, 29.
    Beta (new ed.)   Beta 1 p92. Beta 2 p52-53. Beta 3 p23, 24, 61, 62, 73. Beta 4 p8, 9, 10, 32-33. Beta 5 p22.
                     Beta 6 p2, 27.
    Basic Mathematics   Book 2 p13, 14. Book 3 p94, 95.
                     Book 4 p22, 23.
    Hey Mathematics   Mod 2. Book 5 p8-9.
                     Mod 3. Book 2 p38. Book 3 p36-38. Book 4 p8. Book 5 p19, 21, 36, 37.
                     Mod 4. Book 5 p37, 38.
                     Mod 5. Book 3 p15-17. Book 5 p26-28, 28-32.
                     Mod 6. Book 4 p27-31.
    Key Maths   Level 2. Book 2 p43. Book 5 p67.
    Making Sure of Maths   Book 2 p26. Book 3 p79-81. Book 4 p59, 61-62. Book 5 p76-77.
    Mathematics for Schools   Level 2 (2nd ed.). Book 1 p17.
                     Level 2 (1st ed.). Book 3 p16-17, 35. Book 5 p7-8. Book 7 p64. Book 8 p38.
    Maths Adventure   5. Pupil's Book p80-81.
    Nuffield Maths 5-11   3. Pupils' Book p103-104.
    Primary Mathematics (SPMG)   Stage 2. Workbook 3 p31. Workbook 4 p18-20, 27-28, Card 6a.
                     Stage 3. Textbook p94-95. Workbook p34. Card 9.
                     Stage 4. Textbook p61, 100.
                     Stage 5. Textbook p22. Card 15.
    Towards Mathematics   Core Unit 24 p1, 2.

S   *A World of Mathematics*   Book 2 p44-46. Book 3 p34-35, 47, 49-50, 51-52. Book 5 p14-17.
    Focus Mathematics   Book 2 p94-97, 98-105. Book 8 p67-68.
    Headway Maths   Book 1 p80. Book 2 p80-81. Book 4 p64-65.
    Inner Ring Maths   Book 1 p31. Book 3 p9.
    Mathematics for Life   Book C1 p2-3.
    Maths (Holt)   Book 1 p48. Book 2 p9, 17, 68. Book 3 p52, 53. Workbook 3 p17. 4th Year p44-45.
                5th Year p28-29, 41, 44, 62, 71, 76, 90.
    Maths Matters   Book 1 p6-7, 18. Book 2 p14-15, 44-45.
    Mathsworks   Book 1 p26-29, 51, 60, 73, 76. Tryouts 1 p35.
                Book 2 p77. Tryouts 2 p37.
    Maths You Need   p95, 122-123.

SM   *Check it Again*   Book 5 p4-5, 43-44.
    Four a Day series   Book 10 p19-20.
    Mathematics and Metric Measuring   Book 1 p15-18. Book 2 p18-27, 41-43.
                Book 3 p9-14, 28-31.
    Problems   Third Problems p25, 27-29.

VR9 Line graphs for continuous data.

Use of line graph for continuous data when intermediate points have some meaning.

See also N36　Surveys and generalisations.
AR2,4　Straight line graphs.
VR7　Co-ordinates.
L10, W8　Uneven growth rate.
T13　Journeys not involving constant speed.
Temp. Temperature taken at regular intervals.

P　*Alpha (new ed.)*　Alpha 4 p12.
Beta (new ed.)　Beta 5 p22.
Basic Mathematics　Book 3 p79.
Hey Mathematics　Mod 3. Book 3 p38.
　　　　　　　　Mod 5. Book 5 p27, 40.
Key Maths　Level 2. Book 5 p101-102. Book 6 p121.
Making Sure of Maths　Book 5 p76-78.
Mathematics for Schools　Level 2 (1st ed.). Book 8 p63.
Primary Mathematics (SPMG)　Stage 5. Textbook p86.

S　*A World of Mathematics*　Book 3 p47-48, 51, 52. Book 5 p14-15.
Focus Mathematics　Book 8 p68-72.
Headway Maths　Book 5 p22-23.
Mathematics for Life　Book C3 p14-15.
Maths (Holt)　Book 1 p30-31, 40, 53. Workbook 1 p42-44.
　　　　　　Book 2 p17, 38-39. Book 3 p89. 5th Year p24-26, 42-43.
Mathsworks　Book 1 p61. Book 2 p67.

SM　*Problems*　Third Problems p50.

Sets

Contents

Topics with a sequence of development extending over considerable time.

S1 Sorting and classifying.

Simple selection of sets of objects or pictures according to a single criterion (e.g. colour, shape, size), initially grouping identical items, and then items with a common factor (e.g. the red ones, the long ones).

Temporary recording with ropes, hoops, etc. and more permanent recording using rings and matching lines.

Discussion focusing on ways items are alike, and ways they are different, establishing and refining vocabulary: set, member, group, alike, same, different, etc. and a range of nouns and adjectives.

See also   S1 and S3 are the foundation on which all aspects of mathematics relating to classification depend and build. At the early stages S1 relates particularly to M1,2, N2,3,4, VR1,2,3,4, Sh1,2,3, CV1, A1, L1, W1, T1,2.

P   *Alpha (new ed.)*   Alpha 2 p7.
    Beta (new ed.)   Beta 3 p10-11.
    Basic Mathematics   Book 2 p105, 106.
    Come and Count   Book 1 p15-16. Book 2 p1.
    Hey Mathematics   Mod 1. Book 1 p7-9.
    Key Maths   Level 1 Book 1 p1-12.
    Mathematics for Schools   Level 1. (2nd ed.) Book 1 p1-14, 15-18, 29, 36-38, 39-42. Book 3 p19-20.
    Maths Adventure   Kites 1 p3-8.
                     2. Pupil's Book p46-47.
    Nuffield Maths 5-11   1. Worksheets N1 2·1-2·2.
    Numbers and Words   Book 1 p5.
    Our First School Maths   Book 1 p2-8.
    Towards Mathematics   Core Unit 3 p1.

S   *Focus Mathematics*   Book 1 p7-9. Book 2 p80.

Books for teachers
    Early Mathematical Experiences particularly 'Sand. Raw materials'.
                                 'Towards Number. Apparatus Toys and Games'.
                                 'Outside Activities. The Environment'.
    Mathematics: the first 3 years   p6-8.
    Nuffield Maths 5-11   1. Teachers' Handbook p6-9.

S2 Relations between sets.

Arrow diagrams and mapping according to a prescribed relationship.

(a)   Relations not involving comparison of quantity:

One to one relations

    e.g. Susan $\xrightarrow{\text{likes}}$ baked beans.

        The cat $\xrightarrow{\text{is under}}$ the table.

        Saturday $\xrightarrow{\text{comes after}}$ Friday.

One to many relations

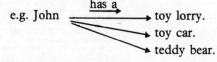

Many to one relations

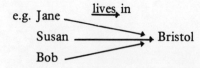

Many to many relations

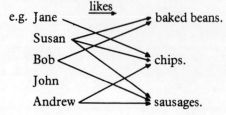

92

(b) Relations involving comparing and ordering two and later more quantities

e.g. Tom $\xrightarrow{\text{is taller than}}$ Susan.

5 > 3 > 1

Reflexive, symmetric and transitive properties (see references to books for teachers).

The equivalent relation and appropriate use of the equals sign

e.g. This book $\xrightarrow[\text{the same as}]{\text{weighs about}}$ this stone (equals sign inappropriate).

See also A great deal of mathematics, including operations on number and algebraic relations, is concerned with relationships. At the early stages S2 relates particularly to the following, where further examples may be found: M1,2,3, N1,4,5,6,7, VR1,2,3,4, Sh1, CV2, A2, L2, W2, T1,2.

P   *Come and Count*   Book 3 p6-9.
        Hey Mathematics   Mod 1. Book 1 p3-6.
                            Mod 3. Book 2 p39.
        Mathematics for Schools   Level 1 (2nd ed.) Book 1 p11-14, 29, 36. Book 3 p19-20, 32, 44. Book 7 p44-45.
                            Level 2 (1st ed.) Book 10 p1-3.
        Maths Adventure   1. Pupil's Book p4.
                            4. Pupil's Book p66.
        Nuffield Maths 5-11   Bronto Books.
                            1. Worksheets N1 1·1-1·6.
        Numbers and Words   Book 7 p28.
        Our First School Maths   Book 3 p14.
        Oxford Middle School Mathematics   Book 1 p14-15, 38-39. Book 2 p74-75.
                            Book 3 p8-9, 89-90.
        Towards Mathematics   Core Unit 3 p2, 6. Core Unit 8 p1-8.

S   *Focus Mathematics*   Book 2 p83-87. Book 7 p16-20.
        Inner Ring Maths   Book 3 p2.
        Maths (Holt)   Book 2 p56-57. Book 3 p12-13, 14, 15.
                            Workbook 3 p5. 5th Year p58.

SM *Four a Day series*   Book 7 p7.

Books for teachers
        Early Mathematical Experiences   All books in the series.
        Mathematics: the first 3 years   p5-6, 24-26, 41-46, 53-55.
        Mathematics: the later Primary years   p35-36.
        Nuffield Maths 5-11   1. Teachers' Handbook p2-6.
                            2. Teachers' Handbook p38-40.

Sorting into disjoint subsets. Inclusion and exclusion. The complement of the set. The empty set.

S3

Sorting and partitioning a mixed collection of items (the universal set) into disjoint subsets and later further subdividing. (Disjoint sets are sets having no items in common.)

Recording pictorially using Venn, Carroll or tree diagrams.

e.g.   *Venn diagram*   *Carroll diagram*   *Tree diagram or decision tree*

3 sided shapes 4 sided shapes

subset of 3 sided shapes

subset of 4 sided shapes

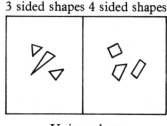

Universal set of shapes

Universal set of shapes

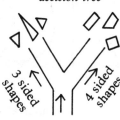

Items enter

Discussion encouraging awareness that the inclusion or exclusion of any single item in a subset depends on the way the subset is defined *and* on the attributes of that item i.e. involves holding in mind both of these aspects at the same time.

The idea of the complement of the set i.e. the unselected items when the universal set has been partitioned into subsets.

The idea of the empty set i.e. a set with no members.

See also   S1 and S3 are the foundation on which all aspects of mathematics relating to classification and grouping depend and build. At the early stages S2 relates particularly to M1,2, N2,3,4, VR1,2,3,4, Sh1,2,3, CV1, A1, L1, W1, T1,2. Later, ideas of place value (PV1-8) depend on an appreciation of the complement of the set.

P   *Alpha (new ed.)*   Alpha 2 p75, 76.
   Beta (new ed.)   Beta 5 p4, 5.
   Basic Mathematics   Book 2 p102, 104.
   Come and Count   Book 4 p1-5.
   Hey Mathematics   Mod 3. Book 4 p14.
   Key Maths   Level 1. Book 1 p13-29, 32-44.
   Making Sure of Maths   Book 1 p103-104. Book 2 p54, 55.
   　　　　　　　　　　　　　　Book 3 p65-68. Book 4 p71-74.
   　　　　　　　　　　　　　　Book 5 p84.
   Mathematics for Schools   Level 1 (2nd ed.). Book 1 p19-35, 43.
   　　　　　　　　　　　　　　　Level 2 (2nd ed.). Book 2 p26.
   Maths Adventure   2. Pupil's Book p48-49.
   　　　　　　　　　　3. Pupil's Book p59.
   　　　　　　　　　　4. Pupil's Book p1.
   Nuffield Maths 5-11   1. Worksheets N1 3·1-3·4.
   Our First School Maths   Book 1 p3, 22-25.
   Oxford Middle School Mathematics   Book 1 p4-7, 32-33, 48-49, 57, 76-79.
   　　　　　　　　　　　　　　　　　　Book 2 p28. Book 3 p88-89.
   Towards Mathematics   Core Unit 23 p1, 4, 7, 11, 12.

S   *A World of Mathematics*   Book 3 p4-6.
   Focus Mathematics   Book 1 p9-12. Book 3 p67-68.
   　　　　　　　　　　　Book 7 p11-12.
   Headway Maths   Book 5 p52.
   Inner Ring Maths   Book 2 p1.
   Maths (Holt)   Book 1 p11. Workbook 1 p7. Book 2 p20.

Books for teachers
   Early Mathematical Experiences   Particularly 'Towards Number. Apparatus, Toys and Games'.
   　　　　　　　　　　　　　　　　　'Outside Activities. The Environment'.
   Mathematics: the first 3 years   p8-14, 30-31.
   Mathematics: the later Primary years   p37-41.
   Nuffield Maths 5-11   1. Teachers' Handbook p9-12.

S4   Intersection of two sets.

Sorting a mixed collection of items (the universal set) into two subsets when those subsets overlap or intersect.

Recording pictorially using Venn, Carroll or tree diagrams.

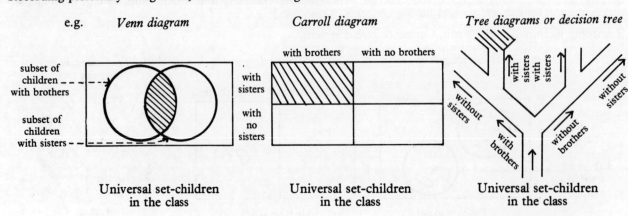

In each diagram the shading refers to the intersection of the sets i.e. children who have brothers *and* sisters.

Discussion of the meaning of statements involving the intersection of two sets e.g. are there any children who want to be in the obstacle race *and* the wheelbarrow race?

The union of two intersecting sets i.e. all the items in either or both of them.

See also N19(3)   Common multiples and divisors.
    N38(1)   Linear programming.
    VR7 Co-ordinates as the intersection of two sets.
    Sh1,2,3,11,14,15,16   Sorting and classifying shapes.
    Sh12 Sorting shapes according to their symmetry.

P *Alpha (new ed.)* Alpha 4 p73.
  Beta (new ed.) Beta 4 p56-57. Beta 5 p34-35, 72, 91.
       Beta 6 p6, 7, 85.
  Basic Mathematics Book 4 p82, 83.
  Hey Mathematics Mod 1. Book 2 p26-27.
       Mod 2. Book 1 p9.
  Making Sure of Maths Book 4 p74. Book 5 p81.
  Mathematics for Schools Level 1 (2nd ed.) Book 7 p28-29.
  Maths Adventure 2. Pupil's Book p49.
       3. Pupil's Book p59, 60, 61. Activity Book p12, 13, 14, 15.
       4. Pupil's Book p3.
  Oxford Middle School Mathematics Book 2 p4-7. Book 3 p4-5, 30.
          Book 4 p4, 6, 95.
  Towards Mathematics Core Unit 23 p2, 3, 5, 12, 13, 14, 15.

S *A World of Mathematics* Book 4 p5-8, 36-38.
  Focus Mathematics Book 3 p34-37, 63-73, 100-105.
  Headway Maths Book 5 p53.
  Inner Ring Maths Book 3 p4.
  Maths (Holt) Book 1 p80. Book 2 p21, 23.
      5th Year p12.
  Mathsworks Book 2 p58-59. Tryouts 2 p28, 29.

Books for teachers
  Mathematics: the first 3 years p14-15.
  Mathematics: the later Primary years p42-43.
  Mathematics: from Primary to Secondary p142-144.

Intersection of three and later more sets. S5

Sorting a mixed collection of items (the universal set) into three and later more subsets when those subsets overlap or intersect.

Recording pictorially using Venn, Carroll or tree diagrams:

     e.g. *Venn diagrams*

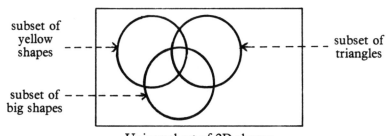

Universal set of 2D shapes

Gradual development to more complex situations e.g.

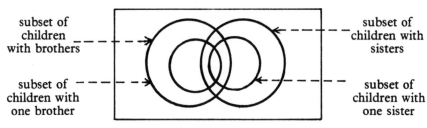

Universal set-children in the class

Use of punched cards to classify. (See-Books for teachers.)

Discussion of the meaning of statements involving the intersection of three or more sets e.g. are there children waiting at my desk who have paid their dinner money but not finished their writing or their maths?

The union of three or more intersecting sets i.e. all the items in either or all of them.

See also   N19(3)   Common multiples and divisors.
           N38(1)   Linear programming.
           Sh1,2,3,11,14,15,16   Sorting and classifying shapes.

P   *Alpha (new ed.)*   Alpha 4 p74.
       Beta (new ed.)   Beta 5 p72, 73. Beta 6 p68-69.
       Basic Mathematics   Book 1 p80. Book 2 p103.
       Making Sure of Maths   Book 5 p82-83.
       Mathematics for Schools   Level 2 (1st ed.) Book 9 p31-35.
       Oxford Middle School Mathematics   Book 1 p32-33, 57, 76-79. Book 3 p16-17, 64-66. Book 4 p5, 7.
       Towards Mathematics   Core Unit 6 p3. Core Unit 23 p6-10, 12-16.

S   *Focus Mathematics*   Book 3 p38-43, 66-73, 106-110.
                              Book 6 p101. Book 7 p7-10.
       Inner Ring Maths   Book 1 p8-9.
       Maths (Holt)   Book 2 p18-19. Workbook 2 p5, 33.
                        Book 3 p5, 96. Workbook 3 p2, 43.
                        4th Year p6-7. 5th Year p32.
       Mathsworks   Tryouts 2 p28. 29.

Books for teachers
       Mathematics: the later Primary years   p43-44.
       Mathematics: from Primary to Secondary   p145-148.

Shape and Space

Contents

⌐--Topics with a sequence of development extending over considerable time.

Sh1 Early concepts and vocabulary associated with shape, space and position.

Introduction to, and extension of vocabulary alongside examination of shape, space and position.

Collecting, sorting and classifying 2D and 3D shapes according to a single attribute e.g. the ones that roll, the ones with straight sides.

Identifying identical or similar shapes.

Drawing straight and curved lines.

Vocabulary associated with shapes: straight, curved, round, flat, sharp, blunt, hollow, open, closed, point, line, edge, corner, side, middle or centre, front, top, bottom, back, face, etc.

Vocabulary associated with position: where, under, between, behind, in front, above, below, over, on, off, by, beside, in, into, inside, next to, near, out, outside, up, down, across, top, bottom, opposite, column, row, etc.

See also VR1,2,3,4,7,8 Column and row in visual representation.
　　　　 S1,3　　Sorting and classifying.
　　　　 S2　　　Relations between sets.
　　　　 S4,5　　Intersection of two and more sets.
　　　　 Sh2,3　Sorting and naming 2D and 3D shapes.
　　　　 A1,2, CV1,2 Handling and sorting 2D and 3D shapes by size.

P　　*Ready for Alpha and Beta (new ed.)*　p10.
　　　Basic Mathematics　Book 1 p67.
　　　Hey Mathematics　Mod 1. Book 1 p17-18. Book 5 p30, 32.
　　　　　　　　　　　Mod 4. Book 5 p2-11, 26-27.
　　　Key Maths　Level 1. Book 1 p27-28, 30, 37. Book 2 p16-18, 29-31. Book 3 p28-31. Book 4 p26-28.
　　　Making Sure of Maths　Book 1 p100.
　　　Mathematics for Schools　Level 1 (2nd. ed.) Book 1 p12, 28-31, 36, 43. Book 3 p17-18, 21-22.
　　　　　　　　　　　　　　Book 7 p28-29, 39, 44-45.
　　　Maths Adventure　1. Pupil's Book p2-3, 21-22. Activity Book p1-3.
　　　　　　　　　　　2. Activity Book p3-5.
　　　　　　　　　　　4. Pupil's Book p1.
　　　Nuffield Maths 5-11　Bronto Books. Set A. Up and Down, Round Red Apple, Set B. Snail's Walk.
　　　　　　　　　　　Set C. 3 buses. In and Out. Set D Bronto visits the dentist. Bronto at the Zoo,
　　　　　　　　　　　Bronto and the rocket.
　　　　　　　　　　　1. Worksheets S1 1·1-1·4.
　　　　　　　　　　　2. Worksheets S2 1·1, 1·3.
　　　　　　　　　　　3. Pupils' Book p6.
　　　Numbers and Words　Book 1 p25. Book 2 p6, 32. Book 4 p1.
　　　　　　　　　　　Book 5 p2-3. Book 6 p15. Book 7 p11.
　　　　　　　　　　　Book 8 p8.
　　　Our First School Maths　Book 3 p23.
　　　Primary Mathematics (SPMG)　Stage 1. Workbook 2 Card 11b.
　　　Towards Mathematics　Core Unit 5 p12.

S　　*Inner Ring Maths*　Book 1 p1. Book 2 p11.
　　　Mathematics for Life　Book A1 p6-7.

Books for teachers
　　　Early Mathematical Experiences　Most books.
　　　Mathematics: the first 3 years　p16-22.
　　　Nuffield Maths 5-11　1. Teachers' Handbook p103-109.
　　　　　　　　　　　2. Teachers' Handbook p81-82.
　　　　　　　　　　　3. Teachers' Handbook p8-9.

Sh2 Sorting and naming 2D shapes.

Circle, triangle, square, rectangle and later kite, polygon, pentagon, hexagon, octagon, etc.

Discussion of common properties: number of sides, etc.

Identification of 2D shapes in the environment.

Drawing and making 2D shapes from Meccano, gummed paper, geoboard, etc. Use of gummed paper shapes to make bigger shapes and pictures.

Abstraction of 2D shapes (faces) from 3D shapes.

See also M2,4 Shapes of coins.
　　　　　N4 Cardinal number — 'threeness' of sides of triangles, etc.
　　　　　N13 Square, rectangular and triangular numbers.
　　　　　S1,3 Sorting and classifying.
　　　　　Sh1 Early concepts and vocabulary.
　　　　　Sh3 Sorting and naming 3D shapes.
　　　　　Sh4 Patterns from shapes.
　　　　　Sh8 Circles.
　　　　　Sh9 Strength of shapes.
　　　　　Sh14,15,16 Further classification of 2D shapes.
　　　　　A1,2 Handling and sorting 2D shapes by size.
　　　　　A3,4,6 etc. Using squares to measure area.

P　　　　*Ready for Alpha and Beta (new ed.)* p27.
　　　　　Alpha (new ed.) Alpha 1 p68.
　　　　　Beta (new ed.) Beta 1 p76.
　　　　　Basic Mathematics Book 1 p70, 71, 83.
　　　　　Hey Mathematics Mod 1. Book 2 p39. Book 3 p40. Book 4 p12. Book 5 p31, 33, 35.
　　　　　　　　　　　　　　Mod 2. Book 4 p40. Book 5 p20.
　　　　　　　　　　　　　　Mod 4. Book 1 p40. Book 5 p16-24.
　　　　　Key Maths Level 1 Book 4 p53-57. Book 5 p53-54. Book 6 p59.
　　　　　　　　　　　Level 2 Book 2 p57-62.
　　　　　Making Sure of Maths Book 1 p64-65, 81-82.
　　　　　Mathematics for Schools Level 1 (2nd ed.) Book 1 p37-38, 39-42. Book 7 p21-22, 42.
　　　　　Maths Adventure 1. Pupil's Book p23, 84-85. Activity Book p17. Card 25.
　　　　　　　　　　　　　2. Activity Book p21.
　　　　　　　　　　　　　3. Card 17, 24.
　　　　　Nuffield Maths 5-11 Bronto Books. Set C. Animal Shapes.
　　　　　　　　　　　　　1. Worksheets S1 3·1-3·4.
　　　　　　　　　　　　　2. Worksheets S2 1·2, 1·4.
　　　　　　　　　　　　　3. Pupils' Book p6-7.
　　　　　Our First School Maths Book 2 p20-21. Book 3 p25.
　　　　　　　　　　　　　　Book 4 p13-15.
　　　　　Oxford Middle School Mathematics Book 1 p23, 40-41.
　　　　　Primary Mathematics (SPMG) Stage 1. Workbook 2 p27-35. Workbook 3 p36-40. Workbook 4,
　　　　　　　　　　　　　　Card 1b, 2b, 3b, 4b.
　　　　　　　　　　　　　　Stage 2. Workbook 1 p34-35.
　　　　　Towards Mathematics Core Unit 5 p1-6, 7, 8, 11.
　　　　　　　　　　　　　Core Unit 10 p5, 6, 7, 8. Core Unit 12 p12, 13.

S　　　　*A World of Mathematics* Book 1 p5-9, 50.
　　　　　Focus Mathematics Book 1 p13. Book 2 p61.
　　　　　Headway Maths Book 1 p18, 81. Book 2 p39, 58, 59.
　　　　　Inner Ring Maths Book 1 p2, 3, 16, 25. Book 2 p13, 14.
　　　　　Maths (Holt) Book 1 p63, 81. Workbook 2 p22.
　　　　　　　　　　　Workbook 3 p15.

Books for teachers
　　　　　Early Mathematical Experiences Most books.
　　　　　Mathematics: the first 3 years p123.
　　　　　Nuffield Maths 5-11 1. Teachers' Handbook p111-113.
　　　　　　　　　　　　　2. Teachers' Handbook p81-82.
　　　　　　　　　　　　　3. Teachers' Handbook p9-10.

Sorting and naming 3D shapes.

Sh3

Cube, cuboid, cylinder, cone, sphere, pyramid and prism.

Discussion of common properties: number of edges, corners, faces, etc.

Identification of 3D shapes in the environment.

Making 3D shapes from plasticine, lego, straws, etc. and from nets i.e. the 2D shape which when folded can be made into a 3D shape.

See also   N and PV sections.   Use of structured apparatus — Dienes etc.
            S1,3   Sorting and classifying.
            Sh1   Early concepts and vocabulary.
            Sh2   Abstraction of 2D shape (face) from 3D shape.
            Sh4   Patterns from shapes.
            Sh11   Further classification of 3D shapes.
            CV1,2   Handling and sorting 3D shapes by size.
            CV4,6, etc.   Using cubes to measure volume.
            A2,11,12   Surface areas from nets.

P   *Ready for Alpha and Beta (new ed.)*   p28.
         Alpha (new ed.)   Alpha 1 p78-79. Alpha 2 p79. Alpha 3 p90.
         Beta (new ed.)   Beta 1 p67-69. Beta 2 p79, 80, 81.
                             Beta 3 p88-89. Beta 5 p80.
         Basic Mathematics   Book 1 p102, 103, 106.
         Hey Mathematics   Mod 1. Book 3 p40. Book 5 p33.
         Key Maths   Level 1. Book 2 p32-34. Book 5 p55. Book 6 p60. Book 7 p59-60.
                        Level 2. Book 4 p56.
         Making Sure of Maths   Book 1 p101-102. Book 2 p73.
                                   Book 3 p84-85.
         Mathematics for Schools   Level 1 (2nd ed.) Book 1 p32-35. Book 3 p16, 19-20. Book 4 p21-22. Book 7 p16-21.
         Maths Adventure   1. Pupil's Book p73, 74. Activity Book p47. Card 16, 17, 18, 19.
                              2. Activity Book p51-57. Card 24.
                              3. Activity Book p25, 31-33.
                              4. Card 20.
                              5. Activity Book p40.
         Nuffield Maths 5-11   1. Worksheets S1 2·1-2·4, 3·6.
                                  2. Worksheets S2 2·1, 2·2, 3·1, 3·2, 3·3, 3·4, 3·5, 3·6.
                                  3. Pupils' Book p63-65.
         Numbers and Words   Book 8 p9.
         Oxford Middle School Mathematics   Book 1 p12-13, 21-22. Book 2 p66.
         Primary Mathematics (SPMG)   Stage 1. Workbook 1. Card 5, 6, 7, 8. Workbook 2. Card 12.
                                         Workbook 4. p35-40.
                                         Stage 2. Workbook 2 p33-37.
         Towards Mathematics   Core Unit 15 p1, 2, 3, 4.

S   *Focus Mathematics*   Book 5 p84-88.
         Headway Maths   Book 1 p19, 81. Book 2 p39.
         Impact Maths   Pupil's Book 1 p44, 45.
         Inner Ring Maths   Book 1 p1, 15. Book 2 p15, 16.
         Maths (Holt)   Book 1 p12-13, 17, 72. Workbook 1 p29-30.
                           Workbook 2 p4-5.

SM   *Check it Again*   Book 5 p41-42.
         Problems   Second Problems p57.

Books for teachers
         Early Mathematical Experiences   'Towards Number. Apparatus, Toys and Games'.
         Mathematics: the first 3 years   p123.
         Nuffield Maths 5-11   1. Teachers' Handbook p109-111, 115-116.
                                  2. Teachers' Handbook p86-89, 98-99.
                                  3. Teachers' Handbook Chapter 14.

Sh4   Patterns from shapes.

Making patterns from 2D and 3D shapes: potato prints, tile patterns, brick walls, etc.

Exploring patterns made by repeating shapes in a straight line (i.e. translation), rotating shapes, reflecting shapes, enlarging and reducing the size of the shape.

Extension of vocabulary associated with movement of shapes: forwards, backwards, move, towards/away from, sideways, round, along, up, left, right, clockwise, anticlockwise, mirror, reflection, direction, etc.

See also   PV1,2   Place value; assumes left/right discrimination.
            Sh2,3   Naming 2D and 3D shapes.
            Sh5,6,8,10,12,13,17,18,19,20   Movement of shapes, lines and points.
            A1,3,5   Early concepts of area. Conservation.
            T4   Observing the clock. Clockwise and anticlockwise.

P   *Key Maths*   Level 1. Book 1 p31. Book 2 p14-15.
    Making Sure of Maths   Book 1 p98-99.
    Mathematics for Schools   Level 1 (2nd ed.) Book 1 p44-46. Book 3 p23. Book 4 p1-2, 37-39. Book 7 p1.
    Maths Adventure   1. Pupil's Book p85. Activity Book p19, 51-52. Card 20.
                   4. Card 18.
    Nuffield Maths 5-11   Bronto Books. Set B. Left-right.
    Oxford Middle School Mathematics   Book 1 p40-41.
    Towards Mathematics   Core Unit 15 p7.

S   *Inner Ring Maths*   Book 1 p4, 5.
    Maths (Holt)   Workbook 1 p20, 21. Workbook 3 p8. 5th Year Workbook p19.

Books for teachers
    Early Mathematical Experiences   'Sand. Raw Materials' p17-18.
                                      'Towards Number. Apparatus, Toys and Games' p18-20.
    Mathematics: the first 3 years   p18, 55-59, 142, 144, 145, 146.

Introduction to tessellations.

Sh5

Experience fitting shapes together without overlapping: tile patterns, etc.

Fitting congruent shapes together without overlapping leading to the discovery of shapes that tessellate i.e. fit together leaving no spaces. Any quadrilateral, any triangle and the regular hexagon are straight-edged 2D shapes that tessellate.

Tessellations involving two different shapes:

    e.g.   regular pentagon and rhombus of related dimensions;
            regular octagon and square of related dimensions.

Tessellations of 3D shapes.

Tessellations in wallpaper, floor tiles, architecture and nature e.g. honey comb.

See also   Sh4   Patterns from shapes.
           Sh8   Circle patterns.
           Sh14,15,16   Further tessellations.
           CV3(2)   Arbitrary units and cubes for measuring volume.
           A3   Arbitrary units and squares for measuring area.

P   *Basic Mathematics*   Book 4 p14-15.
    Hey Mathematics   Mod 4. Book 1 p17-19.
    Making Sure of Maths   Book 1 p98-99.
    Mathematics for Schools   Level 1 (2nd ed.) Book 7 p25-27.
    Maths Adventure   1. Pupil's Book p24.
                   2. Activity Book p44.
                   4 Card 17.
    Nuffield Maths 5-11   2. Worksheets S2. 2·1-2·4.
                       3. Pupils' Book p65, 111.
    Oxford Middle School Mathematics   Book 2 p12-13.
    Primary Mathematics (SPMG)   Stage 4. Textbook p20-21. Card 21, 22.
    Towards Mathematics   Core Unit 5 p13-16. Core Unit 10 p9, 13.
                           Core Unit 15 p8-10, 16.

S   *A World of Mathematics*   Book 2 p25-28.
    Headway Maths   Book 3 p86-87.

Books for teachers
    Mathematics: the first 3 years   p136-140.
    Mathematics: the later Primary years   p95-96, 100-101, 102-103.
    Nuffield Maths 5-11   2. Teachers' Handbook p84-85.

Sh6 Introduction to bilateral symmetry.

Identifying bilateral symmetry in 2D shapes and patterns. Folding and cutting paper, ink blots, string pulling, mirror images, use of kaleidoscope, etc.

Lines of symmetry.

Symmetry in 3D shapes.

Identifying symmetry in the natural and man-made environment.

See also   AR2,5 Symmetrical curved graphs.
             S2   The symmetric relation.
             Sh4   Patterns from reflecting shapes.
             Sh11,14,15,16 Classification and study of 3D and 2D shapes.
             Sh12   Rotational symmetry.
             Sh18   Reflection.

P   *Alpha (new ed.)*   Alpha 2 p10-11. Alpha 3 p76-78.
                         Alpha 4 p49.
     Beta (new ed.)   Beta 3 p15-17. Beta 4 p26-27.
     Basic Mathematics   Book 2 p24-26.
     Hey Mathematics   Mod 3. Book 5 p16.
     Key Maths   Level 1. Book 7 p55-56.
              Level 2. Book 2 p44-47.
     Making Sure of Maths   Book 1 p94-97. Book 2 p65-67.
                          Book 3 p62-64. Book 5 p42-43.
     Mathematics for Schools   Level 1 (2nd ed.) Book 7 p50-53.
                           Level 2 (2nd ed.) Book 1 p56-58.
                           Level 2 (1st ed.) Book 9 p36.
     Maths Adventure   1. Pupil's Book p38-39. Activity Book p30-31.
                     2. Pupil's Book p2, 31. Activity Book p6-7. Card 19.
                     3. Card 20.
     Nuffield Maths 5-11   2. Worksheets S2 5·1-5·4.
                      3. Pupils' Book p8-9.
     Oxford Middle School Mathematics   Book 2 p40-43.
     Primary Mathematics (SPMG)   Stage 2. Workbook 2 Card 8, 9, 10, 11. Workbook 4 p36-40.
                                Stage 3. Textbook p100-102. Workbook p13, 25. Card 57, 59, 61.
                                Stage 5. Textbook p90. Card 59.
     Towards Mathematics   Core Unit 10 p1-2.

S   *A World of Mathematics*   Book 1 p58-59.
     Focus Mathematics   Book 6 p7-19.
     Headway Maths   Book 3 p88-89.
     Inner Ring Maths   Book 2 p8, 9.
     Maths (Holt)   Book 1 p52, 77, 84-85. Workbook 1 p47.
                Book 2 p32, 47. Workbook 2 p37.
                 Workbook 3 p43.

Books for teachers
Early Mathematical Experiences   Particularly 'Space and Shape. Comparisons'. p11.
Mathematics: the first 3 years   p81-86, 141, 142, 143.
Mathematics: the later Primary years   p105-108, 109-110.
Nuffield Maths 5-11   2. Teachers' Handbook p94-97.
                      3. Teachers' Handbook p10-12.

Sh7 Vertical, horizontal and sloping ideas.

Use of home-made plumb line and spirit level to test for vertical and horizontal.

See also   AR2,4,7,9, VR9 Sloping line graphs.
             VR2,3,4,8,9 Vertical and horizontal axes.
             VR7   Co-ordinates.
             Sh10   Right angles. Perpendicular lines.

Circle vocabulary and patterns.

Sh8

Practice in using a pair of compasses. Circle patterns.

Language associated with parts of a circle: radius, diameter, circumference, sector, arc, chord and segment.

The ellipse, parabola, hyperbola, spiral and helix. Curve stitching.

Introduction to the locus idea and its use for drawing straight lines of given length accurately.

See also   AR2,5   Curved graphs. Parabola graphs etc.
           VR5   Pie charts.
           S1,3,4,5   Venn diagrams.
           Sh4   Patterns from shapes.
           Sh5   Introduction to tessellations.
           Sh11   Ellipsoids, paraboloids, etc.
           Sh21   Construction techniques using locus idea.
           Sh22   Circle properties.
           A13, L7,11   Circle area and circumference.
           L4,6   Measuring length.
           L7   Radius as half diameter length.
           T4   The circular clock face and sectors made by clock hands.

Sh9 Rigidity and triangulation.

Exploration of the strength of shapes using Meccano, etc.

Discovery of the triangle as a rigid shape, and its consequent use in the environment for building bridges, etc.

See also   Sh2   Sorting, naming and making 2D shapes.
           Sh14   Classification and study of triangles.
           Sh15,16 Quadrilaterals and polygons. Diagonals.

P   *Alpha (new ed.)*   Alpha 3 p41.
      Beta (new ed.)   Beta 4 p47.
      Basic Mathematics   Book 3 p84, 85.
      Mathematics for Schools   Level 2 (1st ed.) Book 6 p16-17, 53.
      Maths Adventure   2. Pupil's Book p25.
      Primary Mathematics (SPMG)   Stage 5. Textbook p93.
      Towards Mathematics   Core Unit 5 p6.

S   *A World of Mathematics*   Book 2 p34.
      Focus Mathematics   Book 1 p13.
      Maths (Holt)   Book 2 p59. Book 3 p50-51.

Books for teachers
    Mathematics: the later Primary years   p90-94.

Sh 10 Concept of angle. Parallel and perpendicular lines.

Angle as
1.   A measure of turn.
    Complete turn, quarter turn (right angle) and half turn.
    Turning clockwise and anticlockwise.
    North, South, East and West. Use of directional compass.

2.   A measure of the size of a corner.
    Folding a circular piece of paper to make a right angle measure, and comparing angles with this right angle measure.
    Ordering angles by size.
    Identifying right angles, obtuse and acute angles.

Parallel lines. Drawing parallel lines with a set square.

Idea of perpendicular lines.

See also   N5   Ordinal number: 1st, 2nd etc.
           F1,2   Half, quarter, whole one. Addition and subtraction.
           VR5   Pie charts.
           Sh4   Patterns from rotating shapes. Clockwise and anticlockwise.
           Sh7   Vertical, horizontal and sloping.
           Sh12,20 Rotational symmetry. Rotations.
           Sh13   Introduction to degrees.
           Sh14,15 Right angles, parallel lines etc. in triangles and quadrilaterals.
           Sh19   Translations. Parallel lines investigated.
           Sh21   Drawing perpendiculars.
           A12   Area of triangle using perpendicular height.
           L8,9   Maps and plans. Use of directional compass.
           T4,7   Movements of clock hands.

P   *Alpha (new ed.)*   Alpha 1 p56-57. Alpha 2 p41, 63.
                 Alpha 3 p74.
      Beta (new ed.)   Beta 1 p58-60. Beta 2 p36, 37, 43-45.
                 Beta 3 p27, 28. Beta 4 p39.
      Basic Mathematics   Book 1 p72. Book 2 p81, 88, 89, 90, 91, 92. Book 3 p81. Book 5 p72.
      Hey Mathematics   Mod 2. Book 4 p39.
                 Mod 3. Book 5 p10-11.
                 Mod 4. Book 2 p35. Book 4 p36.
                 Mod 5. Book 4 p5-6, 13-16.
      Key Maths   Level 2. Book 2 p39-42. Book 3 p43, 53-54.
      Making Sure of Maths   Book 1 p30-31. Book 2 p56-57, 87-88.
                 Book 3 p38-39.
      Mathematics for Schools   Level 2 (2nd ed.). Book 2 p29-34.
                 Level 2 (1st ed.). Book 3 p51-53, 54.
      Maths Adventure   1. Pupil's Book p40-41, 75. Activity Book p33.
                 2. Pupil's Book p1, 3, 16, 17. Activity Book p22.
      Oxford Middle School Mathematics   Book 2 p24-25, 32-33, 38.

Further classification and study of 3D shapes.

**Sh
11**

Regular and irregular solids.

Regular polyhedra: tetrahedron, cube, octahedron, dodecahedron, and icosahedron.

Irregular polyhedra: cuboids and prisms (other than cubes), pyramids.

Further classification of pyramids: square, triangular pyramids, etc.

Further classification of prisms: triangular, quadrilateral, pentagonal, hexagonal, etc.

Developable and non-developable solids.

Developable solids i.e. solids that can be produced from nets.

Non-developable solids e.g. spheres, ellipsoids, paraboloids.

Properties of these solids investigated and discussed: symmetry, number of vertices, edges, faces, etc.

Cross sections of solids.

See also   S1,3,4,5   Sorting and classifying. Intersection of sets.
                Sh3   Sorting and naming 3D shapes. Nets.
                Sh6   Bilateral symmetry.
                Sh8   The ellipse, parabola, hyperbola etc.
                Sh14,15,16   Triangles, quadrilaterals and other polygons.
                CV9,12   Volume of 3D shapes.
                A11,12   Surface area from nets. Area of cross section.

Sh 12 Introduction to rotational and point symmetry.

Identification of shapes possessing rotational symmetry.

Centre of rotation and order of rotational symmetry.

Point symmetry i.e. when a shape looks the same when rotated through half a revolution.

Relationship investigated between number of lines of symmetry and whether a shape had rotational symmetry.

Sorting shapes possessing bilateral, rotational or point symmetry or a combination of these.

See also   N5   Ordinal number.
            S1,3,4,5   Sorting and classifying. Intersection of sets.
            Sh4   Patterns from rotating shapes.
            Sh6   Bilateral symmetry.
            Sh10   Concept of angle. Right angle.
            Sh14,15,16 Properties of triangles, quadrilaterals and other polygons.
            Sh20   Rotations.

P   *Alpha (new ed.)*   Alpha 4 p50-51.
     Beta (new ed.)   Beta 4 p76-77. Beta 5 p78. Beta 6 p22, 23.
     Making Sure of Maths   Book 5 p44-45. Book 6 p70-72.
     Mathematics for Schools   Level 2. (1st ed.) Book 9 p36, 42.
     Maths Adventure   2. Pupil's Book p31. Activity Book p25-27. Card 20.
                         3. Card 25.
                         4. Pupil's Book p21. Activity Book p26-29.
     Oxford Middle School Mathematics   Book 1 p62. Book 2 p90-93. Book 3 p17.
     Primary Mathematics (SPMG)   Stage 5. Textbook p65-67, 112-113. Card 25, 26.
     Towards Mathematics   Core Unit 10 p3, 4, 10, 12.
                             Core Unit 15 p13, 14, 15.

S   *Focus Mathematics*   Book 6 p20-28.
     Maths (Holt)   Book 2 p40-41. Workbook 3 p43.

Books for teachers
     Mathematics: the later Primary years   p105, 108, 111.

Sh 13 Introduction to degrees.

Use of arbitrary units (e.g. clock minutes) and eventually degrees to measure angles.

Construction and use of a circular protractor with a scale marked in degrees but unnumbered. Later, use of a numbered circular protractor and finally a semi-circular protractor.

Measuring and ordering angles. Estimating size of angle, measuring and recording error. Approximations and limits to accuracy.

The formal naming of angles (e.g. $\angle$ ABC).

Discovery that the sum of the angles on one side of a straight line is 180° and round a point is 360°.

Simple bearings.

Later longitude and latitude.

See also   PV2,4   Place value and counting to 360.
            N15,16,20,21   Addition and subtraction to 360.
            F2   Degree as a fraction of complete turn.
            VR5   Pie charts.
            Sh10   Idea of angle.
            Sh14,15,16 Angles of triangles, quadrilaterals and polygons.
            Sh17   Angles and similarity.
            Sh18,19,20 Angles and congruency.
            Sh19   Corresponding, alternate and vertically opposite angles.
            Sh20   Rotations. Angle of rotation.
            Sh21   Construction techniques.
            Sh22   Angles of shapes inside/outside circles.
            CV8, A6, L6, W7, T6   Limits to accuracy.
            L8,9   Plans and maps.
            L13   Calculating heights. The clinometer.
            T14   World time, longitude and latitude.

P   *Alpha (new ed.)*   Alpha 2 p64, 65. Alpha 3 p64-66, 80-83.
                  Alpha 4 p30, 52-53, 58.
  Beta (new ed.)   Beta 3 p28-30. Beta 4 p38, 52-54, 62-65.
                 Beta 5 p18-19, 42, 43. Beta 6 p18, 20, 67.
  Basic Mathematics   Book 3 p82, 83. Book 5 p70, 71, 73, 74, 75, 76, 79, 80.
  Hey Mathematics   Mod 3. Book 2 p40. Book 4 p40.
                Mod 5. Book 4 p6-13.
                Mod 6. Book 4 p5, 6.
  Key Maths   Level 2. Book 5 p103-105. Book 6 p110-115.
  Making Sure of Maths   Book 3 p35-37. Book 4 p38-40.
                    Book 5 p18-21. Book 6 p33-35.
  Mathematics for Schools   Level 2 (1st ed.) Book 3 p56-57. Book 4 p23-24. Book 5 p31. Book 10 p22.
  Maths Adventure   3. Pupil's Book p4-5, 6. Activity Book p6, 27.
                4. Pupil's Book p4-5. Activity Book p4, 5, 6, 7, 8.
                5. Pupil's Book p12-13, 14. Activity Book p7.
  Oxford Middle School Mathematics   Book 3 p12-15.
  Primary Mathematics (SPMG)   Stage 4. Textbook p84-89. Workbook p8. Card 45.
                       Stage 5. Textbook p56-63. Card 58.
  Towards Mathematics   Core Unit 18 p4-14.

S   *A World of Mathematics*   Book 2 p20-23. Book 3 p28-31.
  Focus Mathematics   Book 4 p35-41. Book 5 p7-32, 151.
  Headway Maths   Book 2 p30-31, 54-55. Book 3 p6-7, 14-15.
               Book 4 p6. Book 5 p70-72.
  Maths (Holt)   Book 2 p76. Book 3 p29, 30, 33.
             Workbook 3 p6, 7. 4th Year Workbook p6, 15.
  Mathsworks   Book 1 p120. Tryouts 1 p59. Book 2 p5.
           Tryouts 2 p1, 2, 3, 32, 33.
  Maths You Need   p124-129.

SM   *Check it Again*   Book 5. p53-54.
  Problems   Third Problems p17.

Books for teachers
  Hey Mathematics   Mod 3. Teachers' Book p43-44, 45.
  Mathematics: the later Primary years   p97-98.
  Mathematics: from Primary to Secondary   p3-8, 108-111.

Classification and study of triangles.   **Sh 14**

Classification of triangles: equilateral, isosceles, scalene and right-angled triangles. Discussion of properties.

Tessellations of triangles.

Investigation and discovery of the angle-sum property of a triangle. Calculations based on this property.

Discovery that the exterior angle of a triangle is equal to the sum of the two interior opposite angles. Calculations based on this property.

See also   N20,21   Addition and subtraction to 180.
          S1,3,4,5   Sorting and classifying. Intersection of sets.
          Sh5   Tessellations.
          Sh6,12   Bilateral and rotational symmetry.
          Sh9   Rigidity and triangulation.
          Sh10   Angles: acute, obtuse etc.
          Sh11   Further classification of 3D shapes.
          Sh13   Degrees. Angle-sum on one side of straight line.
          Sh17   Similar triangles.
          Sh18,19,20   Congruent triangles.
          Sh21   Construction of triangles.
          Sh22   Triangles with circle diameter as base.
          Sh23   Introduction to Pythagoras' theorem.
          A12   Area of triangle.
          L13   Calculating heights using similar triangles.

P   *Alpha (new ed.)*   Alpha 2 p72-74. Alpha 3 p40, 41.
                  Alpha 4 p68-69.
  Beta (new ed.)   Beta 2 p70, 71. Beta 3 p51-53, 87.
                 Beta 4 p38, 66-68. Beta 5 p64.

Basic Mathematics   Book 2 p93.
Hey Mathematics   Mod 5. Book 4 p17-20.
                    Mod 6. Book 4 p2.
Making Sure of Maths   Book 1 p91-92. Book 2 p62-63, 64.
Mathematics for Schools   Level 2 (1st ed.) Book 3 p53, 55. Book 4 p25-26. Book 5 p31, 40. Book 9 p40, 54.
Maths Adventure   3. Pupil's Book p7, 16-17. Activity Book p9, 19.
                    5. Pupil's Book p10. Activity Book p2.
Oxford Middle School Mathematics   Book 2 p27. Book 3 p27.
Primary Mathematics (SPMG)   Stage 3. Textbook p13-15. Workbook p3-4, 21.
                               Stage 5. Textbook p30-34, 120-122. Workbook p11.
Towards Mathematics   Core Unit 5 p10. Core Unit 10 p15, 16.
                        Core Unit 18 p1, 5, 15, 16. Core Unit 20 p1, 3. Core Unit 23 p6, 9, 16.

S   *A World of Mathematics*   Book 6 p28-30.
Focus Mathematics   Book 1 p15-16. Book 5 p24.
Headway Maths   Book 3 p15. Book 4 p7, 12, 22-23.
Maths (Holt)   Workbook 2 p39. Book 3 p29, 42.
                 Workbook 3 p7, 36.
Mathsworks   Book 1 p81. Tryouts 1 p41, 43.
               Book 2 p6, 16, 33.

SM   *Check it Again*   Book 3 p54-55.

Books for teachers
Hey Mathematics   Mod 3. Teachers' Book p45.
Mathematics: the later Primary years   p96, 98-99, 102.

Sh 15   Classification and study of quadrilaterals.

Classification of quadrilaterals: rhombus, parallelogram, trapezium, square, rectangle, kite, arrowhead.

Discussion of properties.

Tessellations of quadrilaterals.

Investigation and discovery of the angle - sum property of a quadrilateral. Calculations based on this property.

See also   N20,21   Addition and subtraction to 360.
           S1,3,4,5   Sorting and classifying. Intersection of sets.
           Sh5   Tessellations.
           Sh6,12   Bilateral and rotational symmetry.
           Sh9   Rigidity and triangulation.
           Sh10   Angles, parallel idea, etc.
           Sh11   Further classification of 3D shapes.
           Sh13   Degrees. Angle - sum round a point.
           Sh17   Similar quadrilaterals.
           Sh18,19,20   Congruent quadrilaterals.
           Sh21   Construction of quadrilaterals.
           Sh22   Cyclic quadrilaterals.
           A7,12   Area of quadrilaterals.

P   *Alpha (new ed.)*   Alpha 1 p69, 70. Alpha 2 p15-16.
                            Alpha 3 p36-37. Alpha 4 p36.
Beta (new ed.)   Beta 1 p74-75, 77. Beta 2 p64-65.
                   Beta 3 p41-43. Beta 4 p46. Beta 5 p21, 56, 57, 58, 72.
Basic Mathematics   Book 3 p86, 87, 88.
Hey Mathematics   Mod 5. Book 4 p17, 21-24.
                    Mod 6. Book 4 p2.
Key Maths   Level 2. Book 3 p44-45.
Making Sure of Maths   Book 2 p58-61, 63-64, 68-69. Book 3 p44-47, 60-61. Book 4 p65-68, 92.
Mathematics for Schools   Level 2 (1st ed.) Book 4 p27-28. Book 5 p38-39, 42. Book 9 p37, 39, 54.
Maths Adventure   2. Pupil's Book p24.
                    3. Pupil's Book p27-30. Activity Book p35. Card 16.
                    4. Pupil's Book p2-3. Activity Book p2-3. Card 16.
                    5. Pupil's Book p7-9, 11. Activity Book p8-9, 37, 41.
Oxford Middle School Mathematics   Book 2 p39. Book 3 p4. Book 4 p6.
Primary Mathematics (SPMG)   Stage 2. Workbook 3 p33-40.
                               Stage 3. Workbook p4, 36-37.
                               Stage 4. Textbook p102, 103, 104, 105. Workbook p18-19. Card 46.
                               Stage 5. Textbook p92, 120-122. Workbook p10. Card 44, 61.
Towards Mathematics   Core Unit 10 p14, 15, 16. Core Unit 18 p1.
                        Core Unit 20 p6. Core Unit 23 p6, 9, 16.

S *Focus Mathematics*   Book 1 p16-17. Book 5 p24, 136-144.
Headway Maths   Book 2 p40-41. Book 3 p84. Book 4 p7, 13, 40-41.
Maths (Holt)   Book 3 p29. Workbook 3 p35, 42.
Mathsworks   Book 2 p16, 20-21. Tryouts 2 p12, 32.

Books for teachers
Mathematics: the later Primary years   p37-43, 100-102.

Classification and study of polygons with more than four sides.

Regular and irregular polygons. Regular and irregular pentagons, hexagons, heptagons, octagons, etc. Discussion of properties: angles, sides, etc.

Investigation and discovery of angle-sum property of polygons. Calculations based on this property.

Tessellations of polygons.

Relationships investigated between number of diagonals, number of corners, number of sides and angles in regular polygons.

See also M4   50p coin as regular heptagon.
N20,21   Addition and subtraction to 360.
AR5   Curved graphs.
S1,3,4,5   Sorting and classifying. Intersection of sets.
Sh5   Tessellations.
Sh6,12   Bilateral and rotational symmetry.
Sh9   Rigidity and triangulation.
Sh11   Further classification of 3D shapes.
Sh13   Degrees. Angle - sum round a point.
Sh14,15   Classification and study of triangles and quadrilaterals.
Sh17   Similar polygons.
Sh18,19,20   Congruent polygons.
Sh21   Construction of polygons.
Sh22   Regular polygons inside and outside circles.
A12   Area of regular polygons.

P *Alpha (new ed.)*   Alpha 4 p39.
Beta (new ed.)   Beta 2 p75. Beta 4 p84. Beta 5 p58.
Basic Mathematics   Book 4 p12, 13.
Hey Mathematics   Mod 4. Book 4 p18.
Mod 6. Book 4 p8-9.
Making Sure of Maths   Book 4 p38-39.
Mathematics for Schools   Level 2 (1st ed.) Book 6 p54. Book 7 p52.
Maths Adventure   2. Pupil's Book p23, 25. Activity Book p19.
3. Pupil's Book p30. Activity Book p44.
5. Activity Book p3.
Oxford Middle School Mathematics   Book 2 p26-27. Book 3 p50, 82-83.
Primary Mathematics (SPMG)   Stage 4. Card 45, 63.
Stage 5. Textbook p67, 90-91. Workbook p12. Card 18, 41.

S *Focus Mathematics*   Book 1 p14. Book 2 p66. Book 5 p25.
Headway Maths   Book 3 p85. Book 4 p51.
Maths (Holt)   Book 3 p77. Workbook 3 p10.

SM *Problems*   Third Problems p34-35.

Books for teachers
Mathematics: the later Primary years   p99-100, 101-104.

Similarity, enlargement and reduction.

Enlargement and reduction of lines and 2D shapes using scale factors and/or co-ordinates.

Investigation of angles and sides of enlarged and reduced simple 2D shapes leading to recognition of similarity.

Applications e.g.   simple surveying, plans and maps (See also L8,9),
photography,
use of microscope and telescope,
finding heights using similar triangles (See also L13).

Investigation of volume, area, length and perimeter relationships of similar 2D and 3D shapes (See also AR4,5, CV11, A9,11,13, L7,11).

Investigation of similar right-angled triangles; discovery of 3:4:5 ratio of the lengths of the three sides of certain similar right-angled triangles.

See also
N13	Square, rectangular and triangular numbers.
N23	Ratio, rate and proportion.
F4	Multiplication of fraction by whole number.
AR9	Gradients of straight line graphs.
VR7	Co-ordinates.
VR8	Block graphs etc. with varied scales.
Sh4,8	Patterns from similar, enlarged and reduced shapes.
Sh13	Degrees.
Sh14,15,16	Triangles, quadrilaterals and other polygons.
Sh23	Pythagoras' theorem.
CV6,7	Cm^3, dm^3, m^3 to measure volume. Relationships between standard units.
A6,8	Cm^2, dm^2, m^2 to measure area. Relationships between standard units.

P   *Beta (new ed.)*   Beta 5 p82, 83.
Basic Mathematics   Book 4 p84.
Hey Mathematics   Mod 6. Book 4 p9.
Making Sure of Maths   Book 4 p90. Book 5 p101.
Mathematics for Schools   Level 2 (1st ed.) Book 8 p51-57. Book 10 p44-48.
Maths Adventure   2. Pupil's Book p71. Card 14.
        3. Pupil's Book p75.
        4. Pupil's Book p23, 53. Activity Book p30-32.
Oxford Middle School Mathematics   Book 2 p60-61. Book 4 p44-45, 56, 58, 72-73.
Primary Mathematics (SPMG)   Stage 3. Workbook p3, 37.
                              Stage 4. Textbook p48-52. Card 18, 33, 34, 52.
                              Stage 5. Textbook p96-98. Card 63.
Towards Mathematics   Core Unit 21 p7, 8, 9, 10. Core Unit 25 p14, 16.

S   *A World of Mathematics*   Book 6 p40-44.
Focus Mathematics   Book 7 p33-38, 40-45.
Headway Maths   Book 5 p58-61.
Inner Ring Maths   Book 3 p11.
Maths (Holt)   Workbook 2 p10-11, 30-31. Book 3 p57, 60, 62. 4th Year p50. 5th Year p4-5.
                5th Year Workbook p41.
Maths Matters   Book 3 p22-23.

Books for teachers
     Mathematics: from Primary to Secondary   p42-45.

Sh 18   Reflection.

Extension of Sh4 and 6. Investigation of the reflection of points, lines and shapes using mirrors.

Symmetry discussed.

Drawing points, lines and shapes on graph paper reflected from one or more 'mirror lines' using co-ordinates.

Comparing angles and sides of original and reflected shapes leading to recognition of congruency.

See also
VR7	Co-ordinates.
Sh13	Degrees.
Sh14,15,16	Triangles, quadrilaterals and other polygons.
Sh19,20	Congruency from translation and rotation.

P   *Alpha (new ed.)*   Alpha 4 p49.
Beta (new ed.)   Beta 5 p62-64. Beta 6 p21, 51, 59, 60, 61.
Making Sure of Maths   Book 4 p69-70. Book 6 p39-41, 67-69.
Mathematics for Schools   Level 2 (1st ed.) Book 6 p58-59. Book 8 p12, 15.
Maths Adventure   4. Pupil's Book p20, 78. Activity Book p22-25.
        5. Pupil's Book p27-28, 31. Activity Book p10-11.
Primary Mathematics (SPMG)   Stage 3. Workbook p12-13, Card 58, 60.
                              Stage 4. Textbook p104, Card 47.
                              Stage 5. Card 60.
Towards Mathematics   Core Unit 10 p11. Core Unit 25 p6, 8, 9.

Books for teachers

Translation i.e. linear movement of points, lines or shapes.

Extension of Sh4. Translation of points, lines and shapes on graph paper using co-ordinates.

Study of angles and sides of original and translated shapes and lines, leading to recognition of congruency, discovery of parallel lines, corresponding, alternate and vertically opposite angles.

Using knowledge of corresponding, alternate or vertically opposite angles to calculate angles associated with parallel and crossing lines.

Translation of points (vectors). Bearings and navigation.

See also   N20,21   Addition and subtraction to 360.
    N27,35   Directed numbers. Simple operations.
    VR7   Co-ordinates.
    Sh5   Tessellations.
    Sh10   Directional compass. Parallel idea.
    Sh13   Degrees. Angle - sum properties of line and point.
    Sh14,15,16   Triangles, quadrilaterals and other polygons. Angle - sum properties.
    Sh18,20   Congruency from reflection and rotation.
    L8,9   Plans and maps.

Books for teachers

Rotation.

Extension of Sh4, 10 and 12. Rotation of lines and shapes on graph paper using co-ordinates.

Investigation of the centre of rotation and angle of rotation.

Investigation of angles and sides of original and rotated shapes leading to the recognition of congruency.

See also   VR7   Co-ordinates.
    Sh5   Tessellations.
    Sh10   Idea of angle.
    Sh13   Degrees.
    Sh18,19   Congruency from reflection and translation.

P   *Beta (new ed.)*   Beta 4 p77. Beta 5 p79. Beta 6 p23, 59, 60, 61.
     Making Sure of Maths   Book 6 p73-77.
     Mathematics for Schools   Level 2 (1st ed.) Book 6 p60-61. Book 8 p13, 14, 15. Book 9 p37.
     Maths Adventure   2. Pupil's Book p3.
                     4. Pupil's Book p22, 78
                     5. Pupil's Book p29-30, 31. Activity Book p12-13.
     Oxford Middle School Mathematics   Book 4 p48-51, 57.
     Towards Mathematics   Core Unit 5 p5. Core Unit 10 p12.
                          Core Unit 15 p13, 14, 15. Core Unit 18 p8.
                          Core Unit 25 p15.

S   *Focus Mathematics*   Book 6 p114-116, 119-120.
     Maths (Holt)   Book 2 p29, 88-90. Book 3 p43.

Books for teachers
     Mathematics: the later Primary years   p112-115.
     Mathematics: from Primary to Secondary   p59-62.

Sh 21   Construction techniques.

Locus idea developed.

Construction of triangles, quadrilaterals and other polygons.

Bisecting angles and lines. Drawing perpendiculars.

See also   N18,30   Dividing numbers by 2.
             Sh8   Introduction to locus idea.
             Sh10   Parallel and perpendicular lines.
             Sh13   Degrees.
             Sh14,15,16   Triangles, quadrilaterals and other polygons.
             Sh22   Construction of cyclic quadrilaterals, etc.
             A12   Area of triangles. Perpendicular height.
             L6   Dimensions of 2D and 3D shapes.
             L13   Construction of triangles to find heights.

P   *Alpha (new ed.)*   Alpha 4 p37.
     Beta (new ed.)   Beta 3 p86. Beta 5 p42, 55, 56, 57, 74-75, 77, 90, 91. Beta 6 p19, 20, 24, 25, 26, 52-54, 88.
     Hey Mathematics   Mod 4. Book 2 p34.
     Making Sure of Maths   Book 3 p41-43, 59. Book 5 p15-17, 22-25, 38.
     Mathematics for Schools   Level 2 (1st ed.) Book 5 p40. Book 9 p55.
     Maths Adventure   4. Card 15.
     Oxford Middle School Mathematics   Book 4 p8-9.
     Primary Mathematics (SPMG)   Stage 5. Textbook p31.

S   *A World of Mathematics*   Book 1 p38-39. Book 2 p35-36.
                                  Book 4 p32, 51-56. Book 6 p44.
     Headway Maths   Book 4 p23. Book 5 p6-9, 24-25.
     Maths (Holt)   Book 2 p55.
     Mathsworks   Book 2 p17, 21. Tryouts 2 p10.

Sh 22   Further study of the properties of the circle.

Investigation of the properties of cyclic quadrilaterals.

Investigation of angle subtended by the diameter.

Regular and irregular shapes inside and outside circles.

Construction techniques developed in Sh21 extended to construction of shapes inside and outside circles.

See also   VR5   Pie charts.
             Sh8   Circles and circle vocabulary.
             Sh13   Degrees.
             Sh14,15,16   Triangles, quadrilaterals and other polygons.
             A13, L11   Circle area and circumference.

P   *Alpha (new ed.)*   Alpha 4 p68.
      Beta (new ed.)   Beta 2 p75. Beta 3 p70. Beta 4 p67.
                    Beta 5 p76, 77, 90. Beta 6 p18, 25, 26, 27, 70-71.
      Making Sure of Maths   Book 3 p58. Book 5 p37, 41.
      Mathematics for Schools   Level 2 (1st ed.) Book 7 p41-44.
      Primary Mathematics (SPMG)   Stage 5. Textbook p28.
      Towards Mathematics   Core Unit 18 p16.

S   *A World of Mathematics*   Book 2 p7.
      Focus Mathematics   Book 8 p53-61.
      Headway Maths   Book 3 p80. Book 5 p26-27.
      Maths (Holt)   Book 2 p48-50. Book 3 p32, 43.

Introduction to Pythagoras' theorem.   **Sh 23**

Investigation of triangles, leading to the discovery that the square on the hypotenuse of the right-angled triangle is equivalent to the sum of the squares on the other two sides.

See also   N26   Powers idea and index notation. Square roots.
            AR3(1)   Generalisations expressed using 'variables'.
            AR3(2)   Substituting numbers into algebraic expressions.
            AR8   Algebraic solution of equations.
            Sh14   Classification and study of triangles.
            Sh17   Similar triangles.
            A7,12   Area of square and triangle.
            L13   Calculating inaccessible heights.

P   *Alpha (new ed.)*   Alpha 4 p70-72.
      Beta (new ed.)   Beta 5 p83-86. Beta 6 p55-58, 88.
      Making Sure of Maths   Book 5 p98. Book 6 p62-66.
      Mathematics for Schools   Level 2 (1st ed.) Book 9 p6-8, 11-12.
      Maths Adventure   5. Pupil's Book p90-92.

S   *Focus Mathematics*   Book 9 p46-56.
      Maths (Holt)   4th Year Workbook p21.
      Mathsworks   Book 2 p14-15, 65. Tryouts 2 p8, 9, 16, 17.

Capacity and Volume

Contents

---- Topics with a sequence of development extending over considerable time.

Early concepts and vocabulary associated with capacity and volume. **CV1**

Introduction to and extension of vocabulary alongside experience handling a wide range of containers and solids. Use of sand, water and other materials to fill containers.

Vocabulary: big, small, enormous, huge, tiny, holds a little/a lot, takes up a little/lot of space, empty, level, full, etc.

See also   S1,3   Sorting and classifying.
             Sh1,3   Sorting and naming 3D shapes.

P   *Come and Measure*   Capacity p1-4.
       Making Sure of Maths   Pink Book p4-5.
       Mathematics for Schools   Level 1 (2nd ed.) Book 1 p7-8.
       Maths Adventure   1. Pupil's Book p72.
       Nuffield Maths 5-11   Bronto Books. Set B. Greedy Pig.
                                     Mini half-as-big.
                                       Set C. 3 buses.
                                       1. Worksheets C1 $1 \cdot 1$-$1 \cdot 2$.
                                       3. Pupils' Book p53.
       Our First School Maths   Book 1 p26-27.

Books for teachers
       Early Mathematical Experiences   'Water. Raw Materials'.
                                                   'Home Corner. The Family'.
                                                   'Outside Activities. The Environment'.
                                                     'Shape and Space. Comparisons'.
       Mathematics: the first 3 years   p16-22.
       Nuffield Maths 5-11   1. Teachers' Handbook p153-154.

Comparing and ordering by capacity and volume. **CV2**

Comparing and ordering the capacity of two and later more containers by pouring sand, water and other 'fillers' from one container to another.

Comparing and ordering the volume of two and later more solids by visual inspection and by displacement i.e. marking the level of a partially filled container, submerging the solid and marking the new level.

Extension of vocabulary: bigger, biggest, smaller, smallest, holds more/less, holds the most/least, takes up more/less/the most/the least space, etc.

Equivalence in capacity and volume.

     'holds about the same as . . .'
     'is about the same size as . . .'

See also   N5   Ordinal number; 1st, 2nd, etc.
             S2   Relations between sets. The equivalent relation.
             CV4   Conservation.

P   *Beta (new ed.)*   Beta 1 p49.
       Come and Measure   Capacity p5-8.
       Mathematics for Schools   Level 1 (2nd ed.) Book 3 p30-33, 51-52.
       Maths Adventure   2. Card 27.
       Nuffield Maths 5-11   1. Worksheets C1 $2 \cdot 1$-$2 \cdot 2$, $4 \cdot 1$.
                                     3. Pupils' Book p51.
       Numbers and Words   Book 1 p20.
       Primary Mathematics (SPMG)   Stage 1. Workbook 4 p24-27.

S   *Focus Mathematics*   Book 5 p82.

Books for teachers
       Early Mathematical Experiences   'Water. Raw Materials'.
                                                   'Home Corner. The Family'.
                                                   'Outside Activities. The Environment'.
                                                     'Space and Shape. Comparisons' p19-21.
       Mathematics: the first 3 years   p74.
       Nuffield Maths 5-11   1. Teachers' Handbook p155, 157.
                                   3. Teachers' Handbook p69-70.

CV3 Use of arbitrary units for measuring capacity and volume.

1. Capacity

Use of arbitrary units (e.g. egg cups of sand, marbles) to measure and order containers by capacity.

Estimating capacity in these units, measuring and recording error.

Use of arbitrary units to calibrate a measuring jar, and use of this jar to measure capacities.

An appreciation of the need for standard units.

See also   PV2   Counting and ordering numbers to 100.
           N5   Ordinal number.
           N9,16   Subtraction to 100.
           F1   Half, quarter, whole one.
           VR8   Scales on measuring instruments.
           S2   Relations between sets.
           Sh13, A3, L3, W3, T3   The need for standard units.
           CV4   Conservation (assumed for measuring jar).

P   *Ready for Alpha and Beta*   p23.
        Alpha (new ed.)   Alpha 1 p66.
        Beta (new ed.)   Beta 1 p49.
        Basic Mathematics   Book 3 p103.
        Come and Measure   Capacity p9-13.
        Hey Mathematics   Mod 2. Book 1 p14.
                                Mod 3. Book 4 p20.
        Key Maths   Level 2. Book 1 p57.
        Making Sure of Maths   Book 1 p70.
        Mathematics for Schools   Level 1 (2nd ed.) Book 4 p54-55.
                                      Level 2 (2nd ed.) Book 2 p50-52.
        Maths Adventure   1. Card 26, 27, 28.
                          2. Card 30.
        Nuffield Maths 5-11   1. Worksheets Cl 3·1, 5·1-5·2.
                              3. Pupils' Book p52-53.
        Numbers and Words   Book 5 p30.
        Our First School Maths   Book 4 p16-17.
        Oxford Middle School Mathematics   Book 1 p54.
        Primary Mathematics (SPMG)   Stage 2. Workbook 1 p31-33. Card 9a, 9b.
        Towards Mathematics   Core Unit 4 p11.

Books for teachers
       Mathematics: the first 3 years   p56, 131.
       Nuffield Maths 5-11   1. Teachers' Handbook p156, 158-160.
                           3. Teachers' Handbook p70, 145.

2. Volume

Use of a wide range of 3D shapes to measure and order solids by volume.

Discussion leading to the use of shapes that tesselate i.e. fit together leaving no spaces.
     e.g.   Cubes. 'This box is about as big as four of these cubes'.

Estimating volume in these units, measuring and recording error.

An appreciation of the need for standard units.

See also   Sh3   Sorting and naming 3D shapes.
           Sh5   Tessellations.
           and topics listed for CV3(1).

P   *Key Maths*   Level 2 Book 4 p57-58.
        Mathematics for Schools   Level 1 (2nd ed.) Book 6 p54-56.
                                  Level 2 (1st ed.) Book 6 p30.
        Maths Adventure   2. Pupil's Book p81. Card 26.
        Nuffield Maths 5-11   3. Pupils' Book p65, 111-112.
        Oxford Middle School Mathematics   Book 2 p76-77.
        Primary Mathematics (SPMG)   Stage 1. Workbook 4 p35.

S   *Impact Maths*   Pupil's Book 1 p50, 51.
        Inner Ring Maths   Book 3 p15.
        Maths (Holt)   Book 2 p46. Workbook 2 p20. 4th Year p70.

Books for teachers
       Mathematics: the first 3 years   p131-134.
       Nuffield Maths 5-11   3. Teachers' Handbook p86.

Conservation of capacity and volume.

Experience leading to the concept of conservation (invariance) of capacity and volume i.e. the idea that capacity and volume are properties independent of other attributes and particularly of shape and length.

Piaget-type experiences with discussion:
> e.g. pouring a fixed amount of water into different sized containers so that the levels are different.
> Building towers with a fixed number of bricks and then altering the shape.

See also   N4, A5, L2, W4   Conservation.
> S2   The equivalent relation.

P   *Come and Measure*   Capacity p17.
> *Mathematics for Schools*   Level 2 (1st ed.) Book 6 p30.
> *Maths Adventure*   1. Card 26.
>   2. Card 28, 30.
> *Nuffield Maths 5-11*   3. Pupils' Book p112.
> *Oxford Middle School Mathematics*   Book 2 p76.
> *Primary Mathematics (SPMG)*   Stage 1. Workbook 2 Card 11a.

S   *Impact Maths*   Pupil's Book 1 p51.

Books for teachers
> *Mathematics: the first 3 years*   p17, 74, 75, 128.
> *Nuffield Maths 5-11*   2. Teachers' Handbook p138-139, 144-145.
>   3. Teachers' Handbook p70-71, 147.

Introduction to litres and millilitres.

Concept of the capacity of one litre, half a litre, quarter of a litre, eventually extended to millilitres. Containers compared by capacity with one litre, etc.

Estimating capacities in litres *or* millilitres, measuring and recording error.

Simple cookery.

Approximations i.e. rounding off measurements.

See also   PV2,4   Counting and ordering numbers to 1,000.
> N5   Ordinal number.
> N9,16,21   Subtraction.
> F1   Half, quarter and whole one.
> S2   Relations between sets.

P   *Alpha (new ed.)*   Alpha 1 p66. Alpha 2 p50.
> *Beta (new ed.)*   Beta 1 p50. Beta 2 p14, 59.
> *Basic Mathematics*   Book 1 p89, 90.
> *Come and Measure*   Capacity p14-16, 21.
> *Hey Mathematics*   Mod 3. Book 3 p15.
> *Key Maths*   Level 2. Book 1 p57-58.
> *Making Sure of Maths*   Introductory Book p49.
>   Book 1 p71-72. Book 2 p47.
> *Mathematics for Schools*   Level 1 (2nd ed.) Book 6 p48.
>   Level 2 (2nd ed.) Book 2 p50, 53.
> *Maths Adventure*   2. Card 29.
>   3. Card 28, 29.
> *Nuffield Maths 5-11*   2. Worksheets C2 1·1, 1·2, 2·1-2·4, 3·1.
>   3. Pupils' Book p109-110.
> *Our First School Maths*   Book 5 p28-29. Book 6 p28-29.
> *Oxford Middle School Mathematics*   Book 1 p55.
> *Primary Mathematics (SPMG)*   Stage 2. Workbook 3 p27-31.
>   Stage 5. Textbook p119.

S   *Mathematics for Life*   Book B2 p6-7.

Books for teachers
> *Nuffield Maths 5-11*   2. Teachers' Handbook p139-143.
>   3. Teachers' Handbook p146-147.

CV6 Introduction to the cubic centimetre, cubic decimetre and cubic metre.

Concept of the volume of one cubic centimetre, one cubic decimetre and one cubic metre.
  Solids compared by volume with one cubic centimetre, etc.

Familiarity with the notation cm³, dm³, m³.

Estimating volume in cm³ *or* dm³ (*or* m³, if practical) measuring and recording error.

Approximations i.e. rounding off measurements.

See also PV2 Counting and ordering numbers to 100.
            N5   Ordinal number.
            N9,16 Subtractions.
            N26   Powers idea and index notation.
            Sh3,17 The cube. Similarity.
            L4   Centimetre, decimetre and metre.

P   *Alpha (new ed.)* Alpha 2 p81. Alpha 3 p90, 91.
      Beta (new ed.) Beta 3 p89.
      Basic Mathematics Book 3 p104.
      Hey Mathematics Mod 6. Book 4 p18.
      Key Maths Level 2. Book 4 p59. Book 5 p84.
      Making Sure of Maths Book 4 p75.
      Maths Adventure 1. Card 29.
      Primary Mathematics (SPMG) Stage 3. Textbook p98-99, Card 51, 52.
                                  Stage 4. Textbook p42.

S   *Focus Mathematics* Book 5 p96-97.
      Headway Maths Book 1 p83.
      Maths (Holt) Book 2 p26.

CV7 Relationships between standard metric units.

Relationships between metric capacity units and relationships between metric volume units. Converting measurements from one standard unit to another using decimal notation when it is understood.

Relationships between metric capacity units and metric volume units.

Relationships investigated between capacity and weight of water leading to the discovery that one litre of water weighs one kilogram.

Addition and subtraction of metric units.

See also PV4,7 Place value. Grouping in 100's and 1,000's.
            PV6,8 Decimal notation.
            N8,9,15,16,20,21 Addition and subtraction of whole numbers.
            N22   Addition and subtraction of decimals.
            N26   Powers idea and index notation.
            AR4   Weight/Volume graph for water.
            Sh17, CV11 Similar, enlarged and reduced cubes.
            CV10 Problems and applications.
            A8, L5 Relationships between standard units.
            W7   Weighing liquids.

P   *Alpha (new ed.)* Alpha 2 p50. Alpha 3 p19. Alpha 4 p21, 76.
      Beta (new ed.) Beta 2 p59. Beta 3 p57, 58. Beta 4 p31, 89.
                      Beta 5 p11. Beta 6 p11, 12.
      Basic Mathematics Book 2 p71. Book 3 p65. Book 4 p65.
                      Book 5 p63, 64, 65.
      Come and Measure Capacity p18-20.
      Hey Mathematics Mod 2. Book 3 p22.
                      Mod 3. Book 2 p4.
                      Mod 4. Book 4 p1-2, 23.
                      Mod 6. Book 4 p17, 21-23.
      Key Maths Level 2. Book 4 p54-55. Book 5 p94, 95. Book 6 p92, 93, 94, 95.
      Making Sure of Maths Book 2 p48, 51. Book 3 p88, 90.
                            Book 4 p76-77.
      Mathematics for Schools Level 2 (1st ed.) Book 8 p30-31.
      Maths Adventure 4. Card 4.

Nuffield Maths 5-11   2. Worksheets C2 3·1-3·2.
Oxford Middle School Mathematics   Book 3 p54-55.
Primary Mathematics (SPMG)   Stage 3. Textbook p36-37.
Stage 4. Textbook p43, 71.
Stage 5. Textbook p47. Card 21.
Towards Mathematics   Core Unit 4 p12. Core Unit 19 p11, 12.

S   *A World of Mathematics*   Book 3 p53. Book 5 p7-8.
Focus Mathematics   Book 5 p111.
Headway Maths   Book 1 p84-85.

SM   *Check it Again*   Book 4 p41-42.
Four a Day series   Book 8 p71. Book 9 p82. Book 10 p74, 87-88.
Number Workbook   Decimals p29.

Measuring capacity and volume using more than one standard unit.   CV8

Estimating capacity or volume, measuring using more than one unit and recording error e.g. 1 litre 250ml. Use of decimal notation when understood.

Use of a range of measuring instruments: measuring jars, dip sticks, displacement cans, etc.

Reading dials or scales.

Approximations (i.e. rounding off measurements) and limits to accuracy.

See also   PV4,7   Place value. Grouping in 100's, 1,000's, etc.
PV6,8   Decimal notation.
N9,16,21   Subtraction of whole numbers.
N22   Subtraction of decimals.
VR8   Scales on measuring instruments.
Sh13, A6, L6, W7, T6   Limits to accuracy.
CV7   Relationships between standard units. Subtraction of metric measurements.

P   *Alpha (new ed.)*   Alpha 4 p21.
Beta (new ed.)   Beta 4 p31. Beta 5 p11. Beta 6 p10.
Come and Measure   Capacity p22-24.
Hey Mathematics   Mod 3. Book 3 p16.
Maths Adventure   4. Card 28.
Primary Mathematics (SPMG)   Stage 4. Textbook p72-73.
Stage 5. Textbook p22, 116. Card 40.

S   *Headway Maths*   Book 1 p86.
Mathematics for Life   Book B2 p4-5.

SM   *Mathematics and Metric Measuring*   Book 6 p4-10.

Volume of a cube and a cuboid.   CV9

Investigation of the volume (V) of a cube or cuboid of length (L), width (W) and height (H) leading to the discovery that

$$V = L \times W \times H$$

Use of this formula to calculate the volumes of cubes and cuboids.

Practical applications.

See also   N17,29,33   Multiplication of whole numbers.
N19(2)   Associative property of multiplication.
N26   Powers idea and index notation.
N31   Multiplication of decimals.
AR3(1)   Generalisations expressed using 'variables'.
AR3(2)   Substituting numbers into algebraic expressions.
AR8   Algebraic solution of equations.
A7   Area of square and rectangle.
L6   Measuring dimensions of 3D shapes.

P   *Alpha (new ed.)*   Alpha 3 p90, 91. Alpha 4 p75, 77.
        Beta (new ed.)   Beta 4 p88-89. Beta 5 p59.
        Basic Mathematics   Book 3 p105. Book 4 p39. Book 5 p61, 62.
        Hey Mathematics   Mod 3. Book 4 p25.
                          Mod 6. Book 4 p18-21, 24, 25, 26.
        Key Maths   Level 2. Book 5 p85-87. Book 6 p80-82, 83, 84.
        Making Sure of Maths   Book 3 p86-87, 89. Book 4 p75-78.
                               Book 5 p72-74. Book 6 p45-47.
        Mathematics for Schools   Level 2 (1st ed.) Book 6 p30, 31-34. Book 9 p3.
        Maths Adventure   3. Pupil's Book p77. Activity Book p53. Card 19, 26.
                          4. Pupil's Book p41. Card 29.
                          5. Pupil's Book p60-61.
        Nuffield Maths 5-11   3. Pupils' Book p112.
        Oxford Middle School Mathematics   Book 2 p78-79. Book 4 p32.
        Primary Mathematics (SPMG)   Stage 4. Textbook p42, 43.
        Towards Mathematics   Core Unit 19 p15, 16.

S   *A World of Mathematics*   Book 3 p36-39. Book 5 p9-10.
        Focus Mathematics   Book 5 p100-102.
        Headway Maths   Book 3 p56-57.
        Maths (Holt)   Book 2 p34-35. 4th Year Workbook p23.
        Mathsworks   Book 1 p115.

SM   *Check it Again*   Book 4 p38-39.
        Four a Day series   Book 10 p84-85, 86-87.
        Mathematics and Metric Measuring   Book 6 p3, 43-44.

CV 10   Focus on problems, applications and everyday use of capacity and volume and metric units.

Problems involving the four number operations.

Medicines, gas and water supplies, capacities of car engines.

Measuring in bulk to find fractional amounts.

Relating units of capacity or volume to other units of measurement:

     e.g.   Unit pricing e.g. 5 litres of petrol at 35p a litre.
           (See M8, and also M11 for gas bills.)
         Measurement of rainfall. (See also L10).
         Petrol consumption: km per litre (See also L10).
         Introduction to density i.e. mass related to volume.

See also   N8,9,15,16,20,21   Addition and subtraction of whole numbers.
            N17,18,29,30,33,34   Multiplication and division of whole numbers.
            N22,31,32   Operations on decimals.
            N23   Ratio, rate and proportion.
            AR4   Straight line graphs.
            CV7   Relationships between standard units. Addition and subtraction.
            L12, W8   Bulk measure to find fractional amounts.
            Imp.   Problems and applications using imperial units.

P   *Alpha (new ed.)*   Alpha 3 p49, 85. Alpha 4 p13.
        Beta (new ed.)   Beta 3 p58. Beta 4 p31.
        Basic Mathematics   Book 1 p90.
        Hey Mathematics   Mod 3. Book 3 p29.
                          Mod 4. Book 4 p1-2.
                          Mod 5. Book 1 p26.
                          Mod 6. Book 3 p26. Book 4 p23-26.
        Key Maths   Level 2. Book 4 p55. Book 6 p84, 93, 96.
        Making Sure of Maths   Book 2 p48. Book 5 p79.
        Mathematics for Schools   Level 2 (1st ed.) Book 5 p63. Book 10 41.
        Primary Mathematics (SPMG)   Stage 3. Card 16, 17.
                                     Stage 4. Textbook p61, 63, 71. Card 35, 60.
                                     Stage 5. Textbook p82.
        Towards Mathematics   Core Unit 19 p2, 3.

S   *A World of Mathematics*   Book 3 p53-55. Book 5 p10.
        Mathematics for Life   Book B2 p2-3. Book B3 p20-21.
        Maths (Holt)   Book 3 p23.
        Mathsworks   Book 1 p42, 56-57, 115. Tryouts 1 p26.
        Understanding Money   Book 2 p68-74, 80-81.

SM *Check it Again*   Book 3 p32.
   Four a Day series   Book 6 p56-57. Book 7 p70-71. Book 9 p83.
   Mathematics and Metric Measuring   Book 6 p44-47.
   Problems   Second Problems p36-37, 52.

Books for teachers
   Hey Mathematics   Mod 3. Teachers's Book p33, 34.

Volume of similar shapes.

Investigation of the relationships between change in dimensions of cubes or similar cuboids and change in volume.

See also   N26   Powers idea and index notation. Square roots.
   AR5   Curved graphs.
   Sh17   Similarity, enlargement and reduction.
   CV9   Volume of cube and cuboid.
   A9   Area of similar shapes.
   A11   Surface area/volume relationships in similar shapes.
   L6   Measuring dimensions of 3D shapes.

P   *Making Sure of Maths*   Book 4 p94.
   Mathematics for Schools   Level 2 (1st ed.) Book 8 p25. Book 10 p46.
   Maths Adventure   2. Pupil's Book p80.
              3. Card 18.
              4. Pupil's Book p55, Card 26.
   Oxford Middle School Mathematics   Book 4 p73.

S   *A World of Mathematics*   Book 5 p16.
   Focus Mathematics   Book 7 p39.

SM   *Mathematics and Metric Measuring*   Book 6 p16-18, 20-23, 24-26.

Volume of a cylinder, prism and later pyramid, sphere and cone.

Investigation of the volume of a cylinder and prism leading to the discovery of generalised formulae.

Use of formulae to calculate volumes of cylinders and prisms, focusing on practical applications.

Later discovery and use of formulae to calculate the volume of a pyramid, sphere and cone.

See also   N17,29,33   Multiplication of whole numbers.
   N19(2)   Associative property of multiplication.
   N26   Powers idea and index notation.
   N31   Multiplication of decimals ('pi' as $3 \cdot 14$).
   F4,6   Multiplication of fractions ('pi' as $^{22}/_7$).
   AR3(1)   Generalisations expressed using 'variables'.
   AR3(2)   Substituting numbers into algebraic expressions.
   AR5   Curved graphs.
   AR8   Algebraic solution of equations.
   Sh3,11   Sorting and naming 3D shapes.
   A7,12,13   Area of square, rectangle, triangle, circle.
   L6,7   Measuring dimensions of 3D shapes.

P   *Alpha (new ed.)*   Alpha 4 p77.
   Beta (new ed.)   Beta 5 p60-61. Beta 6 p72-73.
   Mathematics for Schools   Level 2 (1st ed.) Book 8 p32-33, 34. Book 10 p34-38.
   Maths Adventure   3. Pupil's Book p76. Activity Book p53.
              4. Pupil's Book p37.
              5. Pupil's Book p62. Activity Book p38, 40.
   Oxford Middle School Mathematics   Book 4 p32-33.

S   *A World of Mathematics*   Book 5 p41-44. Book 6 p57.
   Focus Mathematics   Book 5 p103-106, 108-114, 174-175.
   Headway Maths   Book 5 p48-51.
   Mathsworks   Book 1 p113, 115. Book 2 p22, 57.

SM   *Mathematics and Metric Measuring*   Book 6 p27-36, 37-42.

Area

Contents

ᴦ⁻⁻Topics with a sequence of development extending over considerable time.

Early concepts and vocabulary associated with area and surfaces.

A1

Introduction to, and extension of vocabulary alongside experience of surfaces and their sizes.

Experience covering surfaces: crayoning, painting, collage, etc.

Vocabulary: surface, bumpy, rough, smooth, covered, uncovered, gaps, big, small, etc.

See also   S1,3   Sorting and classifying.
                Sh1,2   Sorting and naming 2D shapes.
                Sh4   Shape patterns.

P   *Mathematics for Schools*   Level 1 (2nd ed.) Book 1 p7-8.
            Maths Adventure   2. Card 25.
            Our First School Maths   Book 1 p26-27. Book 2 p20.

Books for teachers
    Early Mathematical Experiences   'Space and Shape. Comparisons' especially p10, 18-19.
    Mathematics: the first 3 years   p16-22, 77.

Comparing and ordering surfaces by area.

A2

Comparing and ordering the sizes of two and later more surfaces visually and by placing one upon another: e.g. more floor than carpet.

Simple 3D shapes (e.g. food packets) opened out and surfaces compared.

Extension of vocabulary: bigger than, biggest, smaller than, smallest, etc.

Equivalence in area: 'has about the same amount of surface as . . .'.

See also   N5   Ordinal number; 1st, 2nd, etc.
                F3   Ordering fractions using fraction diagrams.
                S2   Relations between sets. The equivalent relation.
                Sh3   Nets of 3D shapes.
                A5   Conservation.

P   *Alpha (new ed.)*   Alpha 2 p83.
            Beta (new ed.)   Beta 1 p87.
            Mathematics for Schools   Level 1 (2nd ed.) Book 3 p30-33.
            Maths Adventure   2. Card 21.
            Numbers and Words   Book 3 p1, 20-21. Book 6 p23.
            Primary Mathematics (SPMG)   Stage 1. Workbook 3 p32-35.

Books for teachers
    Early Mathematical Experiences   'Space and Shape. Comparisons' esp. p10-11, 18-19.
    Mathematics: the first 3 years   p81.
    Nuffield Maths 5-11   2. Teachers' Handbook p90.

Use of arbitrary units for measuring area.

A3

Idea of covering a flat surface to find its area.

Measuring and ordering areas by covering them with approximately congruent shapes e.g. hands, beans, geometric shapes.

Discussion leading to the use of shapes that tessellate i.e. fit together leaving no spaces.

Estimating area in these units, measuring and recording error.

The advantages of the square as a unit.

An appreciation of the need for standard units.

See also   PV2   Counting and ordering numbers to 100.
                N5   Ordinal number.
                N9,16   Subtraction to 100.
                F1   Half, quarter, whole one.
                S2   Relations between sets.
                Sh2   Sorting and naming 2D shapes.
                Sh5   Tessellations.
                Sh13, CV3, L3, W3, T3   The need for standard units.

P   *Alpha (new ed.)*   Alpha 2 p83.
      Basic Mathematics   Book 2 p96-97. Book 3 p89.
      Hey Mathematics   Mod 3. Book 3 p33. Book 5 p18.
                        Mod 4. Book 2 p37.
      Key Maths   Level 1. Book 7 p57-58.
                  Level 2. Book 2 p48-49.
      Making Sure of Maths   Book 2 p80-81.
      Mathematics for Schools   Level 2 (2nd ed.) Book 2 p54.
                               Level 2 (1st ed.) Book 5 p54.
      Maths Adventure   2. Pupil's Book p56, 58. Activity Book p35; 39-40.
      Nuffield Maths 5-11   2. Worksheets S2 4·1-4·2.
                           3. Pupils' Book p105-108.
      Oxford Middle School Mathematics   Book 2 p50-52.
      Primary Mathematics (SPMG)   Stage 1. Workbook 4 p28-34.
                                   Stage 2. Workbook 2 p38-39.
      Towards Mathematics   Core Unit 9 p4.

S   *A World of Mathematics*   Book 1 p29-30.
      Focus Mathematics   Book 2 p43-44.
      Maths (Holt)   Book 1 p46. Workbook 1 p31.
                    Workbook 2 p9, 15.

SM   *Four a Day series*   Book 8 p84-85. Book 9 p89.

Books for teachers
      Mathematics: the first 3 years   p79, 147.
      Mathematics: from Primary to Secondary   p28-29.
      Nuffield Maths 5-11   2. Teachers' Handbook p90-92.
                           3. Teachers' Handbook Chapter 23.

A4   Areas of compound plane shapes and irregular shapes.

Measuring and ordering the areas of compound plane shapes (e.g. triangles) and irregular shapes (e.g. leaves) using squared paper or transparent grids and counting squares and parts of squares.

See also   PV2   Counting and ordering numbers to 100.
         N5   Ordinal number.
         F1,2   Half. Addition of halves.
         Sh1,2   Sorting and naming 2D shapes.

P   *Alpha (new ed.)*   Alpha 1 p90.
      Beta (new ed.)   Beta 1 p89.
      Basic Mathematics   Book 2 p97.
      Hey Mathematics   Mod 3. Book 3 p34-35.
                        Mod 4. Book 2 p40.
                        Mod 5. Book 2 p21. Book 4 p40.
      Key Maths   Level 2. Book 2 p49.
      Making Sure of Maths   Book 2 p79.
      Mathematics for Schools   Level 2 (2nd ed.) Book 2 p54, 58.
      Maths Adventure   2. Pupil's Book p57. Activity Book p38.
                        3. Activity Book p43.
      Primary Mathematics (SPMG)   Stage 2. Workbook 2 p40.
      Towards Mathematics   Core Unit 9 p5.

S   *Focus Mathematics*   Book 2 p45-48.
      Impact Maths   Pupil's Book 1 p4-5.
      Maths (Holt)   Book 1 p47, 49.

SM   *Four a Day series*   Book 8 p85-86.

Books for teachers
      Mathematics: the first 3 years   p68.
      Mathematics: from Primary to Secondary   p29-30.

Conservation of area.

Experience leading to the concept of conservation (invariance) of area i.e. the idea that area is a property independent of other attributes and particularly length.

Area distinguished from perimeter and length.

Experience rearranging the parts of a given shape and discussing the area: paper tearing, tangrams, polyominoes, peeling oranges, etc.

Introduction to the term 'area'.

See also   N4, CV4, L2, W4   Conservation.
             F3   Equivalent fractions using fraction diagrams.
             VR5   Pie charts.
             S2   The equivalent relation.
             Sh2,4 2D shapes. Pictures and patterns.
             Sh3   Nets of 3D shapes.
             L7   Curved lines and perimeters.

P   *Alpha (new ed.)*   Alpha 1 p90. Alpha 2 p84.
       Beta (new ed.)   Beta 1 p87. Beta 3 p64.
       Basic Mathematics   Book 2 p99. Book 3 p38.
       Hey Mathematics   Mod 4. Book 5 p29-31.
       Key Maths   Level 2. Book 2 p51.
       Making Sure of Maths   Book 2 p82.
       Mathematics for Schools   Level 1 (2nd ed.). Book 7 p40-41.
                                  Level 2 (2nd ed.). Book 2 p56, 58.
                                  Level 2 (1st ed.). Book 3 p24.
       Maths Adventure   1. Pupil's Book p54-55.
                         2. Activity Book p24. Card 16.
       Nuffield Maths 5-11   3. Pupils' Book p106-108.
       Primary Mathematics (SPMG)   Stage 2. Workbook 4 p32.
       Towards Mathematics   Core Unit 9 p6.

S   *Focus Mathematics*   Book 2 p49-51.
       Headway Maths   Book 3 p53.
       Impact Maths   Pupil's Book 1 p4, 5.
       Maths (Holt)   4th year Workbook p16.

SM *Mathematics and Metric Measuring*   Book 5 p6-8.

Books for teachers
     Early Mathematical Experiences   'Space and Shape. Comparisons' esp. p11.
     Mathematics: the first 3 years   p79, 144, 148.
     Nuffield Maths 5-11   2. Teachers' Handbook p92-93.

Introduction to square centimetre, square decimetre and square metre.

Concept of the area of one square centimetre, one square decimetre and one square metre.

    Areas compared with one square metre, etc.

Familiarity with notation cm^2, dm^2, m^2.

Use of centimetre squared paper, transparent grids, geoboards, etc. to measure the areas of simple plane shapes (e.g. rectangles), compound shapes (e.g. triangles) and irregular shapes (e.g. leaves) in cm^2 by counting squares and parts of squares.

Estimating areas, measuring and recording error.

Approximations (i.e. rounding off measurements) and limits to accuracy.

See also   PV2   Counting and ordering numbers to 100.
             N5   Ordinal number.
             N9,16 Subtraction.
             N13   Arrays. Square numbers.
             N26   Powers idea and index notation.
             F1,2   Half. Addition and subtraction of halves.
             S2   Relations between sets.
             Sh22,17 The square. Similarity.
             Sh13, CV8, L6, W7, T6 Limits to accuracy.
             L4   Centimetre, decimetre and metre.

P   *Alpha (new ed.)*   Alpha 2 p84, 85. Alpha 3 p69, 71.
      Beta (new ed.)   Beta 2 p88, 89. Beta 3 p66, 82.
                      Beta 4 p80.
      Basic Mathematics   Book 2 p98. Book 3 p92-93.
      Hey Mathematics   Mod 3. Book 5 p22, 23, 24, 25, 36.
                      Mod 4. Book 2 p38, 39.
      Key Maths   Level 2. Book 2 p50-51. Book 4 p43-45.
      Making Sure of Maths   Book 2 p83. Book 3 p48-49, 52-53.
      Mathematics for Schools   Level 2 (2nd. ed.) Book 2 p55.
                      Level 2 (1st ed.) Book 3 p21-23, 24.
      Maths Adventure   2. Pupil's Book p58.
                      4. Card 21.
                      5. Pupil's Book p52, 53.
      Oxford Middle School Mathematics   Book 2 p53.
      Primary Mathematics (SPMG)   Stage 2. Workbook 4 p31-35. Card 8.
                      Stage 3. Textbook p16-19, 65-67.
                      Stage 4. Workbook p1, 17.
                      Stage 5. Card 36, 62.
      Towards Mathematics   Core Unit 9 p6, 7.

S   *A World of Mathematics*   Book 1 p30-31.
      Focus Mathematics   Book 2 p54-56.
      Headway Maths   Book 1 p76-77. Book 2 p60, 63.
      Maths (Holt)   Workbook 2 p41. 4th Year p50-51.
      Maths Matters   Book 1 p14.

SM   *Check it Again*   Book 5 p41.
      Four a Day series   Book 9 p90. Book 10 p81-82.
      Mathematics and Metric Measuring   Book 5 p35-38.

Books for teachers
      Mathematics: the first 3 years   p147-149.

A7   Area of a square and a rectangle.

Investigation of the area (A) of a square or rectangle of length (L) and width (W) leading to the discovery that:

$$A = L \times W$$

Use of this formula to calculate the areas of squares, rectangles and later composite shapes involving squares and rectangles.

Calculating the length of one side of a square given the area, and the length of one side of a rectangle given the width and area.

Practical applications.

See also   N8,15,20,22   Addition of whole numbers and decimals.
           N17,18,29,30,31,32,33,34   Multiplication and division of whole numbers and decimals.
           N19(2) Commutative property of multiplication.
           N26   Powers idea and index notation. Square roots.
           AR3(1)   Generalisations expressed using 'variables'.
           AR3(2)   Substituting numbers into algebraic expressions.
           AR3(3)   Simplification of equations.
           AR8   Algebraic solution of equations.
           Sh23   Pythagoras' theorem.
           CV9   Volume of cube and cuboid.
           A9   Area perimeter relationship for square and rectangle.
           A11   Surface area of cube and cuboid. Cross sections.
           A12   Area of triangle, parallelogram, etc.
           L6   Measuring dimensions of 2D shapes.

P   *Alpha (new ed.)*   Alpha 3 p69, 70, 71. Alpha 4 p40, 41.
      Beta (new ed.)   Beta 3 p81, 82. Beta 4 p58, 59, 60, 61.
                      Beta 5 p28.
      Basic Mathematics   Book 2 p99, 100, 101. Book 3 p90-91.
                      Book 4 p34.
      Hey Mathematics   Mod 3. Book 5 p26, 27.
                      Mod 4. Book 4 p39-40.
                      Mod 5. Book 2 p18-23. Book 3 p27.
                      Mod 6. Book 4 p12, 14.
      Key Maths   Level 2. Book 4 p46-47. Book 5 p80, 81, 82, 83. Book 6 p75-76, 77, 78, 79.
      Making Sure of Maths   Book 2 p78-79. Book 3 p49-51. Book 4 p21-22, 23-24. Book 5 p70. Book 6 p42-43.

Mathematics for Schools   Level 2 (2nd ed.) Book 2 p57.
                          Level 2 (1st ed.) Book 4 p22. Book 5 p55-56. Book 6 p22-23. Book 7 p37, 57.
    Oxford Middle School Mathematics   Book 2 p63. Book 4 p20, 22, 23, 67.
    Primary Mathematics (SPMG)   Stage 3. Workbook p38.
                          Stage 5. Textbook p89, 119.
    Towards Mathematics   Core Unit 14 p12-14. Core Unit 19 p13.

S   *A World of Mathematics*   Book 2 p11-12.
    Focus Mathematics   Book 5 p36-38, 44, 47, 49, 50, 51, 52, 53.
    Headway Maths   Book 2 p61-62. Book 3 p24-27.
    Impact Maths   Pupil's Book 1 p46.
    Maths (Holt)   Book 1 p47, 50. Book 2 p31, 35.
                 Book 3 p63.
    Maths Matters   Book 1 p14-15.
    Mathsworks   Tryouts 1 p49. Book 2 p56.
    Maths You Need   p64-65.
    On Our Own Two Feet   Book 5 p5-6.

SM   *Check it Again*   Book 3 p28-30. Book 4 p37-38. Book 5 p38-41.
    Four a Day series   Book 8 p86-88. Book 9 p90-91. Book 10 p82-84.
    Mathematics and Metric Measuring   Book 5 p3-5.

Books for teachers
    Mathematics: from Primary to Secondary   p30-31.

Relationships between standard metric units. Introduction to are, hectare and square kilometre.

A8

Converting measurements from one standard unit to another using decimal notation when it is understood.

Introduction to the larger units of area: the are, hectare and square kilometre. Relationships between all standard units.

Addition and subtraction of metric areas.

See also   PV4,7   Place value. Grouping in 100's, 1,000's etc.
    PV6,8   Decimal notation.
    N8,9,15,16,20,21   Addition and subtraction of whole numbers.
    N13   Arrays. Square numbers.
    N22   Addition and subtraction of decimals.
    N26   Powers idea and index notation.
    Sh17, A9   Similar, enlarged and reduced squares.
    A10   Problems and applications.
    L5   The hectometre and kilometre. Relationships between standard units.

P   *Alpha (new ed.)*   Alpha 4 p41.
    Beta (new ed.)   Beta 6 p37.
    Hey Mathematics   Mod 6. Book 4 p11.
    Key Maths   Level 2. Book 5 p83. Book 6 p79.
    Making Sure of Maths   Book 5 p69.
    Oxford Middle School Mathematics   Book 3 p87.
    Primary Mathematics (SPMG)   Stage 4. Textbook p110. Workbook p17.
                          Stage 5. Card 64.
    Towards Mathematics   Core Unit 19 p13.

Area and perimeter relationships.

A9

Investigation of relationships between area and perimeter, and between area and length of one side of squares and rectangles.

Keeping the perimeter constant, varying the area.

Keeping the area constant, varying the perimeter.

The idea of a maximum area for a given perimeter. Later the discovery of the circle as the shape enclosing the largest area for a given perimeter.

Similar shapes. Area and perimeter of similar shapes plotted graphically and their relationship discussed.
    Area and the length of one side plotted graphically and their relationship discussed.

See also   AR5   Curved graphs.
            Sh17   Similarity, enlargement and reduction.
            CV11   Volume of similar shapes.
            A7   Area of square and rectangle.
            A8   Standard metric units as similar shapes. Relationships.
            A11   Surface area relationships of similar 3D shapes.
            A13   Circle area. Radius/Area relationship.
            L6   Measuring dimensions of 2D shapes.
            L7   Perimeters.

P   *Beta (new ed.)*   Beta 1 p88. Beta 2 p88, 89. Beta 3 p65.
                      Beta 4 p60. Beta 5 p66. Beta 6 p76.
    Basic Mathematics   Book 3 p100, 101.
    Hey Mathematics   Mod 3. Book 5 p13.
    Key Maths   Level 2. Book 4 p47. Book 5 p79, 81, 82, 100.
    Mathematics for Schools   Level 2 (1st ed.) Book 3 p23, 25. Book 6 p54. Book 7 p28-29, 51. Book 8 p28-29, 56.
                      Book 10 p45.
    Maths Adventure   2. Pupil's Book p59, 70, 71.
                      3. Pupil's Book p50.
                      4. Pupil's Book p23, 36. Activity Book p30.
                      5. Pupil's Book p52, 56, 57.
    Oxford Middle School Mathematics   Book 2 p61, 62. Book 4 p72-73.
    Primary Mathematics (SPMG)   Stage 3. Workbook p37, 38.
                          Stage 4. Textbook p115. Card 53, 59.
                          Stage 5. Textbook p30, 96-98. Card 17, 35, 50, 51, 52, 53, 54, 55, 63, 65.
    Towards Mathematics   Core Unit 9 p3.

S   *A World of Mathematics*   Book 5 p14-15.
    Focus Mathematics   Book 7 p37-38, 42.
    Impact Maths   Pupil's Book 1 p6, 46, 47.
    Maths (Holt)   Book 2 p52, 53, 86. 4th Year p51.
                5th Year p4-5. 5th Year Workbook p20-21, 41.

SM   *Four a Day series*   Book 9 p92.
    Mathematics and Metric Measuring   Book 5 p9-13.

Books for teachers
    Hey Mathematics   Mod 3. Teachers' Book p36-37.
    Mathematics: from Primary to Secondary   p31-34, 36-38, 43, 44.

A10 Focus on problems, applications and everyday use of area and metric units.

Problems involving the four number operations.

Planning and implementing enlargements of the area of a flat or house, etc.

Relating units of area to other units of measurement:

    e.g.   Unit pricing. Tiling and carpeting; quantity and costs (See also M8).
          Area/profit relationships in a farm, supermarket, etc. (See also M13).
          Weight of grass seed needed for a given area (See also W8).
          Introduction to the idea of pressure i.e. weight related to area, focusing on applications: tyre pressure, pressure cookers, skis and snow shoes, stiletto heels on lino, atmospheric pressure, etc.

See also   N8,9,15,16,20,21   Addition and subtraction of whole numbers.
            N17,18,29,30,33,34   Multiplication and division of whole numbers.
            N22,31,32   Operations on decimals.
            N23   Ratio, rate and proportion.
            AR4   Straight line graphs.
            A8   Relationships between standard units. Addition and subtraction.
            Weight section: relates to pressure.
            Imp.   Problems and applications using imperial units.

P   *Hey Mathematics*   Mod 5. Book 2 p22-23. Book 4 p40.
                      Mod 6. Book 1 p27-28.
    Key Maths   Level 2. Book 5 p82. Book 6 p78, 84.
    Mathematics for Schools   Level 2 (1st ed.) Book 5 p63. Book 6 p63. Book 7 p63.
    Primary Mathematics (SPMG)   Stage 5. Textbook p118.
    Towards Mathematics   Core Unit 19 p13.

Surface area of a cube and a cuboid.   **A11**

Calculating the surface area of cubes and cuboids by adding together the areas of each face.

> Practical applications e.g area of paper needed to wrap up a parcel.

Finding the area of cross section of cubes and cuboids.

Investigation of the relationships, in cubes and cuboids, between surface area and volume, and surface area and the area of one face or the length of one edge.

See also   N8,15,17,20,22,29,31,33   Multiplication and addition of whole numbers and decimals. Problems involving the use of multiplication and addition.
          AR3(1)   Generalisations expressed using 'variables'.
          AR3(2)   Substituting numbers into algebraic expressions.
          AR3(3)   Simplification of equations.
          AR5   Curved graphs.
          Sh3   Nets of 3D shapes.
          Sh11   Cross sections.
          Sh17   Similarity, enlargement and reduction.
          CV9   Volume of cube and cuboid.
          CV11   Volume and dimension relationships.
          A7   Area of square, rectangle and composite shapes.
          A9   Area and perimeter relationships.
          A12,13   Surface area of prisms, cylinders, etc.
          L6   Measuring dimensions of 3D shapes.

Area of a triangle.   **A12**

Experience dividing rectangles and other quadrilaterals into two triangles leading to the discovery that

$$A = \frac{B \times H}{2}$$ where A is the area of a triangle.
                    B is the length of the base.
                    H is the perpendicular height.

Use of this formula to calculate areas of triangles and later composite shapes involving triangles, rectangles and squares.

Later further investigation leading to the discovery and use of generalised formulae for calculating the area of a parallelogram, rhombus, regular pentagon, regular octagon, etc.

Calculating the surface area of a triangular prism.

Practical applications.

See also N8,15,20,22   Addition of whole numbers and decimals.
           N17,18,29,30,31,32,33,34   Multiplication and division of whole numbers and decimals.
           N19(2) Commutative property of multiplication.
           F4   Multiplication of fraction by whole number.
           AR3(1) Generalisations expressed using 'variables'.
           AR3(2) Substituting numbers into algebraic expressions.
           AR3(3) Simplification of equations.
           Sh10,21   Perpendiculars and their construction.
           Sh11   Nets of 3D shapes.
           Sh14,15,16   Triangles, quadrilaterals and other polygons.
           Sh23   Pythagoras' theorem.
           CV12   Volume of pyramid, etc.
           A7   Area of square and rectangle.
           A11,13 Surface areas of cubes, cuboids, cylinders, etc.
           L6   Measuring dimensions of 2D shapes.

P   *Alpha (new ed.)*   Alpha 4 p43-44, 64, 65.
      Beta (new ed.)   Beta 4 p78-80. Beta 5 p28-29, 88, 89.
                  Beta 6 p37, 38.
      Hey Mathematics   Mod 6. Book 4 p11, 13-17.
      Making Sure of Maths   Book 4 p22-23. Book 5 p67-68. Book 6 p44.
      Mathematics for Schools   Level 2 (1st ed.) Book 5 p57-61. Book 7 p1. Book 9 p58-60.
      Maths Adventure   3. Pupil's Book p54-55.
                  4. Pupil's Book p34-35. Activity Book p34-38.
                  5. Pupil's Book p54-55, 90-91.
      Oxford Middle School Mathematics   Book 3 p37, 62-63. Book 4 p21, 23, 30-31.
      Primary Mathematics (SPMG)   Stage 4. Textbook p18-19.
                  Stage 5. Textbook p24-25, 89. Card 16, 17, 33, 34.

S   *A World of Mathematics*   Book 5 p29-32.
      Focus Mathematics   Book 5 p39-43, 45-46, 48-49, 52.
      Headway Maths   Book 3 p50-52.
      Maths (Holt)   Workbook 2 p40.
      Maths Matters   Book 2 p20-21.
      Mathsworks   Book 1 p112, 113, 114. Book 2 p56, 63.
      Maths You Need   p62-63.

SM *Mathematics and Metric Measuring*   Book 5 p13-25.
Books for teachers
      Mathematics: from Primary to Secondary   p31, 34-36.

A13   Circle area.

Investigation of the relationship between the radius of circles (r) and their areas (A) expressing the relationship in a graph.

Eventual discovery that $A = \pi r^2$ where π is a constant at approximately $3 \cdot 14$.

Use of this formula to calculate areas. Practical applications.

Later use of this formula to calculate the surface area of a cylinder and the surface area of a cone. Practical applications.

See also N22,31   Addition and multiplication of decimals ('pi' as $3 \cdot 14$).
           N26   Powers idea and index notation.
           F4,5,6   Multiplication and addition of fractions ('pi' as $\frac{22}{7}$).
           AR3(1)   Generalisations expressed using 'variables'.
           AR3(2)   Substituting numbers into algebraic expressions.
           AR5   Curved graphs.
           VR5   Pie charts.
           Sh8,22   Circle vocabulary and properties.
           CV12   Volume of cylinder.
           A4,6 Area of circle by counting grid squares.
           A11,12   Surface areas.
           L6,7 Measuring dimensions.
           L11   Circle circumference. 'Pi'.

P *Alpha (new ed.)* Alpha 4 p62, 63.
Beta (new ed.) Beta 5 p53, 54. Beta 6 p37, 39, 70.
Basic Mathematics Book 4 p80, 81. Book 5 p67.
Key Maths Level 2 Book 6 p101-102.
Making Sure of Maths Book 5 p71. Book 6 p49-52.
Mathematics for Schools Level 2 (1st ed.) Book 7 p47-49.
Maths Adventure 4. Pupil's Book p83-84.
Oxford Middle School Mathematics Book 4 p78-79.

S *A World of Mathematics* Book 6 p55-57, 58.
Focus Mathematics Book 7 p87-89.
Headway Maths Book 4 p51, 84-85. Book 5 p46-47.
Maths (Holt) Book 3 p49. 5th Year p10-11.
Mathsworks Book 2 p22, 30-31, 56. Tryouts 2 p17.
Maths You Need p62-63.

SM *Mathematics and Metric Measuring* Book 5 p26-30.

Length and Distance

Contents

┌----Topics with a sequence of development extending over considerable time.

Early concepts and vocabulary associated with length, height, depth and distance. L1

Introduction to, and extension of vocabulary, alongside experience of length, height, depth and distance.

Terms like big and small become refined through discussion so that more specific words like long, short, fat, thin, thick, wide, narrow, slim, high, low, tall, short, deep, shallow, far and near are understood and used.

See also S1,3   Sorting and classifying.
           T4   Distinguishing clock hands.

P   *Come and Measure*   Length p2.
    Hey Mathematics   Mod 1. Book 5 p37.
    Mathematics for Schools   Level 1 (2nd ed.) Book 1 p7-8.
    Maths Adventure   1. Card 11.
    Nuffield Maths 5-11   Bronto Books. Set B. Mini half-as-big. Set C. 3 buses. Set D. Bronto at the fair.
                  1. Worksheets L1 1·1-1·2.
    Numbers and Words   Book 1 p1-3. Book 3 p5, 31.
    Our First School Maths   Book 1 p26-29. Book 2 p20.

Books for teachers
    Early Mathematical Experiences   Most books.
    Mathematics: the first 3 years   p16-22.
    Nuffield Maths 5-11   1. Teachers' Handbook p88-91.

Comparing and ordering by length. Conservation. L2

Comparing and ordering the length of two and later more objects by matching them from a baseline. Extension of vocabulary: longer, longest, shorter, shortest, etc. (See L1 for vocabulary list).

Comparing and ordering heights, depths and distances. Extension of vocabulary: higher, highest, lower, lowest, further, furthest, nearer, nearest, etc.

Equivalence in length, height, depth and distance. 'is about as long as' etc.

Experience leading to the concept of conservation (invariance) of length i.e. the idea that length is a property independent of other attributes, particularly volume and area.

    e.g.   A table can be about as long as a piece of cotton.
          A curled up piece of string is as long as that piece of string spread out.

See also N4, CV4, A5, W4   Conservation.
           N5   Ordinal number; 1st, 2nd, etc.
           F3   Ordering fractions using fraction diagrams.
           VR1,2,3,4,8   Comparing and ordering quantities expressed linearly.
           S2   Relations between sets. The equivalent relation.
           T4   Comparing length of clock hands.

P   *Come and Measure*   Length p2-7.
    Hey Mathematics   Mod 1. Book 1 p10-12.
    Key Maths   Level 1 Book 2 p1-11. Book 4 p58.
    Making Sure of Maths   Pink Book p6. Green Book p16.
                  Introductory Book p27-28.
    Mathematics for Schools   Level 1 (2nd ed.) Book 1 p9-10. Book 3 p30-33, 43-50. Book 4 p1-2.
    Maths Adventure   1. Pupil's Book p8.
             2. Card 12.
    Nuffield Maths 5-11   Bronto Books. Set A. Comparing with Bronto. Set D. Bronto visits the dentist.
                  1. Worksheets L1 2·1-2·2, 4·1-4·3. S1 1·2.
    Numbers and Words   Book 2 p10. Book 5 p10-11.
    Our First School Maths   Book 2 p8-9, 32.
    Oxford Middle School Mathematics   Book 1 p14-15.
    Primary Mathematics (SPMG)   Stage 1. Workbook 1 p31-36. Card 4. Workbook 2 p22.

Books for teachers
    Early Mathematical Experiences   'Space and Shape. Comparisons' p17-18, 21-22.
    Mathematics: the first 3 years   p76-77.
    Nuffield Maths 5-11   1. Teachers' Handbook p92-96, 97-99.

L3 Use of arbitrary units.

1. Use of body units.

Use of body units (e.g. span, pace, reach) to measure and order items by length.

Estimating length, height, depth and distance in these units, measuring and recording error.

Comparison of equivalent measurements of different children using these units leading to an appreciation of the need for standard units.

See also PV2   Counting and ordering numbers to 100.
              N5   Ordinal number.
              N9,16 Subtraction to 100.
              F1   Half, quarter, whole one.
              S2   Relations between sets.
              Sh13, CV3, A3, W3, T3 The need for standard units.

P   *Alpha (new ed.)* Alpha 1 p38.
       Beta (new ed.) Beta 1 p18-19.
       Basic Mathematics Book 1 p14.
       Come and Measure Length p8-14.
       Key Maths Level 1 Book 4 p58-59.
                         Level 2 Book 1 p52.
       Making Sure of Maths Book 1 p38.
       Mathematics for Schools Level 1 (2nd ed.) Book 4 p3-5.
       Maths Adventure 1. Pupil's Book p9. Card 12, 13.
                         2. Card 11.
       Nuffield Maths 5-11 1. Worksheets L1 6·1-6·2.
                         2. Worksheets L2 1·1.
                         3. Pupils' Book p16-18.
       Our First School Maths Book 3 p20-22.
       Primary Mathematics (SPMG) Stage 1. Workbook 2 p24-26. Card 10b. Workbook 3 p22.
       Towards Mathematics Core Unit 4 p1.

S   *A World of Mathematics* Book 1 p12.
       Focus Mathematics Book 3 p48-52.
       Maths (Holt) Book 2 p9.

SM *Mathematics and Metric Measuring* Book 1 p3-4, 5-6.

Books for teachers
     Mathematics: the first 3 years p103.
     Nuffield Maths 5-11 1. Teachers' Handbook p101-102.
                         2. Teachers' Handbook p73.
                         3. Teachers' Handbook Chapter 4.

2. Use of unmarked and calibrated sticks.

Use of unmarked sticks and other objects as measuring units: rods, straws, matchboxes, etc.

Use of body or other non-standard units to calibrate sticks or string as measuring instruments.

Estimating length, height, depth and distance in these units, measuring and recording error.

An appreciation of the need for standard units.

See also PV, N Sections   Use of structural apparatus (e.g. Cuisenaire) where length represents number.
              L2   Conservation (assumed for calibrated sticks).
              Temp. Use of thermometer where length represents temperature,
              and topics listed for L3(1).

P   *Hey Mathematics* Mod 1. Book 5 p40.
       Key Maths Level 1. Book 5 p60.
       Mathematics for Schools Level 2 (2nd ed.) Book 1 p16.
       Maths Adventure 1. Card 14.
       Nuffield Maths 5-11 1. Worksheets L1 3·1, 5·1-5·2.
       Numbers and Words Book 8 p15-17.
       Oxford Middle School Mathematics Book 1 p18-19.
       Primary Mathematics (SPMG) Stage 1. Workbook 2 p23.

Books for teachers
     Mathematics: the first 3 years p78-79.
     Nuffield Maths 5-11 1. Teachers' Handbook p96-97, 99-101.

Introduction to metres and centimetres. **L4**

Concept of the length of one metre, one decimetre and one centimetre. Lengths, heights and depths compared with one metre, etc.

Estimating lengths, heights, depths and distances in metres *or* decimetres *or* centimetres, measuring and recording error.

Approximations i.e. rounding off measurements.

See also PV2 Counting and ordering numbers to 100.
        N5   Ordinal number.
        N9,16 Subtraction.
        F1   Half, quarter, whole one.
        S2   Relations between sets.
        CV6, A6 Introduction to cubic cm, square cm, etc.

P   *Alpha (new ed.)* Alpha 1 p39-42.
    Beta (new ed.) Beta 1 p20, 30-31. Beta 2 p12, 13, 80.
            Beta 3 p33.
    Basic Mathematics Book 1 p15, 16. Book 2 p47.
    Come and Measure Length p15-18.
    Hey Mathematics Mod 1. Book 5 p34.
            Mod 2. Book 2 p7, 9, 23. Book 3 p7, 22, 35. Book 4 p9, 20, 23. Book 5 p14, 16, 19.
            Mod 3. Book 5 p15.
    Key Maths Level 1. Book 4 p60. Book 6 p19-20.
            Level 2. Book 1 p53-56.
    Making Sure of Maths Introductory Book p29.
            Book 1 p39-40, 46-47, 49. Book 2 p42-44.
    Mathematics for Schools Level 1 (2nd ed.) Book 4 p6-8. Book 6 p24-25.
            Level 2 (2nd ed.) Book 1 p15, 17.
            Level 2 (1st ed.) Book 3 p2, 3, 4, 19, 20. Book 8 p38.
    Maths Adventure 1. Pupil's Book p52-53. Card 15.
            2. Activity Book p17. Card 13.
    Nuffield Maths 5-11 2. Worksheets L2 2·1-2·3, 3·1, 4·1, 5·1.
            3. Pupils' Book p18, 19, 80-82, 84.
    Our First School Maths Book 4 p26-28. Book 5 p19-22. Book 6 p15-16, 17.
    Oxford Middle School Mathematics Book 1 p20, 36, 37.
    Primary Mathematics (SPMG) Stage 1. Workbook 3 p22-26. Card 8.
            Stage 2. Workbook 1 p24-25. Workbook 2 p25-27. Card 5.
              Workbook 3 p22-23, 24, 26.
            Stage 3. Textbook p49. Workbook p11. Card 20.
            Stage 5. Textbook p18, 53. Card 12, 32.
    Towards Mathematics Core Unit 4 p2-4, 5, 6.

S   *A World of Mathematics* Book 1 p12-13, 18.
    Headway Maths Book 1 p10.
    Inner Ring Maths Book 3 p16.
    Mathematics for Life Book A1 p30-32.
    Maths (Holt) Book 1 p33. Workbook 1 p26.

SM *Check it Again* Book 1 p33. Book 2 p29-30.
    Four a Day series Book 6 p53-54.
    Mathematics and Metric Measuring Book 1 p5, 7.

Books for teachers
    Nuffield Maths 5-11 2. Teachers' Handbook p73-78.
            3. Teachers' Handbook Chapters 4 and 18.

Relationships between standard metric units. Introduction to millimetre, hectometre and kilometre. **L5**

Converting measurements from one standard unit to another using decimal notation when it is understood:
    e.g. 1m 30cm, 130cm or 1·30m.

Introduction to millimetre, hectometre and kilometre. Relationships between all standard units.

Addition and subtraction of metric lengths.

L6 Measurements using more than one standard unit.

Estimating length, height, depth or distance, measuring using more than one unit and recording error e.g. 1 metre 45 cm. Use of decimal notation when understood.

Selecting the appropriate units for measuring a given length, height, depth or distance.

Use of a wide range of measuring devices: trundle wheel, calipers, etc. Reading the scales.

Measuring and drawing simple 2D shapes. Measuring 3D shapes. Idea of dimensions.

Approximations (i.e. rounding off measurements) and limits to accuracy.

See also   PV2,4,7   Place value. Grouping in 10's, 100's, 1,000's, etc.
           PV5,6,8   Decimal notation.
           N9,16,21   Subtraction of whole numbers.
           N22   Subtraction of decimals.
           VR8   Scales on measuring instruments.
           Sh2,3,11,14,15,16   Sorting and naming shapes.
           Sh8,21   Use of locus idea for accurate drawing of straight lines, and 2D shapes.
           Sh13, CV8, A6, W7, T6   Limits to accuracy.
           CV6, A6,8   Dimensions of standard volume and area units.
           CV9,11,12, A7,9,11,12,13   Measuring dimensions needed to calculate volume and area.
           L5   Relationships between standard units. Subtraction of metric lengths.
           L7   Measuring dimensions needed for perimeters.

P   *Ready for Alpha and Beta (new ed.)*   p21.
       Alpha (new ed.)   Alpha 2 p27. Alpha 3 p16, 17. Alpha 4 p19, 60.
       Beta (new ed.)   Beta 2 p29, 30, 31. Beta 3 p34, 36.
                          Beta 4 p28. Beta 5 p8, 14. Beta 6 p9.
       Basic Mathematics   Book 1 p81.
       Come and Measure   Length p22-24.
       Hey Mathematics   Mod 4. Book 3 p37-40.
       Making Sure of Maths   Book 4 p18.
       Mathematics for Schools   Level 1 (2nd ed.) Book 6 p26.
                                   Level 2 (1st ed.) Book 5 p27-29, 32.
       Maths Adventure   2. Pupil's Book p15. Card 15.
                          3. Card 13
                          4. Pupil's Book p38. Card 11.
       Nuffield Maths 5-11   3. Pupils' Book p19
       Oxford Middle School Mathematics   Book 1 p27. Book 2 p10, 11. Book 4 p19.
       Primary Mathematics (SPMG)   Stage 3. Textbook p50. Workbook p10.
                                      Stage 4. Textbook p78, 79, 80. Workbook p7. Card 25.
                                      Stage 5. Textbook p43, 100, 116. Card 23, 37, 38.
       Towards Mathematics   Core Unit 4 p6, 15. Core Unit 14 p1, 2, 3.
                               Core Unit 15 p12.

       A World of Mathematics   Book 4 p30-33.
       Focus Mathematics   Book 2 p69-71.
       Headway Maths   Book 1 p68-69. Book 2 p73-74.
       Mathematics for Life   Book A2 p30-32.
       Maths (Holt)   Book 1 p32, 42-43. Workbook 1 p27.
                        Book 2 p68. Workbook 2 p6, 7.
       Mathsworks   Tryouts 1 p18.
       Maths You Need   p47, 48, 49.

SM   *Four a Day series*   Book 9 p71.
         Mathematics and Metric Measuring   Book 1 p8, 9, 12, 13, 14, 15-21.
         Problems   Second Problems p9, 15.

Curved lines and perimeters.   L7

Measuring curved lines and perimeters.

Calculating perimeters given the dimensions. Calculating length of one side given the perimeter and other necessary dimensions.

Investigating the relationships between the perimeter of a square, rectangle and equilateral triangle and the lengths of their sides.

Circles. Measuring the radius and diameter of circles and investigating their relationship. Measuring circle circumference using string, etc.

See also   N8,9,15,16,20,21   Addition and subtraction of whole numbers.
           N22   Addition and subtraction of decimals.
           N23   Ratio, rate and proportion.
           AR3(1)   Generalisations expressed using 'variables'.
           AR3(2)   Substituting numbers into algebraic expressions.
           AR3(3)   Simplification of equations.
           AR4   Straight line graphs.
           AR8   Algebraic solution of equations.
           Sh8   Circle vocabulary.

CV12, A13, L11   Measuring radius and diameter for volume, area and circumference calculations.
A5   Conservation. Area distinguished from perimeter.
A9   Area/perimeter relationships.
L5   Addition and subtraction of metric lengths.
L8,9   Plans and maps.
L11   Circle circumference.

P   *Alpha (new ed.)*   Alpha 1 p54. Alpha 2 p61.
         Beta (new ed.)   Beta 2 p35, 87. Beta 3 p35, 63, 70.
                            Beta 4 p60.
         Basic Mathematics   Book 2 p47, 48, 49, 73, 80. Book 3 p98, 99.
         Come and Measure   Length p20-21.
         Hey Mathematics   Mod 2. Book 2 p13, 23. Book 4 p9, 23. Book 5 p25.
                            Mod 3. Book 5 p12, 13.
                            Mod 4. Book 4 p35.
                            Mod 6. Book 4 p3, 12, 13, 14.
         Key Maths   Level 2 Book 4 p36, 40-43, 47. Book 5 p77, 78, 81. Book 6 p73-74.
         Making Sure of Maths   Book 1 p48. Book 2 p76-77.
         Mathematics for Schools   Level 1 (2nd ed.) Book 6 p27.
                            Level 2 (2nd ed.) Book 1 p17, 20, 21.
                            Level 2 (1st ed.) Book 3 p21, 22, 23. Book 4 p10, 11, 46-49, 51, 53, 54. Book 5 p32.
         Maths Adventure   4. Pupil's Book p38.
         Nuffield Maths 5-11   2. Worksheets L2 4·2.
                            3. Pupils' Book p83.
         Our First School Maths   Book 5 p23-24. Book 6 p16, 18.
         Oxford Middle School Mathematics   Book 1 p74-75. Book 2 p11, 34, 68-69, 70.
                            Book 3 p32. Book 4 p21, 67.
         Primary Mathematics (SPMG)   Stage 1. Workbook 2 Card 10a.
                            Stage 2. Workbook 2 Card 4, 5. Workbook 3 p24.
                            Stage 3. Workbook p11. Card 21.
                            Stage 4. Textbook p49-52, 102, 105, 114. Workbook p18. Card 33, 34.
                            Stage 5. Textbook p18, 30, 54-55. Card 41, 55.
         Towards Mathematics   Core Unit 9 p1-3. Core Unit 15 p12.

S   *A World of Mathematics*   Book 1 p51-52.
         Focus Mathematics   Book 2 p23-24, 72-73. Book 4 p105-107.
         Headway Maths   Book 1 p11. Book 2 p41. Book 3 p24-27.
                            Book 4 p50.
         Impact Maths   Pupil's Book 1 p46.
         Inner Ring Maths   Book 2 p27, 28.
         Maths (Holt)   Book 1 p32. Workbook 1 p28. Workbook 2 p6, 7.
                            Book 3 p41. 4th Year Workbook p20.
         Maths You Need   p49, 59-60.

SM   *Check it Again*   Book 5 p37, 38-41.
         Four a Day series   Book 8 p60-64. Book 9 p74-77. Book 10 p68-70.
         Mathematics and Metric Measuring   Book 1 p10.
         Problems   Third Problems p19-20.

Books for teachers
         Hey Mathematics   Mod 3. Teachers' Book p35.
         Mathematics: the first 3 years   p69, 77-78, 104-106.
         Nuffield Maths 5-11   2. Teachers' Handbook p76-77.
                            3. Teachers' Handbook p111-112.

L8   Plans and maps with scales of one-to-one.

Idea of a plan or map as a bird's eye view.

Drawing and interpreting plans or maps with no explicit scale, and with a one-to-one scale e.g. 1cm. represents 1km.

Ordnance Survey maps, etc.

See also   N1   One-to-one correspondence.
           N23   Ratios.
           AR4   Straight line graphs.
           VR1,2,3,4   Representation of quantity with one-to-one scale.
           VR7   Co-ordinates.
           S2   The equivalent relation.
           Sh10,13,19   Directional compass, bearings and navigation.
           Sh17   Similarity, enlargement and reduction.
           Sh21   Construction techniques.

Plans and maps with varied scales. L9

Plans and maps with scales other than one-to-one e.g. 5 cm. represents 1 km. Drawing and interpreting plans or maps with scales.

Contour maps.

See also   PV1,2,4,7   Place value grouping experiences. Idea of 1 representing 5, 10, 100, 1,000, etc.
            N17,18,19,29,30   Multiplication and division.
            N23   Ratios.
            F4   Multiplication of fraction by whole number.
            VR8   Representing quantity using scales
            and selected topics listed for L8.

S *A World of Mathematics* Book 3 p31. Book 4 p12. Book 6 p47.
Focus Mathematics Book 2 p18-21. 26. Book 7 p43.
Headway Maths Book 4 p52-55, 80.
Impact Maths Pupil's Book 1 p47.
Mathematics for Life Book B1 p24-25. Book B2 p22-23, 26-27.
Maths (Holt) Workbook 1 p28. Book 2 p76. Book 3 p61, 68-70, 88. 5th Year p27, 52-54. 5th Year Workbook p9.
Maths Matters Book 1 p24-25. Book 2 p8-9, 30-31.
Book 3 p16-17, 20-21.
Mathsworks Book 1 p83, 84-85. Tryouts 1 p44, 57, 58, 59.
Book 2 p5, 62. Tryouts 2 p2, 33.
Maths You Need p50-53, 61, 106-107.
On Our Own Two Feet Book 3 p14.

SM *Check it Again* Book 4 p43-44. Book 5 p46-47, 48-50, 51-52.
Mathematics and Metric Measuring Book 1 p10, 34-36, 43-45.
Problems Third Problems p24.

L10 Focus on problems, applications and everyday use of length and metric units.

Problems involving the four number operations.

Clothes and shoe sizes, heights above and below sea level, etc.

Reading and understanding distance tables, as in the back of road atlases.

Relating units of length to other units of measurement
e.g. Unit pricing e.g. 6 metres of material at £1·85 a metre. (See also M8).
Public transport costs: distance related to cost (See also AR6). See T12, AR6 for duration of trip related to cost.
Petrol consumption: Km per litre (See also CV10).
Growth rate: height related to time (See also VR9). See W8, VR9 for weight related to time.
Measurement of rainfall (See also CV10).
For speed, i.e. distance related to time, see T13.

See also N8,9,15,16,20,21 Addition and subtraction of whole numbers.
N17,18,29,30,33,34 Multiplication and division of whole numbers.
N22,31,32 Operations on decimals.
N23 Ratio, rate and proportion.
N27,35 Directed numbers. Operations. (heights above and below sea level.)
AR4 Straight line graphs.
VR7 Co-ordinates: (use of distance tables).
L5 Relationships between standard units. Addition and subtraction.
Imp. Problems and applications using imperial units.

P *Alpha (new ed.)* Alpha 1 p42. Alpha 3 p85. Alpha 4 p13, 14.
Beta (new ed.) Beta 2 p32. Beta 6 p9.
Basic Mathematics Book 3 p66.
Hey Mathematics Mod 2. Book 4 p36. Book 5 p11.
Mod 5. Book 1 p23, 27. Book 4 p3.
Mod 6. Book 1 p10-11. Book 4 p30-31, 32.
Key Maths Level 2. Book 4 p35. Book 5 p70, 71. Book 6 p10, 72.
Making Sure of Maths Book 2 p46. Book 3 p30. Book 4 p19-20.
Book 5 p7, 79.
Mathematics for Schools Level 2 (1st ed.) Book 5 p9, 10, 11, 12, 63.
Maths Adventure 2. Pupil's Book p65.
Oxford Middle School Mathematics Book 2 p72-73. Book 3 p18, 42.
Primary Mathematics (SPMG) Stage 4. Textbook p78, 79, 82, 113. Card 35, 38, 57.
Stage 5. Textbook p82. Card 12, 32, 42, 43.
Towards Mathematics Core Unit 14 p8, 10. Core Unit 19 p2, 3.

S *A World of Mathematics* Book 3 p12.
Headway Maths Book 3 p22. Book 5 p14, 41-43.
Mathematics for Life Book A1 p14-15. Book A2 p24-25, 28-29, 30-31. Book B2 p24-25. Book B3 p30-32.
Book C3 p8-9.
Maths (Holt) Book 1 p4. Book 2 p27, 70. Book 3 p37.
4th Year p68, 74.
Maths Matters Book 1 p22-23. Book 3 p8-9.
Mathsworks Book 1 p42. Tryouts 1 p20. Book 2 p12, 67.
Maths You Need p60-61, 111-112.
Understanding Money Book 2 p9-12, 69-74, 80-81.

SM *Check it Again* Book 2 p30-31. Book 3 p27-28. Book 5 p45-46.
Four and Day series Book 7 p64. Book 8 p56. Book 10 p67-68.
Problems Second Problems p51. Third Problems p54, 62.

Circle circumference.

Investigation of the relationship between the diameter (D) or radius of a circle and its circumference (C) as measured using string etc. Discovery that $\frac{C}{D}$ is constant for all circles.

Circumferences and diameters plotted on a graph and use of the graph to find the approximate value of 'pi' (π).

Use of formula C = π D to calculate circumference

See also   N19(2) Commutative property of multiplication.
          N23   'pi' as a ratio.
          N31   Multiplication of decimals ('pi' as 3·14).
          F4   Multiplication of fraction by whole number ('pi' as $^{22}/_7$).
          AR3(1) Generalisations expressed using 'variables'.
          AR3(2) Substituting numbers into algebraic expressions.
          AR4,9 Straight line graphs.
          Sh8   Circle vocabulary.
          A13   Circle area ('pi'). Surface area of cylinder.
          L7   Measuring circumference, diameter and radius.

P   *Alpha (new ed.)*   Alpha 3 p56-57. Alpha 4 p61, 63.
       Beta (new ed.)   Beta 4 p85-86. Beta 5 p51, 52.
       Basic Mathematics   Book 4 p78, 79, 80. Book 5 p66.
       Key Maths   Level 2. Book 6 p98-100.
       Making Sure of Maths   Book 5 p38-39. Book 6 p48-49.
       Mathematics for Schools   Level 2 (2nd ed.) Book 1 p21.
                                       Level 2 (1st ed.) Book 4 p52, 54. Book 7 p45-46, 49. Book 10 p43.
       Maths Adventure   3. Card 14.
                        4. Pupil's Book p82. Card 13.
                        5. Pupil's Book p15. Activity Book p14.
       Oxford Middle School Mathematics   Book 3 p33. Book 4 p24-25.
       Primary Mathematics (SPMG)   Stage 4. Card 37.
                                    Stage 5. Textbook p29. Card 20, 31.

S   *A World of Mathematics*   Book 5 p52-55.
       Focus Mathematics   Book 7 p81-86.
       Headway Maths   Book 3 p79-81. Book 4 p50.
       Maths (Holt)   Book 3 p56. 4th Year p27.
       Mathsworks   Book 1 p116-117.

SM   *Mathematics and Metric Measuring*   Book 1 p31-33.

Very large distances and very small lengths.

Distances across the world and in space. Light years.

Micrometer and feeler gauges for very small lengths.

Measuring in bulk to find fractional lengths by simple proportion
     e.g.   measuring the thickness of 100 sheets of paper and then calculating the approximate thickness of one sheet.

See also   PV4,7   Place value.
          PV5,6,8   Decimal notation.
          N18,30,32,34   Division of whole numbers and decimals.
          N23   Ratio, rate and proportion.
          CV10, W8   Bulk measure to find fractional amounts.
          L5   Relationships between standard units.
          T13   Light years.
          T14, M10   World time. Planning and costing overseas trips.

P   *Beta (new ed.)*   Beta 4 p10.
       Hey Mathematics   Mod 6. Book 4 p32-34.
       Mathematics for Schools   Level 2 (1st ed.) Book 5 p16, 17, 18.
       Maths Adventure   2. Card 22.
                        3. Pupil's Book p36-37. Card 11.
                        4. Card 13.
       Primary Mathematics (SPMG)   Stage 4. Textbook p82. Card 56.

SM   *Mathematics and Metric Measuring*   Book 1 p28-30.
        Problems   Second Problems p17.

L13 Tall and inaccessible heights and distances.

Investigation of methods of determining heights or distances that are not readily measurable e.g. height of a tall tree, width of a river.

Calculating heights using similar triangles. Use of the clinometer.

Hill gradients.

See also N23   Ratio, rate and proportion.
          AR9   Gradients of straight line graphs.
          Sh13 Degrees.
          Sh17 Similar triangles.
          Sh21 Construction techniques.
          Sh23 Pythagoras' theorem.
          L8,9 Maps and plans. Scales.

P   *Alpha (new ed.)*   Alpha 3 p17. Alpha 4 p82-86.
      Beta (new ed.)   Beta 5 p38-39, 90. Beta 6 p66, 91.
      Making Sure of Maths   Book 5 p46, 64-66.
      Mathematics for Schools   Level 2 (1st ed.) Book 7 p2-5. Book 9 p56-57.
      Maths Adventure   4. Card 12.
      Oxford Middle School Mathematics   Book 4 p46-47.

S   *A World of Mathematics*   Book 6 p42-43.
      Focus Mathematics   Book 4 p120-136. Book 7 p43-45.
      Headway Maths   Book 5 p60-61.
      Maths (Holt)   Book 3 p57.
      Mathsworks   Book 1 p82. Book 2 p4, 6, 63.
                     Tryouts 2 p3.

SM   *Mathematics and Metric Measuring*   Book 1 p37-46.

Mass and Weight

Contents

Topics with a sequence of development extending over considerable time.

W1 Early concepts and vocabulary associated with mass and weight.

Introduction to, and extension of vocabulary alongside experience holding objects. Investigation of objects that float or sink. Experience pushing and pulling, introducing the idea of weight as a force.

Vocabulary: light, heavy, lift, drop, fall, float, sink, push, pull, hard to push, etc.

See also   S1,3   Sorting and classifying.

P   *Come and Measure*   Mass p2.
Nuffield Maths 5-11   1. Worksheets W1 1·1-1·2.
Numbers and Words   Book 2 p17.

Books for teachers
Early Mathematical Experiences   'Sand. Raw Materials' esp. p14-18.
'Towards Number. Apparatus, Toys and Games'
'Outside Activities. The Environment'.
Mathematics: the first 3 years   p18-22.
Nuffield Maths 5-11   1. Teachers' Handbook p117, 118-119.

W2 Comparing and ordering by weight.

Comparing and ordering by weight two and later more objects using hands.

Use of see-saws, home-made scales (e.g. coat hanger scales) and later balance-type scales for ordering objects by weight.

Extension of vocabulary: heavier, heaviest, lighter, lightest, weighs more/less, weighs the most/least, etc.

Equivalence in weight: 'weighs about the same as'.

See also   N5   Ordinal number: 1st, 2nd, etc.
S2   Relations between sets. The equivalent relation.
W4   Conservation.

P   *Alpha (new ed.)*   Alpha 1 p63.
Beta (new ed.)   Beta 1 p37, 38.
Basic Mathematics   Book 1 p85.
Come and measure   Mass p2-7, 9.
Hey Mathematics   Mod 1. Book 5 p36.
Making Sure of Maths   Introductory Book p38.
Book 1 p73.
Mathematics for Schools   Level 1 (2nd ed.) Book 3 p34-36.
Maths Adventure   1. Card 2.
Nuffield Maths 5-11   Bronto Books. Set A. Comparing with Bronto.
1 Worksheets W1 2·1-2·2, 2·3-2·6, 2·7-2·8, 4·1, 4·4.
3. Pupils' Book p37.
Numbers and Words   Book 7 p26-27.
Our First School Maths   Book 3 p4-6. Book 4 p25.
Primary Mathematics (SPMG)   Stage 1. Workbook 2 p36-40. Card 13. Workbook 4 Card 6b.

SM   *Mathematics and Metric Measuring*   Book 2 p3-6, 29-30.

Books for teachers
Early Mathematical Experiences   'Sand. Raw Materials' esp. p14-18.
'Towards Number. Apparatus, Toys and Games'
'Outside Activities. The Environment'.
'Space and Shape. Comparisons' esp. p18-19.
Mathematics: the first 3 years   p70-72.
Nuffield Maths 5-11   1. Teachers' Handbook p119-121, 122, 123-124, 127.
3. Teachers' Handbook p50-52.

W3 Use of arbitrary units.

Use of arbitrary units (e.g. marbles, beans) to weigh and order objects by weight using balance-type scales.

Estimating weight in these units, measuring and recording error.

An appreciation of the need for standard units.

See also PV2 Counting and ordering numbers to 100.
         N5 Ordinal number.
         N9,16 Subtraction to 100.
         F1 Half, quarter, whole one.
         S2 Relations between sets.
         Sh13, CV3, A3, L3, T3 The need for standard units.

P *Alpha (new ed.)* Alpha 1 p64.
    Beta (new ed.) Beta 1 p38.
    Come and Measure Mass p10.
    Mathematics for Schools Level 1 (2nd ed.). Book 4 p56. Book 6 p44-46.
    Maths Adventure 1. Card 3.
                2. Card 1, 2.
    Nuffield Maths 5-11 1. Worksheets W1 $3 \cdot 1$-$3 \cdot 2$, $4 \cdot 2$-$4 \cdot 3$.
                          3. Pupils' Book p38-39, 40.
    Our First School Maths Book 4 p24.
    Oxford Middle School Mathematics Book 1 p34-35.
    Primary Mathematics (SPMG) Stage 1. Workbook 4 p20-23. Card 5a, 5b, 6a.
                                     Stage 4. Card 29.
                                     Stage 5. Card 66.
    Towards Mathematics Core Unit 4 p7.

S *Maths (Holt)* Book 1 p23.

SM *Mathematics and Metric Measuring* Book 2 p7-11.

Books for teachers
    Mathematics: the first 3 years p70-72.
    Nuffield Maths 5-11 1. Teachers' Handbook p124-126, 127-130.
                          3. Teachers' Handbook p54, 135.

Conservation of weight.   **W4**

Experience leading to the concept of conservation (invariance) of weight i.e. the idea that weight is a property independent of other attributes, especially size;

    e.g. the weight of a long sausage-shaped piece of plasticene is equivalent to the weight of that same piece of plasticene when spherical.

Ordering 'mystery parcels' by weight, when weight does not necessarily relate to size.

See also S2 The equivalent relation.
         N4, CV4, A5, L2 Conservation

P *Alpha (new ed.)* Alpha 1 p63.
    Beta (new ed.) Beta 1 p69.
    Come and Measure Mass p8, 11-12, 16-17, 21.
    Maths Adventure 1. Card 1.
    Nuffield Maths 5-11 1. Worksheets W1 $2 \cdot 8$.
                          3. Pupils' Book p39, 40.
    Primary Mathematics (SPMG) Stage 1. Workbook 4 p23.

Books for teachers
    Nuffield Maths 5-11 1. Teachers' Handbook p121-122.
                          2. Teachers' Handbook p101.
                          3. Teachers' Handbook p52-54.

Introduction to kilograms and grams.   **W5**

Concept of the weight of one kilogram, 500 grams, 100 grams and one gram. Objects compared by weight with one kilogram, etc.

Estimating weight in kilograms *or* grams, measuring and recording error.

Simple cookery.

Approximations i.e. rounding off measurements.

See also   PV2,4   Counting and ordering numbers to 1,000.
              N5   Ordinal number.
              N9,16,21 Subtraction.
              F1   Half, quarter, whole one.
              S2   Relations between sets.

P   *Alpha (new ed.)*   Alpha 1 p64. Alpha 2 p47, 48. Alpha 4 p20.
     Beta (new ed.)   Beta 1 p39. Beta 2 p14, 48.
     Basic Mathematics   Book 1 p86, 88.
     Come and Measure   Mass p13-18, 20.
     Hey Mathematics   Mod 2. Book 2 p18. Book 3 p26. Book 4 p16-18.
     Key Maths   Level 2. Book 1 p59-60. Book 2 p4.
     Making Sure of Maths   Introductory Book p39.
                        Book 1 p74.
     Mathematics for Schools   Level 1 (2nd ed.) Book 4 p57. Book 6 p47.
                        Level 2 (2nd ed.) Book 2 p15.
                        Level 2 (1st ed.) Book 3 p2, 3, 4, 32, 34-35.
     Maths Adventure   1. Card 4, 5.
                     3. Card 4, 5.
     Nuffield Maths 5-11   2. Worksheets W2 1·1-1·4, 2·1-2·2, 3·1-3·2.
                     3. Pupils' Book p41, 101, 102, 103, 104.
     Our First School Maths   Book 5 p25-27. Book 6 p19-21.
     Oxford Middle School Mathematics   Book 1 p44.
     Primary Mathematics (SPMG)   Stage 2. Workbook 1 p27-30. Card 8a, 8b. Workbook 4 p27, 28. Card 6.
                        Stage 5. Card 15.
     Towards Mathematics   Core Unit 4 p8-9.

M   *Four a Day series*   Book 7 p67.

Books for teachers
     Nuffield Maths 5-11   2. Teachers' Handbook p102-108.
                     3. Teachers' Handbook p54. Chapter 22.

W6 Relationships between standard metric units.

Converting weights from one standard unit to another using decimal notation when it is understood, e.g. 1 kg 300 g, 1,300 g or 1·300 kg.

The economic use of weights for weighing objects.

Addition and subtraction of metric weights.

See also   PV7   Place value. Grouping in 1,000's.
              PV8   Decimal notation.
              N8,9,15,16,20,21 Addition and subtraction of whole numbers.
              N22   Addition and subtraction of decimals.
              W8   Problems and applications.
              W9   Weighing objects in air and water.
              W10   Metric tonne, milligram, etc.

P   *Alpha (new ed.)*   Aipha 1 p65. Alpha 2 p47, 48, 49. Alpha 3 p18.
     Beta (new ed.)   Beta 2 p14, 48, 49. 50. Beta 3 p44.
                  Beta 5 p12.
     Basic Mathematics   Book 1 p87. Book 2 p67, 69, 72.
                     Book 3 p63, 64. Book 4 p63, 64, 66.
     Come and Measure   Mass p19.
     Hey Mathematics   Mod 3. Book 5 p39.
                   Mod 4. Book 3 p18, 19. Book 4 p23.
                   Mod 6. Book 1 p29-30.
     Key Maths   Level 2. Book 2 p4. Book 4 p48, 49, 50. Book 5 p90, 91. Book 6 p89, 91.
     Making Sure of Maths   Book 1 p75-76. Book 2 p49-50, 52.
                      Book 3 p32-33.
     Mathematics for Schools   Level 2 (2nd ed.) Book 2 p16-18.
                        Level 2 (1st ed.) Book 3 p33, 36-37. Book 7 p10, 11, 12.
     Maths Adventure   1. Pupil's Book p88.
                     2. Pupil's Book p40, 41.
                     4. Pupil's Book p40.
     Nuffield Maths 5-11   3. Pupils' Book p102.
     Primary Mathematics (SPMG)   Stage 2. Workbook 4 p29-30.
                        Stage 3. Textbook p20, 21.
                        Stage 4. Card 61.
                        Stage 5. Textbook p46. Card 21.
     Towards Mathematics   Core Unit 14 p11.

S   *A World of Mathematics*   Book 1 p56-57. Book 3 p23-25.
  Headway Maths   Book 1 p62.
  Impact Maths   Pupil's Book 1 p56.
  Maths (Holt)   Book 2 p15. 5th Year p58-59.
        5th Year Workbook p23, 31, 34.
  Maths Matters   Book 1 p21.
  Maths You Need   p88-90.

SM   *Check it Again*   Book 1 p40. Book 3 p31. Book 4 p40.
  Four a Day series   Book 6 p55-56. Book 7 p66, 67-68, 68-69.
        Book 8 p65, 67, 68-69. Book 9 p79-80.
        Book 10 p70-71.
  Number Workbook   Decimals p31.
  Problems   Second Problems p30.

Books for teachers
  Hey Mathematics   Mod 3. Teachers' Book p31-32.
  Mathematics: the first 3 years   p111.

Weighing using more than one standard unit.   **W7**

Estimating weight, measuring using more than one unit and recording error e.g. 1kg 625kg. Use of decimal notation when understood.

Weighing liquids. Subtracting weight of container from total weight.

Use of a wide range of weighing instruments: spring balance, kitchen scales (dial type), bathroom scales, etc. Reading the dials.

Approximations (i.e. rounding off measurements) and limits to accuracy.

See also   PV7   Place value. Grouping in 1,000's.
      PV8   Decimal notation.
      N9,16,21   Subtraction of whole numbers.
      N22   Subtraction of decimals.
      AR4   Straight line graphs. Spring stretch/weight relationship.
      VR8   Scales on measuring instruments.
      Sh13, CV8, A6, L6, T6   Limits to accuracy.
      CV7, AR4   Relationship weight/volume of water.
      W6   Relationships between standard unts. Subtraction of metric weights.
      W9   Weighing objects in air and water.

P   *Alpha (new ed.)*   Alpha 1 p65. Alpha 2 p49. Alpha 3 p18.
        Alpha 4 p20.
  Beta (new ed.)   Beta 2 p49, 51. Beta 3 p44, 45, 46.
        Beta 4 p8, 30. Beta 5 p14. Beta 6 p13, 76.
  Basic Mathematics   Book 3 p62.
  Come and Measure   Mass p22-23.
  Key Maths   Level 1 Book 7 p53.
        Level 2 Book 1 p59. Book 3 p14. Book 4 p48-50. Book 6 p90.
  Making Sure of Maths   Book 2 p53.
  Mathematics for Schools   Level 2 (1st ed.) Book 5 p30. Book 10 p39-40.
  Maths Adventure   2. Card 3, 4, 5.
        3. Card 1.
  Oxford Middle School Mathematics   Book 1 p45.
  Primary Mathematics (SPMG)   Stage 3. Textbook p71-74. Card 38, 39.
        Stage 4. Textbook p40. Card 30.
        Stage 5. Textbook p23, 100, 116. Card 24.
  Towards Mathematics   Core Unit 4 p10.

S   *Headway Maths*   Book 1 p63.
  Mathematics for Life   Book B2 p10-11.

SM   *Check it Again*   Book 4 p41.
  Four a Day series   Book 8 p66. Book 10 p72.
  Mathematics and Metric Measuring   Book 2 p18-25, 26-27, 34-36, 40-45.

Books for teachers
  Mathematics: the first 3 years   p73, 110.

W8 Focus on problems, applications and everyday use of weight and metric units.

Problems involving the four number operations.

Net and gross, wet and dry weights, calories and dieting.

Idea of average weight.

Varying the yield in cookery by varying the ingredient quantities.

Relating units of weight to other units of measurement:
  e.g. Unit pricing e.g. 7 kg of potatoes at 16p a kg (See also M8).
  Weight of coins related to their value (See also AR6).
  Weight of grass seed needed for given area: weight related to area (See also A10).
  Growth rate: weight related to time (See also VR9). For height related to time see L10, VR9.
  For weight of a given substance related to its volume, see CV7 and AR4.
  For introduction to density i.e. weight related to volume, see CV10.
  For introduction to pressure i.e. weight related to area, see A10.
  For introduction to specific gravity, see W9.

See also M11   Post office services: parcel costs, etc.
  N8,9,15,16,20,21   Addition and subtraction of whole numbers.
  N17,18,29,30,33,34   Multiplication and division of whole numbers.
  N22,31,32   Operations on decimals.
  N23   Ratio, rate and proportion.
  N37   Average.
  AR4   Straight line graphs.
  W6   Relationships between standard units. Addition and subtraction.
  Imp   Problems and applications using imperial units.

P   *Alpha (new ed.)*   Alpha 1 p65.
  Beta (new ed.)   Beta 2 p50. Beta 3 p46. Beta 4 p30.
      Beta 5 p12. Beta 6 p13, 40.
  Basic Mathematics   Book 1 p88. Book 2 p70. Book 3 p69.
  Come and Measure   Mass p24.
  Hey Mathematics   Mod 2. Book 4 p16.
      Mod 3. Book 1 p27. Book 3 p29. Book 5 p40.
      Mod 4. Book 3 p19.
      Mod 6. Book 1 p24. Book 2 p10.
  Key Maths   Level 2. Book 4 p53. Book 5 p92, 93. Book 6 p87, 89, 91.
  Making Sure of Maths   Book 3 p33. Book 4 p25-26. Book 5 p6, 79.
  Mathematics for Schools   Level 2 (1st ed.) Book 5 p9, 10. Book 8 p64.
  Maths Adventure   3. Pupil's Book p47. Card 3.
      4. Card 3.
      5. Pupil's Book p41.
  Nuffield Maths 5-11   3. Pupils' Book p39.
  Primary Mathematics (SPMG)   Stage 2. Workbook 2 p27. Workbook 4 Card 7.
      Stage 3. Textbook p93, 95. Card 9, 10, 11.
      Stage 4. Textbook p41, 62. Card 38.
      Stage 5. Textbook p23, 79.
  Towards Mathematics   Core Unit 19 p8, 13.

S   *Headway Maths*   Book 1 p62. Book 4 p10-11.
  Inner Ring Maths   Book 3 p21.
  Mathematics for Life   Book A1 p28-29. Book B2 p8-9, 10-13.
      Book B3 p22-23. Book C3 p14-15.
  Maths (Holt)   Book 2 p30, 38-39, 67. Book 3 p7.
      4th Year p68. 5th Year p58-59, 70, 86-87
      5th Year Workbook p25-26, 40.
  Maths Matters   Book 1 p4-5, 20-21.
  Mathsworks   Book 1 p42. Tryouts 1 p11, 37, 38, 39, 40.
      Book 2 p24-27, 33. Tryouts 2 p13, 15.
  Maths You Need   p90-93.

SM   *Check it Again*   Book 3 p31.
  Four a Day series   Book 7 p70. Book 8 p69.
      Book 9 p81, 83. Book 10 p72.
  Mathematics and Metric Measuring   Book 2 p16-17, 18-28, 31-33, 46-47.
  Problems   Second Problems p31, 54.
      Third Problems p55.

Gravity pull. Mass and weight.

Weight as the force of gravity on a mass.

The idea of weightlessness.

Weighing objects in air and then water and comparing the results. The idea of upthrust.

Introduction to specific gravity (relative density).

See also N9,16,21 Subtraction of whole numbers.
  N22 Subtraction of decimals.
  N23 Ratio, rate and proportion.
  CV10 Introduction to density.
  W6 Subtraction of metric weights.
  W10 Plimsoll line.

P *Alpha (new ed.)* Alpha 4 p26.
  Maths Adventure 3. Card 2.

S *A World of Mathematics* Book 4 p27, 29.

SM *Mathematics and Metric Measuring* Book 2 p37-39.

Books for teachers
  Nuffield Maths 5-11 1. Teachers' Handbook p117.
    2. Teachers' Handbook p100.

Very large and very small weights.

Introduction to the metric tonne, focusing on practical applications: maximum loads in lorries, cranes, lifts, etc., weight restrictions on bridges.

The Plimsoll line.

Introduction to the milligram, microgram and megagram focusing on practical applications of these units e.g. medicines and tablets.

Relationships between these units and the kilogram and gram.

Weighing in bulk to find fractional weights, e.g. weighing 100 grains of rice and then calculating the approximate weight of one grain.

See also PV4,7 Place value. Grouping in 100's, 1,000's, etc.
  PV6,8 Decimal notation.
  N18,30,32,34 Division of whole numbers and decimals.
  N23 Ratio, rate and proportion.
  CV10, L12 Bulk measure to find fractional amounts.
  W6 Relationships between kg and g.
  W9 Weighing objects in air and water.

P *Alpha (new ed.)* Alpha 4 p23.
  Beta (new ed.) Beta 4 p30. Beta 5 p10. Beta 6 p13.
  Basic Mathematics Book 3 p68. Book 4 p63.
  Hey Mathematics Mod 6. Book 2 p10.
  Key Maths Level 2. Book 5 p88, 89. Book 6 p88.
  Mathematics for Schools Level 2 (1st ed.) Book 10 p42.
  Maths Adventure 3. Card 3.
    4. Card 1, 2, 5.
  Oxford Middle School Mathematics Book 3 p87.
  Towards Mathematics Core Unit 19 p12.

S *Maths (Holt)* 5th Year p46.

SM *Four a Day series* Book 10 p73.
  Mathematics and Metric Measuring Book 2 p14-15.
  Problems Second Problems p54
    Third Problems p14.

Books for teachers
  Hey Mathematics Mod 3. Teachers' Book p32.

Time

Contents

Topics with a sequence of development extending over considerable time.

Early concepts and vocabulary associated with ordering events in time and continuity.　T1

Discussion about past, present and future events extending vocabulary.

Verbal and pictorial flow accounts of the cycle of the day and of routine activities e.g. getting up in the morning.

Vocabulary: (a) day, night, morning, afternoon, evening, special times e.g. dinnertime.
　　　　　(b) when, before, after, now, then, soon, nearly, next, still, during, past, beginning, middle, end, yesterday, today, tomorrow, sometimes, occasionally, never, always, till, until, since, once, twice, etc.

See also　N5　　Ordinal number: 1st, 2nd, etc.
　　　　　VR6　　Flow charts.
　　　　　S2　　Relations between sets.

P　*Come and Measure*　Time p1-6, 8-9.
　　Mathematics for Schools　Level 1 (2nd ed.) Book 7 p43.
　　　　　　　　　　　　　Level 2 (1st ed.) Book 6 p1-2.
　　Nuffield Maths 5-11　1. Worksheets T1 1·1-1·2, 2·1-2·2.
　　Numbers and Words　Book 2 p14.

Books for teachers
　　Early Mathematical Experiences　'The Passage of Time. Rhymes and Stories'.
　　Mathematics: the first 3 years　p86-87.
　　Nuffield Maths 5-11　1. Teachers' Handbook p132-135.

Early concepts and vocabulary associated with duration. Comparing and ordering durations.　T2

Introduction to and extension of vocabulary alongside experience of duration: quick, slow, a long time, a short time, early, late, etc.

Comparison of time taken to do simple activities.
　　e.g.　running a fixed distance, completing a simple assault course.

　　Extension of vocabulary: faster, fastest, slower, slowest, quicker, quickest, etc.

Equivalent duration: 'takes about the same time as . . .'.

Vocabulary associated with age: old, new, young, older, oldest, newer, newest, younger, youngest.

See also　N5　　Ordinal number: 1st, 2nd, etc.
　　　　　S1,3　　Sorting and classifying.
　　　　　S2　　Relations between sets. The equivalent relation.

P　*Come and Measure*　Time p17, 21, 23-24.
　　Maths Adventure　4. Card 6.
　　Nuffield Maths 5-11　1. Worksheets T1 3·1.

Books for teachers
　　Early Mathematical Experiences　'Water. Raw Materials'.
　　　　　　　　　　　　　　'Outdoor Activities. The Environment'.
　　　　　　　　　　　　　　'Space and Shape. Comparisons'.
　　Nuffield Maths 5-11　1. Teachers' Handbook p135-136.

Use of arbitrary units to measure duration.　T3

Use of various devices and units to measure and order durations. Clapping, skipping, etc. leading to the use of historical devices e.g. candle clocks, sand clocks, water clocks, pendulums.

Estimating duration in these units, measuring and recording error.

An appreciation of the need for standard units.

See also PV2   Counting and ordering numbers to 100.
          N5   Ordinal number.
          N9,16 Subtraction to 100.
          F1   Half, quarter, whole one.
          S2   Relations between sets.
          Sh13, CV3, A3, L3, W3   The need for standard units.

P *Basic Mathematics*   Book 2 p74.
       Come and Measure   Time p10-11.
       Hey Mathematics   Mod 2. Book 1 p22.
       Mathematics for Schools   Level 1 (2nd ed.) Book 6 p35-36.
       Maths Adventure   1. Card 7, 8, 9, 10.
                           2. Card 8, 10.
       Nuffield Maths 5-11   1. Worksheets T1 3·2.
       Our First School Maths   Book 3 p31. Book 5 p6.
       Oxford Middle School Mathematics   Book 1 p97.

SM *Mathematics and Metric Measuring*   Book 3 p15-17, 18-22, 22-27.

Books for teachers
        Mathematics: the first 3 years   p87.
        Mathematics; the later Primary years   p12.
        Nuffield Maths 5-11   1. Teachers' Handbook p136-137.
                                2. Teachers' Handbook p111-112.

T4 Observing the clock. Special times.

Observing the clock and the movements of the clock hands.

Recognition of o'clock times and relating special times (e.g. dinner time) to the clock face.

See also N5   Ordinal number.
          Sh4   Clockwise and anticlockwise.
          Sh8   Circles and circle vocabulary.
          Sh10 Idea of angle.
          L1,2 Long, short, longer, shorter (clock hands).
          T7   Telling the time.

P *Ready for Alpha and Beta (new ed.)*   p9.
       Come and Measure   Time p12.
       Key Maths   Level 1. Book 4 p45.
       Making Sure of Maths   Yellow Book p10, 14.
                                Introductory Book p14.
       Mathematics for Schools   Level 1 (2nd ed.) Book 6 p39. Book 7 p1.
       Maths Adventure   2. Card 7.
       Nuffield Maths 5-11   Bronto Books. Set C. Bronto Time.
                               2. Worksheets T2 2·1, 2·2, 3·1.
                               3. Pupils' Book p91.
       Numbers and Words   Book 6 p27-29. Book 8 p1.
       Our First School Maths   Book 3 p28-30.

S *Mathematics for Life*   Book A1 p20-21.

SM *Blackie's Practice Workbook*   Book 2 p3, 5.
        Four a Day series   Book 4 p52.

Books for teachers
        Early Mathematical Experiences   'The Passage of Time. Rhymes and Stories'.
        Nuffield Maths 5-11   2. Teachers' Handbook p113-115, 124-125.
                                3. Teachers' Handbook p123-124.

T5 Days of the week and months of the year.

The names of the days of the week and the months of the year, emphasizing the continuous cycle.

Days and months related to events, e.g. Monday as dinner money day; birthday months and festival months.

Working days: shops, offices, etc.

Idea of daily, weekly and monthly.

Simple scientific understanding of day and night and lunar month.

See also M7   Opening days of shops.
         M11,12,13 Weekly and monthly payments.
         N5   Ordinal number.
         VR6   Flow charts.
         T8   The calendar and the seasons.

P *Basic Mathematics*   Book 1 p94.
       Come and Measure   Time p6-8, 19-20.
       Hey Mathematics   Mod 3. Book 4 p39.
       Key Maths   Level 1 Book 6 p58.
       Mathematics for Schools   Level 1 (2nd ed.) Book 6 p42-43.
       Maths Adventure   1. Pupil's Book p58, 60.
                          2. Pupil's Book p39.
       Nuffield Maths 5-11   1. Worksheets T1 4·1-4·2.
       Numbers and Words   Book 6 p10-12.
       Our First School Maths   Book 6 p25.

S *A World of Mathematics*   Book 1 p42-43. Book 2 p49.
       Maths Matters   Book 2 p14-15, 24-25.
       On Our Own Two Feet   Book 1 p9, 10.

SM *Check it Again*   Book 2 p33-34.
        Four a Day series   Book 10 p20.
        Problems   Third Problems p29.

Books for teachers
       Early Mathematical Experiences: 'Sand. Raw Materials' p4.
                                          'The Passage of Time. Rhymes and Stories'.
       Nuffield Maths 5-11   1. Teachers' Handbook p137-140.
                              2. Teachers' Handbook p112, 121.

Seconds, minutes and hours.   **T6**

Concept of the duration of a second, a minute and later an hour.

Timing activities e.g. how many pages of a book can be turned over in 5 seconds, 20 seconds, 1 minute?

Estimating duration, measuring and recording error.

Approximations and limits to accuracy.

Relationships between seconds, minutes and hours.

Addition and subtraction of standard time units.

See also PV1   Number bases. Grouping in 60's.
         PV2,4   Counting and ordering numbers to 100, 1000.
         N8,9,15,16,20,21   Addition and subtraction.
         N14   Multibase arithmetic.
         F4   ½ hour as 30 minutes, etc.
         Sh13, CV8, A6, L6, W7   Limits to accuracy.
         T7,10,11   Telling the time.
         T12   Application and problems.
         T13   Speed.

P *Alpha (new ed.)*   Alpha 2 p22. Alpha 3 p28.
       Beta (new ed.)   Beta 2 p61.
       Come and Measure   Time p14-16, 18, 22.
       Hey Mathematics   Mod 4. Book 5 p39.
       Mathematics for Schools   Level 1 (2nd ed.) Book 6 p40-41.
       Maths Adventure   1. Card 24.
                          2. Card 6, 9.
                          3. Card 6, 7, 8, 10.
                          4. Card 9, 10.
       Oxford Middle School Mathematics   Book 1 p98.
       Primary Mathematics (SPMG)   Stage 2. Workbook 2 p10. Workbook 3 Card 5, 6.
                                      Stage 4. Textbook p100.
                                      Stage 5. Textbook p21, 117.

SM *Four a Day series*   Book 8 p74. Book 9 p85. Book 10 p75.
        Mathematics and Metric Measuring   Book 3 p3-8, 9-14, 28-31.

Books for teachers
       Early Mathematical Experiences   'The Passage of Time. Rhymes and Stories'.
       Nuffield Maths 5-11   2. Teachers' Handbook p121.

T7 Telling the time.

Gradual development of the ability to tell the time on the circular clock face.

Grandfather clocks, cuckoo clocks, clocks with Roman numerals, etc.

Calculations related to telling the time e.g. how long is it from 10 to 4 till 5 past 4?

Clocks that are fast or slow.

Opening times of shops, offices, etc.

See also   M7   Opening days and times of shops.
             PV2   Place value to 30.
             PV3(2) Roman numerals.
             N8,9,15,16   Addition and subtraction.
             N13, 19(3)   Counting in 5's.
             N27,35   Directed numbers. Simple operations. ('To' and 'past' times.)
             F1,2   Fractions. Simple addition and subtraction.
             Sh13   Clock minutes as arbitrary units for measuring angles.
             T4   Observing the clock. 'O' clock' times.
             T6   Seconds, minutes and hours.
             T10,11   12 and 24 hour clock times.

P   *Ready for Alpha and Beta (new ed.)*   p16, 17.
       Beta (new ed.)   Beta 2 p60.
       Basic Mathematics   Book 1 p59-61. Book 3 p20.
       Hey Mathematics   Mod 1. Book 4 p5, 11, 28.
       Key Maths   Level 1. Book 4 p46-47. Book 5 p56-58. Book 6 p49, 51. Book 7 p51.
                  Level 2. Book 1 p27-30. Book 5 p110
       Making Sure of Maths   Introductory Book p15.
                  Book 1 p78-80.
       Mathematics for Schools   Level 1 (2nd ed.) Book 6 p37-39. Book 7 p2-4.
       Maths Adventure   1. Pupil's Book p28-29. Activity Book p23. Card 6.
       Nuffield Maths 5-11   2. Worksheets T2 $3\cdot2$-$3\cdot4$, $4\cdot1$-$4\cdot4$, $5\cdot1$-$5\cdot2$.
                  3. Pupils' Book p47-50, 91-92, 95.
       Numbers and Words   Book 8 p2-3.
       Our First School Maths   Book 4 p31-32. Book 5 p7-8. Book 6 p26-27.
       Primary Mathematics (SPMG)   Stage 1. Workbook 1 p37-40. Workbook 3 p27-31.
                  Stage 2. Workbook 2 p28-32. Card 6, 7.
                  Stage 3. Textbook p10.

S   *Headway Maths*   Book 1 p7, 48.
       Inner Ring Maths   Book 1 p5.
       Mathematics for Life   Book A1 p22-25. Book A2 p18-19.
       Maths (Holt)   Workbook 2 p36. Workbook 3 p40.
                5th Year Workbook p30.

SM   *Blackie's Practice Workbooks*   Book 2 p4, 6. Book 4 p7-8, 20-21.
                  Book 5 p3-4, 13-14.
       Four a Day series   Book 4 p53. Book 5 p61-62. Book 8 p76.

Books for teachers

       Hey Mathematics   Mod 3. Teachers' Book p39.
       Nuffield Maths 5-11   2. Teachers' Handbook p115-118, 120, 124-125.
                  3. Teachers' Handbook. Chapters 10 and 20.

T8 The calendar and the seasons.

Understanding of and experience using the calendar. Relating days on the calendar to events:
    e.g.   planting seeds or bulbs and observing growth;
           gestation period and growth of pets/babies.

The number of days in each month.

The number of days in a year. Leap years.

Ways of writing the date e.g. $4\cdot3$ or 4/3 as equivalent to March 4th.

The seasons. Variation in the length of the day according to the season.

See also   PV1   Number bases. Grouping in 7's.
             PV2,4 Counting and ordering numbers to 31 and 366.
             N5   Ordinal number for the date.
             N13, 19(3) Counting in 7's.
             VR2,3,4,8,9 Ordered block graphs, etc.
             VR6   Flow charts.
             VR7   Co-ordinates for use of calendar.
             T5   Names of days and months.

P   *Alpha (new ed.)*   Alpha 1 p36-37. Alpha 2 p53. Alpha 3 p31.
      Beta (new ed.)   Beta 1 p62-63, 93. Beta 2 p22. Beta 3 p22.
                    Beta 4 p14.
      Basic Mathematics   Book 1 p95.
      Come and Measure   Time p19.
      Hey Mathematics   Mod 3. Book 2 p29. Book 3 p17.
      Key Maths   Level 1. Book 4 p52. Book 6 p58.
                  Level 2. Book 2 p52-54. Book 5 p112.
      Making Sure of Maths   Book 3 p14.
      Mathematics for Schools   Level 2 (1st ed.) Book 8 p44.
      Maths Adventure   1. Pupil's Book p61, 82.
                  2. Pupil's Book p42.
                  4. Card 8.
      Nuffield Maths 5-11   2. Worksheets T2 6·1-6·2.
      Our First School Maths   Book 6 p24.
      Primary Mathematics (SPMG)   Stage 3. Textbook p68-70.
                           Stage 4. Textbook p60.
                           Stage 5. Textbook p20, 117.
      Towards Mathematics   Core Unit 19 p1.

S   *A World of Mathematics*   Book 1 p44.
      Headway Maths   Book 2 p33.
      Inner Ring Maths   Book 2 p23.
      Mathematics for Life   Book A1 p10-13. Book B2 p14-15.
      Maths (Holt)   Workbook 1 p32-33. 4th Year p87.
               5th Year Workbook p8.

SM   *Check it Again*   Book 2 p36-38. Book 3 p39-41.
                 Book 4 p49-50. Book 5 p34-35.
      Four a Day series   Book 8 p78-79. Book 9 p88. Book 10 p77-78.
      Problems   Second Problems p8. Third Problems p3.

Books for teachers
      Early Mathematical Experiences   'The Passage of Time. Rhymes and Stories'.
      Nuffield Maths 5-11   2. Teachers' Handbook p122-123.

Years.   T9

Idea of annual, biennial and perennial.

Dates of birth and ages of children and adults.

Awareness of one's life, past, present and future in perspective. Time lines of a life marking birth, arrival at school, the present time, leaving school, eventual retirement and death.

Later extension of period of time considered to the century, dates in history, BC and AD times.

See also   PV2,4,7   Place value. Ordering numbers by size.
             N5   Ordinal number.
             N8,9,15,16,20,21   Addition and subtraction.
             N27,35 Directed numbers. Simple operations.
             F1,2,4 Fractions of a year in ages.
             VR8, L8,9 Scales for time lines
             L12, T13 Light years.

P   *Alpha (new ed.)*   Alpha 2 p53. Alpha 3 p31. Alpha 4 p16.
      Beta (new ed.)   Beta 4 p14.
      Basic Mathematics   Book 1 p95.
      Hey Mathematics   Mod 2. Book 5 p32.
                 Mod 3. Book 3 p9. Book 4 p17.
                 Mod 5. Book 1 p19. Book 5 p12.
      Key Maths   Level 2. Book 1 p22. Book 2 p54.
      Maths Adventure   1. Pupil's Book p12.
                  2. Pupil's Book p38.

S   *Focus Mathematics*   Book 1 p33-36, 87.
         Inner Ring Maths   Book 1 p31.
         Maths (Holt)   Book 1 p31.
         Maths Matters   Book 2 p14-15.
         On Our Own Two Feet   Book 4 p1.

SM   *Check it Again*   Book 1 p37-38. Book 3 p40-41. Book 4 p50-51.
         Four a Day series   Book 7 p71. Book 8 p72.
         Problems   Third Problems p3.

Books for teachers
         Mathematics; the later Primary years   p73-74.

T10   12 hour digital clock times; a.m. and p.m.

More precise recording of the time

    12 hour digital clock times e.g. 4·55;

    a.m. and p.m.

Calculations based on 12 hour digital clock times e.g. how long is it from 4·55 p.m. till 5·30 p.m.?

Use of timetables based on 12 hour digital clock times.

See also   PV2   Place value to 100.
            N8,9,15,16,20,21   Addition and subtraction.
            N14   Multibase arithmetic.
            N27,35 Directed numbers. Simple operations.
            T6   Minutes and hours.
            T7   Telling the time.
            T11   24 hour clock.

P   *Alpha (new ed.)*   Alpha 1 p13, 14. Alpha 2 p21. Alpha 3 p28.
         Beta (new ed.)   Beta 1 p32-33, 93. Beta 2 p17, 60, 61.
                             Beta 3 p21. Beta 4 p13. Beta 5 p15.
         Basic Mathematics   Book 1 p62. Book 2 p75, 76, 77.
         Hey Mathematics   Mod 2. Book 5 p4, 7, 18, 32.
                              Mod 3. Book 1 p13. Book 2 p36. Book 4 p11, 12.
                              Mod 4. Book 5 p40.
         Key Maths   Level 1. Book 7 p50.
                        Level 2. Book 3 p55-57. Book 5 p109.
         Making Sure of Maths   Book 2 p18. Book 3 p15.
         Mathematics for Schools   Level 2 (2nd ed.) Book 1 p47-51. Book 2 p47-49.
         Nuffield Maths 5-11   2. Worksheets T2 4·5, 4·6.
                                  3. Pupils' Book p92-95.
         Oxford Middle School Mathematics   Book 1 p99.
         Primary Mathematics (SPMG)   Stage 3. Textbook p11-12, 44-47. Card 18, 19.
                                         Stage 4. Textbook p16-17. Card 19, 20.
                                         Stage 5. Textbook p100.

S   *A World of Mathematics*   Book 1 p44.
         Focus Mathematics   Book 1 38-39, 45-46, 90-91.
         Headway Maths   Book 1 p61.
         Inner Ring Maths   Book 1 p6. Book 2 p2.
         Mathematics for Life   Book A2 p20-21, 22-23. Book B1 p26-27.
         Maths Matters   Book 1 p2-3, 12-13, 19.
         On Our Own Two Feet   Book 1 p9, 11, 13-14. Book 3 p17-21.

SM   *Check it Again*   Book 1 p38-39. Book 2 p32-33, 34-36.
                             Book 3 p35-38. Book 4 p47-48.
         Four a Day series   Book 7 p72-74. Book 8 p73-74, 75, 76-77.
                                Book 9 p84, 85. Book 10 p75.
         Problems   Second Problems p2, 55, 58.
                       Third Problems p13, 26.

Books for teachers
         Hey Mathematics   Mod 3. Teachers' Book p40-41.
         Nuffield Maths 5-11   2. Teachers' Handbook p119.
                                  3. Teachers' Handbook p63.

24 hour clock times.

Relating traditional clock times and 12 hour digital clock times to the 24 hour clock e.g. 10 to 6, and 5·50 p.m. as 17·50.

Calculations based on the 24 hour clock e.g. how long is it from 23·30 till 00·10?

Use of time tables based on the 24 hour clock.

See also PV2 Place value to 100.
          N8,9,15,16,20,21 Addition and subtraction.
          N14 Multibase arithmetic.
          N27,35 Directed numbers. Simple operations.
          T6 Minutes and hours.
          T7 Telling the time.
          T10 12 hour digital clock times.

P   *Alpha (new ed.)* Alpha 2 p51-52. Alpha 3 p30. Alpha 4 p17.
     Beta (new ed.) Beta 2 p69. Beta 3 p59-60. Beta 4 p42-43.
                  Beta 5 p15. Beta 6 p8.
     Basic Mathematics Book 3 p21-23.
     Hey Mathematics Mod 3. Book 1 p14, 23. Book 2 p5, 7. Book 4 p37.
                  Mod 5. Book 5 p34-35.
                  Mod 6. Book 1 p9-10. Book 2 p40.
     Key Maths Level 2. Book 3 p57. Book 5 p108, 111.
     Making Sure of Maths Book 3 p15-16. Book 4 p11-13. Book 5 p9-10.
     Mathematics for Schools Level 2 (1st ed.) Book 3 p16-18. Book 5 p7. Book 8 p45. Book 9 p30. Book 10 p43.
     Maths Adventure 2. Pupil's Book p54.
                  3. Pupil's Book p14-15. Activity Book p11, 17.
     Oxford Middle School Mathematics Book 2 p14-15.
     Primary Mathematics (SPMG) Stage 4. Textbook p37-39, 74-77. Card 27, 28, 41, 42.
                  Stage 5. Textbook p20, 117. Card 13, 14.
     Towards Mathematics Core Unit 9 p8, 9. Core Unit 16 p13.
                  Core Unit 19 p1.

S   *A World of Mathematics* Book 2 p49-52.
     Focus Mathematics Book 1 p40-44, 92-93.
     Headway Maths Book 2 p28-29. Book 3 p62.
                  Book 5 p66.
     Impact Maths Pupil's Book 1 p57.
     Inner Ring Maths Book 1 p7.
     Mathematics for Life Book B1 p28-29.
     Maths (Holt) Book 1 p51, 75. Workbook 1 p12.
                  Book 2 p66. Workbook 3 p41.
                  4th Year p69. 4th Year Workbook p31.
                  5th Year Workbook p24, 36.
     Maths Matters Book 2 p6-7. Book 3 p4-5, 28-29.
     Maths You Need p96-97, 98-100.
     On Our Own Two Feet Book 2 p16-17, 18. Book 3 p11-13, 25-26.
                  Book 5 p18-20.
     Understanding Money Book 1 p65-68.

SM *Check it Again* Book 4 p48-49. Book 5 p32-33.
     Four a Day series Book 8 p75. Book 9 p86-87. Book 10 p76.
     Mathematics and Metric Measuring Book 3 p46-47.
     Problems Third Problems p12, 16.

Focus on problems, applications and everyday use of time and standard time units.

Problems involving the four number operations.

The realistic planning of a day, week, etc.

Relating units of time to other units of measurement

    e.g. Unit pricing (See also M8).
           Telephone costs on STD (See also M11).
           Time sheets, time work and wages (See also M12).
           Parking charges.

Public transport costs: duration of trip related to cost(See also AR6). See L10 for distance related to cost of trip.

Temperature measured at regular intervals (See also Temp.)

For regular payments — rent, rates, HP, etc. see M11, 13.

For growth rate — weight related to time, see W8, VR9.

            — height related to time, see L10, VR9.

For speed i.e. distance related to time, see T13.

See also   N8,9,15,16,20,21   Addition and subtraction.
                N14   Multibase arithmetic.
                N17,18,29,30,31,32,33,34   Multiplication and division of whole numbers and decimals.
                N23   Ratio, rate and proportion.
                AR4   Straight line graphs.
                VR6   Flow charts.
                T6   Relationships between standard units. Addition and subtraction.

P   *Basic Mathematics*   Book 3 p28. Book 5 p48.
      Hey Mathematics   Mod 2. Book 3 p11, 18. Book 4 p4, 7.
                        Mod 3. Book 1 p27. Book 3 p32.
      Making Sure of Maths   Book 1 p80. Book 2 p17. Book 3 p15.
      Maths Adventure   2. Pupil's Book p55.
      Oxford Middle School Mathematics   Book 3 p19.
      Towards Mathematics   Core Unit 19 p1.

S   *A World of Mathematics*   Book 6 p46.
      Focus Mathematics   Book 1 p40.
      Headway Maths   Book 2 p14-15.
      Mathematics for Life   Book A1 p20-25. Book B1 p18-19, 20-23.
                             Book C1 p8-11, 28-29, 30-31.
                             Book C3 p16-17.
      Maths (Holt)   5th Year p90.
      Maths Matters   Book 1 p28-29. Book 2 p10.
      Mathsworks   Book 1 p51, 57.

SM   *Problems*   Third Problems   p27-28

T13   Introduction to speed.

Idea of speed as distance related to time.

Measuring and comparing times taken to walk and run a fixed distance.

Constant speed.

   Distance and time plotted graphically (See also AR4).

Discovery and use of formula: $\text{Speed (S)} = \dfrac{\text{Distance (D)}}{\text{Time (T)}}$

Bicycle, car, train, boat and aeroplane speeds.

Journeys involving constant speeds which periodically change

   e.g.   cycling to the station and then travelling by train to London.

   Such journeys plotted graphically.

Idea of average speed.

Petrol consumption of cars at different speeds.

Stopping distances of cars at different speeds taken from The Highway Code (See also AR5).

Large speeds e.g. speed of sound (Concorde). Light years (See also L12).

Knots.

Introduction to the idea of acceleration and deceleration i.e. change in speed per unit of time (See also AR5).

See also   N23   Ratio, rate and proportion.
                N37   Average.
                AR3(1)   Generalisations expressed using 'variables'.
                AR3(2)   Substituting numbers into algebraic expressions.
                AR8   Algebraic solution of simple equations.
                AR9   Gradients of straight line graphs.
                L4,5,6,12   Measurement of distance. Standard metric units.

P *Alpha (new ed.)* Alpha 3 p29, Alpha 4 p14.
   Beta (new ed.) Beta 2 p32. Beta 3 p67. Beta 4 p8, 29, 34.
        Beta 5 p9, 23, 65. Beta 6 p14.
   Basic Mathematics Book 2 p78-79. Book 3 p29-32, 60, 61, 72, 79. Book 4 p55, 56, 68, 69, 70, 71.
        Book 5 p57-60, 82-85.
   Hey Mathematics Mod 2. Book 5 p8-9.
        Mod 3. Book 4 p9. Book 5 p37, 38.
        Mod 4. Book 5 p39.
        Mod 6. Book 3 p46-47.
   Key Maths Level 2. Book 2 p5. Book 5 p47, 48. Book 6 p116-122.
   Making Sure of Maths Book 2 p90. Book 5 p50-51, 78.
   Mathematics for Schools Level 2 (1st ed.) Book 7 p53. Book 8 p46-50, 63. Book 10 p43.
   Maths Adventure 3. Card 9.
        4. Pupil's Book p72-74. Card 7.
        5. Pupil's Book p76.
   Oxford Middle School Mathematics Book 3 p42, 58.
   Primary Mathematics (SPMG) Stage 3. Textbook p50.
        Stage 4. Card 36, 43.
        Stage 5. Textbook p80, 86-88.
   Towards Mathematics Core Unit 14 p15, 16. Core Unit 22 p16.

S *A World of Mathematics* Book 2 p45-46. Book 4 p13. Book 6 p22-25, 47.
   Focus Mathematics Book 8 p27-37.
   Headway Maths Book 3 p63-64. Book 4 p78-79. Book 5 p22-23, 44.
   Maths (Holt) Book 1 p5, 75, 92. Workbook 1 p2-3.
        Book 2 p4-5, 13, 16. Workbook 2 p2, 36.
        Book 3 p89. 4th Year p11, 20-22.
        5th Year p89. 5th Year Workbook p36.
   Mathsworks Book 1 p59-60, 118-119. Tryouts 1 p26, 27, 57, 58. Book 2 p66.
   Maths You Need p101-102, 108.

SM *Check it Again* Book 4 p45-46. Book 5 p44-45.
   Four a Day series Book 8 p80-83. Book 9 p93-94.
        Book 10 p78-80.
   Mathematics and Metric Measuring Book 3 p33-40.
   Problems Third Problems p63.

World time. BST and GMT.   **T14**

World time zones, longitude and latitude and the International Date Line.

See also M10 Planning and costing overseas holidays.
     N27,35 Directed numbers. Simple operations.
     Sh13 Longitude and latitude.
     L12 Distances across the world.

P *Alpha (new ed.)* Alpha 4 p16.
   Beta (new ed.) Beta 4 p13.
   Basic Mathematics Book 5 p81.
   Hey Mathematics Mod 2. Book 3 p31.
   Making Sure of Maths Book 4 p11.
   Towards Mathematics Core Unit 19 p1.

S *A World of Mathematics* Book 4 p42-44.
   Headway Maths Book 5 p70-73.
   Mathematics for Life Book B2 p16-17.
   Maths (Holt) Book 3 p91.

Books for teachers
   Mathematics: from Primary to Secondary p111-114.

Imperial Units.

⌐---**Imp**   Imperial units in common use. Applications.

Temperature.

⌐---**Temp**   Measuring temperature. Applications.

⌐---Topics with a sequence of development extending over considerable time.

Use of imperial units for measuring capacity, volume, area, length and weight.

Imp

Concepts of the imperial units still in common use, and experience measuring in these units.

Relationships between imperial and metric units. Conversion graphs.

Applications and problems involving imperial units.

See also   PV1,3   Number bases. Grouping in 12's, 16's, etc.
           PV2   Counting and ordering numbers to 100.
           N14   Multibase arithmetic.
           AR4   Conversion graphs.
           See Temp. for Fahrenheit and Celsius temperatures, and CV, A, L and W sections.

P   *Hey Mathematics*   Mod 6. Book 4 p40.

S   *Focus Mathematics*   Book 3 p52-58.
      Maths (Holt)   Book 1 p42. 5th Year p68.

SM   *Mathematics and Metric Measuring*   Book 1 p47.
      Problems   Third Problems p64, 65.

Measurement of temperature.

Temp

Measuring and recording temperatures in degrees Celsius using different kinds of thermometers. Temperatures above and below zero.

Recording temperatures at regular intervals. Temperature charts.

Knowledge of the range of room, outdoor and body temperatures, the range of air temperatures around the world, boiling and freezing points of water and the temperatures of ice.

Average temperature.

Problems and everyday applications: central heating thermostats, cost-effectiveness of fuel, cooking temperatures, fridge and deep-freeze temperatures, etc.

The relationship between degrees Celsius and Fahrenheit. Conversion graphs.

See also   PV2,4   Counting and ordering to 100 and above.
           N15,16   Addition and subtraction to 100. Use of 100 number line.
           N23   Ratio, rate and proportion.
           N27,35   Directed numbers. Simple operations.
           N37   Average.
           AR4   Conversion and other straight line graphs.
           AR7   Graphs with directed numbers.
           VR8   Reading the scales on measuring instruments.
           VR9   Line graphs for continuous data.
           L3(2)   Arbitrary units (in mercury thermometer, length represents temperature).
           T12   Temperature related to time.

P   *Alpha (new ed.)*   Alpha 2 p23. Alpha 3 p34-35. Alpha 4 p12.
      Beta (new ed.)   Beta 3 p79-80. Beta 4 p55. Beta 5 p13.
      Basic Mathematics   Book 3 p26-27.
      Hey Mathematics   Mod 5. Book 1 p7-12. Book 5 p8-9.
      Key Maths   Level 2 Book 1 p62. Book 5 p101-103.
      Mathematics for Schools   Level 2 (1st ed.) Book 8 p1.
      Maths Adventure   3. Pupil's Book p65, 78.

S   *Headway Maths*   Book 2 p78.
      Inner Ring Maths   Book 1 p31.
      Maths (Holt)   Book 1 p53. Workbook 1 p44. Book 2 p35.
                     Workbook 3 p17.
      Mathsworks   Book 1 p88. Book 2 p38. Tryouts 2 p18.
      Maths You Need   p119-120.

SM   *Check it Again*   Book 5 p36.
      Problems   Third Problems p43, 49-51.

Books for teachers
      Hey Mathematics   Mod 3. Teachers' Book p38-39.

Appendix I

Why teach mathematics?

The following are aims given by various educationalists. Several of these aims are interdependent. There is no suggested order of priority.

I **Utilitarian aims** i.e. those with a direct and obvious external reference.

1. To equip the child to cope with the mathematical demands of everyday life.
   (a) 'Survival skills'. These refer to a minimum level of mathematical competence necessary in our society.
   (b) More diverse skills, increasing the options — relating to leisure, buying a house, etc.
   (c) To create a buffer of objectivity so that the individual is better able to resist manipulation and insensitive planning.
2. To provide the 'tool skills' for other learning (e.g. craft, science, engineering, history, geography, business studies) and for future employment (e.g. a nurse will need to use capacity measures for medicines).
3. To provide the skills necessary for qualifying tests and examinations as a gateway to further education and/or employment.
4. To equip the child to understand and communicate quantifiable ideas.

II **More generalised aims.**

5. To develop the mind. To establish and practise disciplined thought and flexible reasoning.
6. To develop an awareness of the basic structure of mathematics, an appreciation of mathematical pattern and the ability to identify relationships.
7. To encourage an awareness of the part mathematics has played in man's control over his environment.
8. To encourage system, care and perseverance as work habits.
9. To maintain and encourage curiosity. The sustaining of the wish to learn is considered by many educationalists to be implicit in the concept of education.
10. Affective aims
    (a) To provide a source of aesthetic and creative pleasure.
    (b) To encourage a positive attitude towards, and confidence in, mathematics.

Appendix II

Mathematical concepts, skills and facts. Why are concepts so important?

What is a mathematical concept?
It is an all-round understanding of a mathematical notion or process.

Concepts vary in kind and complexity and may be acquired to a greater or lesser degree. They are usually developed by concrete experience of an idea alongside relevant vocabulary in a wide range of different situations. Precision in assessment of the extent to which a concept has been acquired is difficult because of its abstract nature, and we have to rely on evidence from behaviour in different situations.

Mathematical skills and facts.
A *skill* is the practical ability to perform a task. It is learned, depends on memory and may involve concepts to a greater or lesser extent. Thus a child may have the skill necessary to perform the multiplication operation 3×4, and this skill may or may not involve a full grasp of the concepts 3, 4 or of multiplication. Many animals are capable of learning skills but they are not thought to acquire concepts. The acquisition of a skill can be more easily assessed than a concept as it is behavioural, though assessment of the extent to which it is conceptually based and has been generalised is more difficult.

A mathematical *fact* is an item of assumed mathematical truth. Thus in the example above, $3 \times 4 = 12$ is a fact and the ability to find the correct answer a skill. A fact can be learned, may involve memory alone — as with a parrot — or be based on a skill and/or understanding of the concepts involved. Facts, if known, can be obtained by recall, and therefore knowledge of facts can be fairly easily assessed.

Skills and facts that are not based on a grasp of underlying concepts are limited in use to the situations in which they were learned. Most of the aims listed in Appendix I imply a conceptual approach to learning, as skills and facts lacking a conceptual foundation cannot be readily applied in varied contexts, whether to real-life applications or such mathematical extensions as the identification of patterns and relationships.

A child with a conceptually based skill will still need further practice applying it in varied situations — e.g. problems and applications — so that it is generalised and can be confidently applied in future. The developmental relationship between the acquisition of concepts, the learning and generalisation of skills and the learning of facts can be represented thus —

Concepts acquired ⟶

Skills learned and generalised ⟶

facts learned ⟶

Readers will reach their own conclusions from the following extract from The Assessment of Performance Unit's survey of 11 year old children.

'One subtraction item . . . gave a car mileometer reading at the beginning and end of a holiday and asked for the distance driven to be calculated. The before and after numbers of miles were displayed as shown here.

| 0 | 0 | 9 | 7 | 5 | miles |

| 0 | 1 | 1 | 2 | 5 | miles |

The results of the computations of the whole numbers sub-category would have suggested a facility of around 50 per cent with these sizes of numbers, but the item obtained a facility of around 35 per cent, perhaps due to the unusual form of display with the smaller number at the top' (APU, 1980a). (The facility value refers to the percentage of those presented with the item who answered it correctly.)

Appendix III

Worth Considering? Looking more analytically at new schemes and books by Norman Cawley.

A *Fitting the teacher and the school.*

1. Are the author's priorities reasonably in line with your own: i.e. the balance between social survival, basic mathematical skills, and activities that inform, stimulate or extend?

2. Alternatively, does it fit an existing gap, adding to some aspect of your scheme that is not well covered at present?

3. Is it essentially a topic book to be used to support a scheme?

4. Does the scheme work as part of the overall curriculum of the school? For example, if you are considering a remedial series, would success with it help a pupil towards coping with the mainstream requirements? It may well be that the school uses a general scheme, which you believe does not have enough to offer for your withdrawal group as a long term direction. If so, you can decide, consciously, not to direct your work towards a return to such work. What you have to accept and face is that this may turn a temporary retardation into a permanent separation for particular children.

5. How does it fit your beliefs about how children learn most effectively? If you believe in 'learning by doing', say, does the scheme give plenty of opportunity for practical activity? If you are committed to pupils working individually, do the planning and pattern of the exercises provide for this, without a lot of need for explanatory 'chalk and talk'?

6. Is it well structured, with a coherent development? Do the activities at a later stage depend on what has been covered earlier? Are the early activities based on realistic assumptions about your usual intake? Does the planning 'spiral', i.e. return to early topics in order to consolidate, generalise and extend them?

7. Is there a good balance, in your eyes, between the 'pure' work, with numbers and symbols, and the 'applied', the social and other contexts in which they are used? Are the links between the two made evident for pupils?

8. If you intend to use the books as your basic scheme, are there sufficient practice examples and a good coverage of the major significant areas? If not, what will you use to supplement it?

9. Does the scheme fit in with the way you, and your school, operate? If the books suggest a lot of open-ended investigations, everyone is going to get very frustrated if you are tied to a tight timetable of if you do not have ready access to apparatus. This may be the reason why some of the primary schools use the 'Fletcher' scheme but ignore the Resource Books' suggestions for exploratory activity and merely have pupils working steadfastly through pupils' books which are only intended to check and supplement.

10. Are they durable and, particularly with work cards, well organised and practical?

11. Is there adequate support for the non-specialist teacher? Is there a manual which gives plenty of additional suggestions? Does the manual square with your view of the teacher's role; equipment organiser, guide, occasional reference point, diagnostician, etc? Are the links between the manual and the stages of the scheme clear and evident or is it just a vague spread of semi-philosophical rambling?

12. How much will the new approach cost, taking into account your class size, any necessary supplementary material and apparatus?

(1) This is a revised version of the original article, published by Inner London Education Authority in *Struggle; mathematics for low attainers* Vol. 2 Winter 79/80. It is reproduced here with the permission of the author and the ILEA.

B *Fitting the pupils.*

1. Are the books right for the general developmental level of the majority? Are they for example dependent on you for explanations and the next step simply because most of your pupils are 'concrete operational'?

2. Have they been designed to promote and support a positive attitude? When they are introducing new topics and concepts are they staged to give the maximum opportunity for initial success?

3. Is there leeway for your full ability range? Is there enough material to reinforce the learning, sufficiently carefully staged for even the least able or least secure? Are there applications relevant to all your pupils? Are there also suggestions for open ended exploration?

4. Are the activities related to the interests and eventual needs of most of the pupils? Are the things you think they ought to know clearly connected with the things they feel they want to know?

5. Do the books look lively and inviting? This has to be done without going over the top so that it is still clear what the pupil has to do.

6. Does the scheme ring the changes in what the pupils are required to do? Maths lessons will keep that much more momentum if there is plenty of variety in the kind of question and the kind of answer that is expected.

7. Are there always 'right' answers, or is there some encouragement of divergent thinking? Maths, we believe, should be creative and enjoyable, even if it does make marking a problem sometimes.

8. Is the maths spread across the curriculum and are links made with other subjects? This might involve you in using support materials that are not maths books at all, such as *Science 5-13* series, published by Macdonald.

9. Does the scheme develop a basic mathematical vocabulary? Are both the reading and the mathematical levels appropriate to the majority of the pupils? Sometimes books go the other way and become infantile, patronising or confusing. It's clearly a fine balance.

10. How much will pupils learn from using the scheme and how much will they merely be occupied? It may be helping them if they can prove they can do the sums, but not all the time.

11. Are there any assessments or checks suggested at different stages? That not only helps you to keep track of how pupils are learning or failing, but it is a valuable way of 'keying in' newcomers to your group, at something like their appropriate level.

12. Are the author's ideas practical, in classroom terms, for the age group or ability level you are teaching? This is particularly relevant when you are considering work cards or schemes linked with apparatus. The best test is to try out representative pages or particular specimen cards at the inspection copy stage.

In the end, there never is a perfect scheme, only an uneasy set of compromises. These, perhaps, are less likely to matter if you are consciously aware of them at the time of purchase. At least, such awareness gives you a chance to redress the balance at a later stage.

Appendix IV

Assessment of understanding of Place Value to 100 (PV2).

This is offered as an example of a group criterion referenced test that could be devised by a teacher. See page 9.

This example obviously assumes a level of reading proficiency; if children have reading difficulties parts could be read out by the teacher but not of course the numerals.

1. What number is one more than
    - 17?
    - 19?
    - 34?
    - 59?
    - 90?

2. What number is one less than
    - 14?
    - 20?
    - 48?
    - 71?
    - 90?

3. Another way of writing 42 is ☐ tens and ☐ units.

4. Put a ring round the largest number.
    34, 43, 19, 28

5. Write the numeral for eighteen
    forty three
    eighty one

6. Round off these numbers to the nearest 10. The first one has been done for you.

    28 ⟶ 30
    42 ⟶
    64 ⟶
    88 ⟶

7. Harry had 52 sweets. He gave away 10. How many did he have left?

8. Which of the following does not show another way of writing 75?
    70 + 5
    50 + 25
    50 + 17
    65 + 10

Appendix V

List of Referenced Materials

For full details see publisher's catalogue.
For publisher's address see list of publishers.
For precise explanation of groupings **P**, **S** and **SM** see page 7.

P (Primary)

Ready for Alpha and Beta (new ed.)	T. R. Goddard	
Alpha 1-4 (new ed.)	J. W. Adams	
Beta 1-4 (new ed.)	R. P. Beaumont	Schofield and Sims
Beta 5 (new ed.)	B. Clayton, K. A. Oakley, Ed. T. R. Goddard	
Beta 6 (new ed.)	B. Clayton, Ed. T. R. Goddard	
Basic Mathematics Books 1-5	A. L. Griffiths	Oliver and Boyd
Come and Count Books 1-6	M. E. Williams	Macmillan
Come and Measure Length, Time, Capacity, Mass	M. E. Williams	Macmillan
Hey Mathematics Modules 1-6. Books 1-5 in each module	Ed. J. Boucher	Holt, Rinehart and Winston (formerley published by Caffrey Smith)
Key Maths Level 1. Books 1-7 Level 2. Books 1-6	A. L. Griffiths	Oliver and Boyd
Making Sure of Maths Pink, Green, Yellow, Blue Books Introductory Book Books 1-6	C. D. Cormack, I. F. Fraser T. F. Watson and T. A. Quinn	Holmes McDougall
Mathematics for Schools Level 1 (2nd ed.) Books 1-7 Level 2 (2nd ed.) Books 1-2 Level 2 (1st ed.) Books 3-10 (some omissions in later books)	H. Fletcher et al.	Addison-Wesley
Maths Adventure Kites 1-7 1-5. Pupil's Books, Activity Books, Cards	J. Stanfield	Evans
Nuffield Maths 5-11 Bronto Books: Sets A,B,C,D 1. Worksheets 2. Worksheets 3. Pupils' Book	Gen. ed. E. A. Albany	Longman
Numbers and Words Books 1-8	A. Duncan	Ward Lock
Our First School Maths Books 1-6	C. Edwards, D. Newton, D. Smith	Collins
Oxford Middle School Mathematics Books 1-4	D. Paling, J. Hiscocks, W. Nickels	Oxford University Press
Primary Mathematics Stages 1-2. Workbooks. Cards. Stages 3-5. Textbooks. Workbooks. Cards.	Scottish Primary Mathematics Group.	Heinemann
Towards Mathematics Core Units 1-25	D. Sturgess, J. Glenn	Schofield and Sims

S (Secondary)

A World of Mathematics Books 1-6	G. Marshall	Nelson
Focus Mathematics Books 1-10 (omissions in later books)	S. W. Burton, A. C. Nicholls	Pergamon
Headway Maths Books 1-5	R. Hollands, H. Moses	Hart-Davis
Impact Maths Pupil's Book 1 (9 years upwards)	J. Stanfield, J. Cwirko-Godycki	Evans
Inner Ring Maths Books 1-3	M. Holt	Benn
Mathematics for Life Books A1-3, B1-3, C1-3	N. Moore, A. Williams	Oxford University Press
Maths 1-3. Workbooks 1-3 4th Year. 4th Year Workbook 5th Year. 5th Year Workbook	M. Holt	Macmillan
Maths Matters Books 1-3	J. Chester, E. Harper, G. Price.	Addison-Wesley
Mathsworks Books 1-2 Tryouts 1-2	M. Holt, A. Rothery	Longman
Maths You Need	A. Ferguson	Nelson
On Our Own Two Feet Books 1-5	M. Thomas	Heinemann
Understanding Money Books 1-2	P. Connah	Macmillan

SM (Support Material)

Blackie's Practice Workbooks Books 1-5	G. Pemberton	Blackie
Check it Again Books 1-5	J. Hulbert, W. Wiles	Heinemann
Four a Day series (metric ed.) Books 4-10	A. L. Griffiths	Oliver and Boyd
Mathematics and Metric Measuring Books 1-6	P. W. Cordin	Macmillan
Number Workbook Addition, Subtraction, Multiplication, Division, Decimals, Fractions.	J. G. Saunders	Nelson
Problems (decimal and metric ed.) First, Second and Third Problems	K. A. Hesse	Longman

Books for teachers

Early Mathematical Experiences
Water. Raw Materials
Towards Number. Apparatus, Toys
  and Games
The Passage of Time. Rhymes and
  Stories
Home Corner. The Family
Outdoor Activities.
  The Environment
Space and Shape. Comparisons
	Schools Council (1978)	Addison-Wesley

Hey Mathematics Teacher's Book. Module 3	J. Boucher (1978)	Holt, Rinehart and Winston (formerly published by Caffrey Smith)
Mathematics: the first 3 years	Nuffield/British Council (1970)	
Mathematics: the later Primary years	Nuffield/British Council (1972)	Chambers, Murray, Wiley
Mathematics: from Primary to *Secondary*	Nuffield/British Council (1978)	
Nuffield Maths 5-11		Longman
1. Teachers' Handbook	W. Moore (1979)	
2. Teachers' Handbook	M. Williams, W. Moore (1979)	
3. Teachers' Handbook	P. Latham, P. Truelove (1980)	

Appendix VI
Record Sheets

A format for detailed record sheet of child's experiences and attainments.

Summary chart of a child's mathematical attainments.*

Class mathematics record sheets:

       5-8 years. *

       8-12 years. Sections I* and II.*

*Additional copies of these record sheets may be obtained from
NARE Publications, NARE Central Office, 2 Lichfield Road, Stafford ST17 4JX.

A format for detailed record sheet of child's experiences and attainments.

TIME		Learning experiences incl. detailed reference to any published materials used.		Outcome: attainment , specific difficulties, general comments. (√if succeded with minimum help.)
		Date		
T1	Early concepts/vocab. associated with ordering events in time and continuity.			
				Date of mastery:
T2	Ordering by duration.			
				Date of mastery:
T3	Use of arbitrary units to measure duration. The need for standard units.			
				Date of mastery:
T4	Observing the clock. Special times and o'clock times.			
				Date of mastery:
T5	Seconds, minutes and hours.			
				Date of mastery:
T6	Days and months.			
				Date of mastery:

etc.

© Joanna Turnbull 1981

SUMMARY CHART OF A CHILD'S MATHEMATICAL ATTAINMENTS

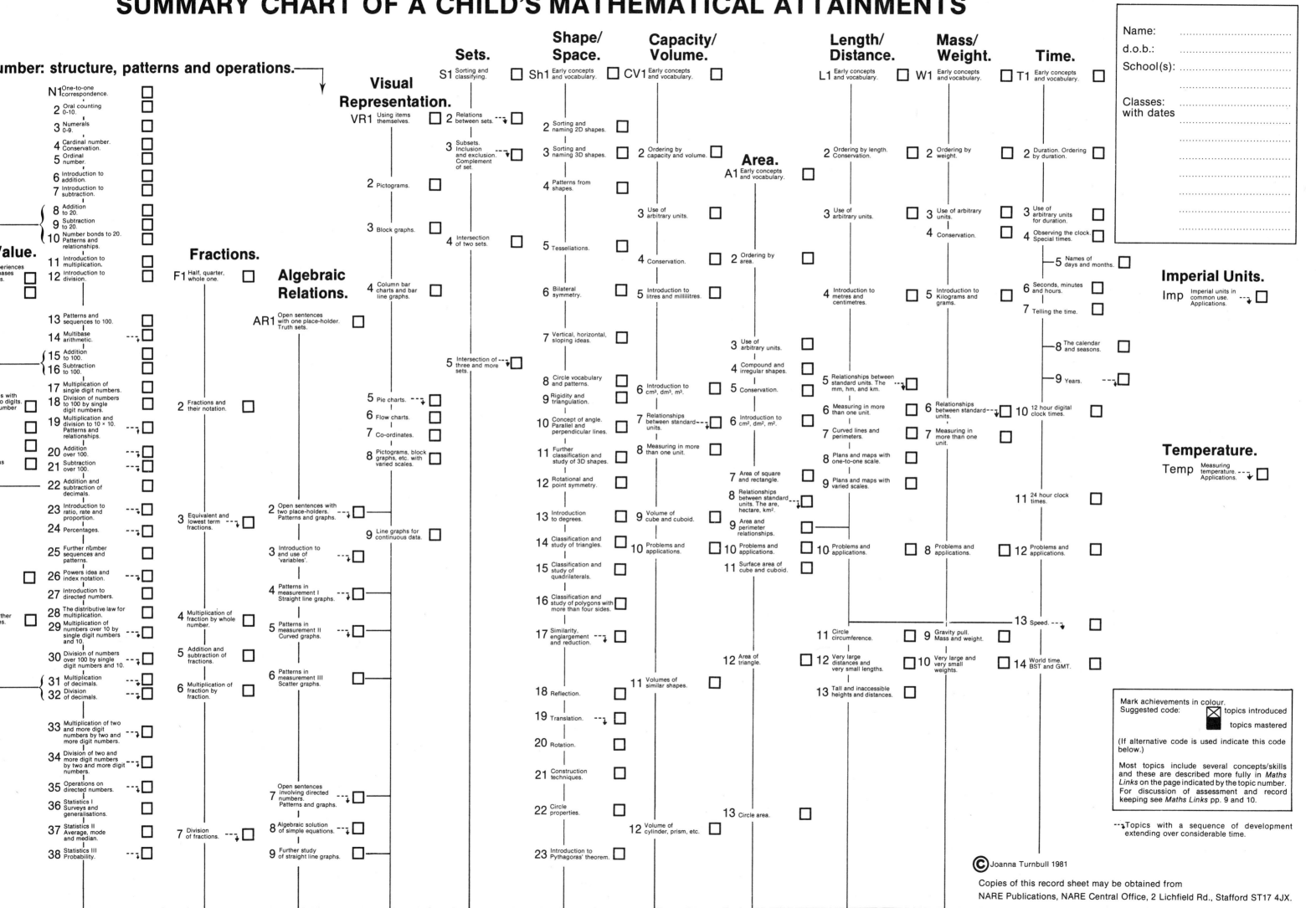

Number: structure, patterns and operations.

- N1 One-to-one correspondence.
- 2 Oral counting 0-10.
- 3 Numerals 0-9.
- 4 Cardinal number. Conservation.
- 5 Ordinal number.
- 6 Introduction to addition.
- 7 Introduction to subtraction.
- 8 Addition to 20.
- 9 Subtraction to 20.
- 10 Number bonds to 20. Patterns and relationships.
- 11 Introduction to multiplication.
- 12 Introduction to division.
- 13 Patterns and sequences to 100.
- 14 Multibase arithmetic.
- 15 Addition to 100.
- 16 Subtraction to 100.
- 17 Multiplication of single digit numbers.
- 18 Division of numbers to 100 by single digit numbers.
- 19 Multiplication and division to 10 × 10. Patterns and relationships.
- 20 Addition over 100.
- 21 Subtraction over 100.
- 22 Addition and subtraction of decimals.
- 23 Introduction to ratio, rate and proportion.
- 24 Percentages.
- 25 Further number sequences and patterns.
- 26 Powers idea and index notation.
- 27 Introduction to directed numbers.
- 28 The distributive law for multiplication.
- 29 Multiplication of numbers over 10 by single digit numbers and 10.
- 30 Division of numbers over 100 by single digit numbers and 10.
- 31 Multiplication of decimals.
- 32 Division of decimals.
- 33 Multiplication of two and more digit numbers by two and more digit numbers.
- 34 Division of two and more digit numbers by two and more digit numbers.
- 35 Operations on directed numbers.
- 36 Statistics I Surveys and generalisations.
- 37 Statistics II Average, mode and median.
- 38 Statistics III Probability.

Value.
(experiences/ases...)
(with... digits. number...)
(... ther ...s.)

Fractions.

- F1 Half, quarter, whole one.
- 2 Fractions and their notation.
- 3 Equivalent and lowest term fractions.
- 4 Multiplication of fraction by whole number.
- 5 Addition and subtraction of fractions.
- 6 Multiplication of fraction by fraction.
- 7 Division of fractions.

Algebraic Relations.

- AR1 Open sentences with one place-holder. Truth sets.
- 2 Open sentences with two place-holders. Patterns and graphs.
- 3 Introduction to and use of 'variables'.
- 4 Patterns in measurement I Straight line graphs.
- 5 Patterns in measurement II Curved graphs.
- 6 Patterns in measurement III Scatter graphs.
- 7 Open sentences involving directed numbers. Patterns and graphs.
- 8 Algebraic solution of simple equations.
- 9 Further study of straight line graphs.

Visual Representation.

- VR1 Using items themselves.
- 2 Pictograms.
- 3 Block graphs.
- 4 Column bar charts and bar line graphs.
- 5 Pie charts.
- 6 Flow charts.
- 7 Co-ordinates.
- 8 Pictograms, block graphs, etc. with varied scales.
- 9 Line graphs for continuous data.

Sets.

- S1 Sorting and classifying.
- 2 Relations between sets.
- 3 Subsets. Inclusion and exclusion. Complement of set.
- 4 Intersection of two sets.
- 5 Intersection of three and more sets.

Shape/Space.

- Sh1 Early concepts and vocabulary.
- 2 Sorting and naming 2D shapes.
- 3 Sorting and naming 3D shapes.
- 4 Patterns from shapes.
- 5 Tessellations.
- 6 Bilateral symmetry.
- 7 Vertical, horizontal, sloping ideas.
- 8 Circle vocabulary and patterns.
- 9 Rigidity and triangulation.
- 10 Concept of angle. Parallel and perpendicular lines.
- 11 Further classification and study of 3D shapes.
- 12 Rotational and point symmetry.
- 13 Introduction to degrees.
- 14 Classification and study of triangles.
- 15 Classification and study of quadrilaterals.
- 16 Classification and study of polygons with more than four sides.
- 17 Similarity, enlargement and reduction.
- 18 Reflection.
- 19 Translation.
- 20 Rotation.
- 21 Construction techniques.
- 22 Circle properties.
- 23 Introduction to Pythagoras' theorem.

Capacity/Volume.

- CV1 Early concepts and vocabulary.
- 2 Ordering by capacity and volume.
- 3 Use of arbitrary units.
- 4 Conservation.
- 5 Introduction to litres and millilitres.
- 6 Introduction to cm³, dm³, m³.
- 7 Relationships between standard units.
- 8 Measuring in more than one unit.
- 9 Volume of cube and cuboid.
- 10 Problems and applications.
- 11 Volumes of similar shapes.
- 12 Volume of cylinder, prism, etc.

Area.

- A1 Early concepts and vocabulary.
- 2 Ordering by area.
- 3 Use of arbitrary units.
- 4 Compound and irregular shapes.
- 5 Conservation.
- 6 Introduction to cm², dm², m².
- 7 Area of square and rectangle.
- 8 Relationships between standard units. The are, hectare, km².
- 9 Area and perimeter relationships.
- 10 Problems and applications.
- 11 Surface area of cube and cuboid.

Length/Distance.

- L1 Early concepts and vocabulary.
- 2 Ordering by length. Conservation.
- 3 Use of arbitrary units.
- 4 Introduction to metres and centimetres.
- 5 Relationships between standard units. The mm, hm, and km.
- 6 Measuring in more than one unit.
- 7 Curved lines and perimeters.
- 8 Plans and maps with one-to-one scale.
- 9 Plans and maps with varied scales.
- 10 Problems and applications.
- 11 Circle circumference.
- 12 Very large distances and very small lengths.
- 13 Tall and inaccessible heights and distances.

Mass/Weight.

- W1 Early concepts and vocabulary.
- 2 Ordering by weight.
- 3 Use of arbitrary units.
- 4 Conservation.
- 5 Introduction to Kilograms and grams.
- 6 Relationships between standard units.
- 7 Measuring in more than one unit.
- 8 Problems and applications.
- 9 Gravity pull. Mass and weight.
- 10 Very large and very small weights.

Time.

- T1 Early concepts and vocabulary.
- 2 Duration. Ordering by duration.
- 3 Use of arbitrary units for duration.
- 4 Observing the clock. Special times.
- 5 Names of days and months.
- 6 Seconds, minutes and hours.
- 7 Telling the time.
- 8 The calendar and seasons.
- 9 Years.
- 10 12 hour digital clock times.
- 11 24 hour clock times.
- 12 Problems and applications.
- 13 Speed.
- 14 World time. BST and GMT.

Imperial Units.

- Imp Imperial units in common use. Applications.

Temperature.

- Temp Measuring temperature. Applications.

Name: ....

d.o.b.: ....

School(s): ....

Classes: with dates

Mark achievements in colour.
Suggested code: ⊠ topics introduced
☐ topics mastered

(If alternative code is used indicate this code below.)

Most topics include several concepts/skills and these are described more fully in *Maths Links* on the page indicated by the topic number. For discussion of assessment and record keeping see *Maths Links* pp. 9 and 10.

--- Topics with a sequence of development extending over considerable time.

© Joanna Turnbull 1981

Copies of this record sheet may be obtained from
NARE Publications, NARE Central Office, 2 Lichfield Rd., Stafford ST17 4JX.

CLASS MATHEMATICS RECORD SHEET : 5 — 8 YEARS.

GENERAL NUMBER/OPERATIONS	Fractions	Algebraic Relations	VISUAL REPRESENTATION	SETS	SHAPE/SPACE	CAPACITY/VOLUME	AREA	LENGTH/DISTANCE	MASS/WEIGHT	TIME	

GENERAL NUMBER/OPERATIONS
- 3 Numerals 0 – 9.
- 4 Cardinal number. Conservation.
- 5 Ordinal number.
- 6/8 7/9 Addition to 20.
- Subtraction to 20.
- 10 Number bonds to 20. Patterns and relationships.
- 11 Introduction to multiplication.
- 12 Introduction to division.
- 13 Patterns and sequences to 100.
- (14) Introduction to multibase arithmetic.
- 15 Addition to 100.
- 16 Subtraction to 100.
- 17 Multiplication of single digit numbers.
- 18 Division of numbers to 100 by single digit numbers.
- (19) Multiplication and division to 10x10. Patterns and relationships.

Fractions (F)
- 1 Half, quarter, whole one.
- 2 Fractions and their notation.

Algebraic Relations (AR)
- 1 Open sentences with place-holder. Truth sets.

VISUAL REPRESENTATION (VR)
- 1 Using items themselves.
- 2 Pictograms.
- 3 Block graphs.
- 4 Column bar charts and bar line graphs.
- (5) Introduction to pie charts.
- 6 Flow charts.
- 7 Co-ordinates.
- 8 Pictograms, block graphs, etc. with varied scales.

SETS (S)
- 1 Sorting and classifying.
- 2 Relations between sets.
- 3 Subsets. Inclusion and exclusion. Complement of set.
- 4 Intersection of two sets.

SHAPE/SPACE (Sh)
- 1 Early concepts and vocabulary.
- 2 Sorting and naming 2D shapes.
- 3 Sorting and naming 3D shapes.
- 4 Patterns from shapes.
- 5 Tessellations.
- 6 Bilateral symmetry.
- 7 Vertical, horizontal, sloping ideas.
- 8 Circle vocabulary and patterns.
- 9 Rigidity and triangulation.

CAPACITY/VOLUME (CV)
- 1 Early concepts and vocabulary.
- 2 Ordering by capacity and volume.
- 3 Use of arbitrary units.
- 4 Conservation.
- 5 Introduction to litres and millilitres.
- 6 Introduction to cm³, dm³, m³.
- (7) Relationships between standard units.

AREA (A)
- 1 Early concepts and vocabulary.
- 2 Ordering by area.
- 3 Use of arbitrary units.
- 4 Compound and irregular shapes.
- 5 Conservation.
- 6 Introduction to cm², dm², m².

LENGTH/DISTANCE (L)
- 1 Early concepts and vocabulary.
- 2 Ordering by length. Conservation.
- 3 Use of arbitrary units.
- 4 Introduction to metres and centimetres.
- (5) Relationships between standard units. The mm, cm, m and km.
- 6 Measuring in more than one unit.
- 7 Curved lines and perimeters.

MASS/WEIGHT (W)
- 1 Early concepts and vocabulary.
- 2 Ordering by weight.
- 3 Use of arbitrary units.
- 4 Conservation.
- 5 Introduction to kilograms and grams.
- (6) Relationships between standard units.

TIME (T)
- 1 Early concepts and vocabulary.
- 2 Duration. Ordering by duration.
- 3 Use of arbitrary units for duration.
- 4 Observing the clock. Special times.
- 5 Names of days and months.
- 6 Seconds, minutes and hours.
- 7 Telling the time.
- 8 The calendar and seasons.
- (9) Years.
- 10 12 hour digital clock times.

NAME

Mark achievements in colour.

Suggested Code: ⊠ topics introduced. ■ topics mastered.

Most topics include several concepts/skills and these are described more fully in *Maths Links* on the page indicated by the topic number. Ringed numbers denote topics which are unlikely to be mastered at this stage. For discussion of assessment and record-keeping see *Maths Links* pages 9 and 10.

..d, Stafford ST17 4JX.

CLASS MATHEMATICS RECORD SHEET : 8 — 12 YEARS. SECTION I

| PLACE VALUE | GENERAL NUMBER/OPERATIONS | FRACTIONS | ALGEBRAIC RELATIONS | VISUAL REPRESENTATION | SETS | |

PLACE VALUE (PV)
1. Grouping experiences. Number bases with two digits.
2. Place value to 100.
3. Number bases with more than two digits. Alternative number systems.
4. Place value to 1000.
5. Tenths as decimals.
6. Hundredths as decimals.
7. Thousands, millions, etc.
8. Third and further decimal places.

GENERAL NUMBER/OPERATIONS (N)
1. One-to-one correspondence. Rational counting 0 – 10.
2/3. Numerals 0 – 9.
4. Cardinal number. Conservation.
5. Ordinal number.
6/8, 7/9. Addition to 20.
10. Subtraction to 20.
11. Number bonds to 20. Patterns and relationships.
12. Introduction to multiplication.
13. Introduction to division.
14. Patterns and sequences to 100.
15. Multibase arithmetic.
16. Addition to 100.
17. Subtraction to 100.
18. Multiplication of single digit numbers.
19(1). Division of two digit numbers by single digit numbers.
19(2). Division as the inverse of multiplication.
19(3). Commutativity and associativity.
20. Patterns.
21. Addition over 100.
22. Subtraction over 100.
23. Addition and subtraction of decimals.
24. Introduction to ratio, rate and proportion.
25. Percentages.
26. Further number sequences and patterns.
27. Powers idea and index notation.
28. Introduction to directed numbers.
29. The distributive law for multiplication.
30. Multiplication of numbers over 10 by single digit numbers and 10.
31. Division of numbers over 100 by single digit numbers and 10.
32. Multiplication of decimals.
33. Division of decimals.
34. Multiplication of two and more digit numbers by two and more digit numbers.
35. Division of two and more digit numbers by two and more digit numbers.
36. Operations on directed numbers.
37. Statistics I. Surveys and generalisations.
38. Statistics II. Average, mode and median. Statistics III. Probability.

FRACTIONS (F)
1. Half, quarter, whole one.
2. Fractions and their notation.
3. Equivalent and lowest term fractions.
4. Multiplication of fractions by whole number.
5. Addition and subtraction of fractions.
6. Multiplication of fractions.
7. Division of fractions.

ALGEBRAIC RELATIONS (AR)
1. Open sentences with one place-holder. Truth sets.
2. Open sentences with two place-holders. Patterns and graphs.
3(1). Introduction to and use of variables. Forming algebraic expressions.
3(2). Substituting numbers in algebraic expressions.
3(3). Simplification of algebraic expressions.
4. Patterns in measurement I. Straight line graphs.
5. Patterns in measurement II. Curved graphs.
6. Patterns in measurement III. Scatter graphs.
7. Open sentences involving directed numbers. Patterns and graphs.
8. Algebraic solution of simple equations.
9. Further study of straight line graphs.

VISUAL REPRESENTATION (VR)
1/2. Using items themselves. Pictograms.
3. Block graphs.
4. Column bar charts and bar line graphs.
5. Pie charts.
6. Flow charts.
7. Co-ordinates.
8. Pictograms, block graphs, etc., with varied scales.
9. Line graphs for continuous data.

SETS (S)
1. Sorting and classifying.
2. Relations between sets.
3. Subsets. Inclusion and exclusion. Complement of set.
4. Intersection of two sets.
5. Intersection of three and more sets.

NAME

Mark achievements in colour.

Suggested code: ⊠ topics introduced.
◼ topics mastered.

Most topics include several concepts/skills and these are described more fully in *Maths Links* on the page indicated by the topic number.
For discussion of assessment and record-keeping see *Maths Links* pages 9 and 10.

ad, Stafford ST17 4JX.

CLASS MATHEMATICS RECORD SHEET : 8 — 12 YEARS. SECTION II

SHAPE/SPACE														CAPACITY/VOLUME												AREA													LENGTH/DISTANCE														MASS/WEIGHT										TIME															IMPERIAL UNITS in common use	TEMPER-ATURE		NAME
Concept of angle. Parallel and perpendicular lines.	Further classification and study of 3D shapes.	Rotational and point symmetry.	Introduction to degrees.	Classification and study of triangles.	Classification and study of quadrilaterals.	Classification and study of polygons with more than four sides.	Similarity, enlargement and reduction.	Reflection.	Translation.	Rotation.	Construction techniques.	Circle properties.	Introduction to Pythagoras' theorem.	Early concepts/vocabulary. Ordering by capacity and volume.	Use of arbitrary units.	Conservation.	Introduction to litres and millilitres.	Introduction to cm³, dm³, m³.	Relationships between standard units.	Measuring in more than one unit.	Volume of cube and cuboid.	Problems and applications.	Volume of similar shapes.	Volume of cylinder, prism, etc.	Early concepts/vocabulary. Ordering by area.	Use of arbitrary units.	Compound and irregular shapes.	Conservation.	Introduction to cm², dm², m².	Area of square and rectangle.	Relationships between standard units. The are, hectare, km².	Area and perimeter relationships.	Problems and applications.	Surface area of cube and cuboid.	Area of triangle.	Circle area.	Early concepts/vocabulary. Ordering by length. Conservation.	Use of arbitrary units.	Introduction to metres and centimetres.	Relationships between standard units. The mm, hm and km.	Measuring in more than one unit.	Curved lines and perimeters.	Plans and maps with one-to-one scale.	Plans and maps with varied scales.	Problems and applications.	Circle circumference.	Very large distances and very small lengths.	Tall and inaccessible heights and distances.	Early concepts/vocabulary. Ordering by weight.	Use of arbitrary units.	Conservation.	Introduction to kilograms and grams.	Relationships between standard units.	Measuring in more than one unit.	Problems and applications.	Gravity pull. Mass and weight.	Very large and very small weights.	Early concepts/vocabulary. Ordering by duration.	Use of arbitrary units for duration.	Observing the clock.	Names of days and months.	Seconds, minutes and hours.	Telling the time.	The calendar and seasons.	Years.	12 hour digital clock times.	24 hour clock times.	Problems and applications.	Speed.	World time. BST and GMT.	Measuring using standard units. Relationships between units.	Problems and applications.	Measuring temperature in standard units.	Problems and applications.	NAME
10	11	12	13	14	15	16	17	18	19	20	21	22	23	CV 1/2	3	4	5	6	7	8	9	10	11	12	A 1/2	3	4	5	6	7	8	9	10	11	12	13	L 1/2	3	4	5	6	7	8	9	10	11	12	13	W 1/2	3	4	5	6	7	8	9	10	T 1/2	3	4	5	6	7	8	9	10	11	12	13	14	Imp	Temp	NAME

Mark achievements in colour.

Suggested code:

⊠ topics introduced.

■ topics mastered.

Most topics include several concepts/skills and these are described more fully in *Maths Links* on the page indicated by the topic number.

For discussion of assessment and record-keeping see *Maths Links* pages 9 and 10.

d, Stafford ST17 4JX.

Bibliography

General

Assessment of Performance Unit (1980a) *Mathematical Development. Primary Survey Report No. 1*   HMSO

Assessment of Performance Unit (1980b) *Mathematical Development. Secondary Survey Report No. 1*   HMSO

Williams, E. M. and Shuard, H. (1970) *Primary Mathematics Today New Metric Edition*   Longman

Assessments

Checkpoints Assessment Cards (Primary Pack)   Inner London Education Authority

O and B Maths Test   Oliver and Boyd

Profile of Mathematical Skills   Norman France   Nelson

Yardsticks   Nelson

Publishers' Addresses

Addison-Wesley Publishers Ltd., 53 Bedford Square, London WC1B 3BR.

Benn (Ernest) Ltd., Sovereign Way, Tonbridge, Kent TN9 1RW.

Blackie and Son Ltd., Western Cledderns Road, Bishopbriggs, Glasgow G64 2NZ.

Chambers (W and R) Ltd., 11 Thistle Street, Edinburgh EH2 1DG.

Collins (William) Sons and Co. Ltd., P.O. Box 39, Glasgow G4 0NB.

Evans Brothers Ltd., Montague House, Russell Square, London WC1B 5BX.

Hart-Davis Educational Ltd., (Granada Publishing Ltd.) P.O. Box 9, 29 Frogmore, St. Albans, Herts AL2 2NF.

Heinemann Educational Books Ltd., The Windmill Press, Kingswood, Tadworth, Surrey KT20 6BR.

HMSO Books, Atlantic House, Holborn Viaduct, London EC1P 1BN.

Holmes McDougall Ltd., Allander House, 137-141 Leith Walk, Edinburgh EH6 8NS.

Holt, Rinehart and Winston Ltd., 1 St. Anne's Road, Eastbourne, East Sussex BN21 3UN.

Inner London Education Authority, Learning Materials Service, Publishing Centre, Highbury Station Road, London N1 1SB.

Longman Group Ltd., Longman House, Burnt Mill, Harlow, Essex CM20 2JE.

Macmillan Education Ltd., Houndmills, Basingstoke, Hampshire RG21 2XS.

Murray (John) Ltd., 50 Albemarle Street, London W1X 4BD.

NARE Central Office, 2 Lichfield Road, Stafford ST17 4JX.

Nelson (Thomas) and Sons Ltd., Nelson House, Mayfield Road, Walton-on-Thames, Surrey KT12 5PL.

Oliver and Boyd Ltd., Robert Stevenson House, 1-3 Baxters Place, Leith Walk, Edinburgh EH1 3AF.

Oxford University Press, Clarendon Press, Walton Street, Oxford OX2 6DP.

Pergamon Press Ltd., Headington Hill Hall, Oxford OX3 0BW.

Schofield and Sims Ltd., Dogley Mill, Fenay Bridge, Huddersfield HD8 0NQ.

Ward Lock Educational Co. Ltd., 47 Marylebone Lane, London W1M 6AX.

Index